Comprehensive English

REVIEW TEXT

SEVENTH EDITION

Harold Levine

AMSCO

When ordering this book, please specify:
either **R 627 P** *or* COMPREHENSIVE ENGLISH

AMSCO SCHOOL PUBLICATIONS, INC.
315 Hudson Street / New York, N.Y. 10013

Dedicated to the memory of
Albert Beller (1906–1995)
Publisher, editor, and students' advocate

ISBN 1-56765-030-9
NYC Item 56765-030-8

Copyright © 1996 by Amsco School Publications, Inc.

6 7 8 9   00 99 98

Preface to the Seventh Edition

The aim of this *Comprehensive English Review Text* is to provide students with the materials and guidance they need to pass the Comprehensive Examination in English with a score they can be proud of. Among the services the book offers are the following:

* It conducts students through a typical test in every one of the examination areas—listening, vocabulary, spelling, reading, the literature essay, and the composition—with an abundance of exercises and practice materials to improve proficiency in each of these areas.

* It offers practical hints for finding the answer to each of the sixty multiple-choice questions in the examination.

* It prepares students for the writing demands of the examination by teaching them how to plan and write a literature essay and a composition that meet the stated requirements. In addition, it provides model literature essays and model compositions for every choice that the examination offers.

The following literary works have been added to the appendix entitled *A Little Anthology of Short Stories, Poems, and Essays* (pages 151–184):

"When in Disgrace with Fortune and Men's Eyes" by William Shakespeare
"When I Heard the Learn'd Astronomer" by Walt Whitman
"Opportunity" by Edward Rowland Sill
"The Gettysburg Address" by Abraham Lincoln
"The Hibernation of the Woodchuck" by Alan Devoe

Students should supplement their preparation for the literature essay test by reading some of the short literary works in the *Little Anthology*. An example of how to use these works in a literature essay appears on page 130.

To perfect their writing, students should study and correct common errors in standard written English that their predecessors have made in literature essays and compositions. One way to do this is to complete the exercises on pages 131, 139, 141, and 146, using *A Review of Correct Usage* (page 185) as a reference tool.

Harold Levine

Contents

The Comprehensive Examination in English
... in a nutshell

The examination requires you to

1. Listen to a passage and answer ten printed questions testing your understanding of the passage.   *10 credits*

2. Choose the correct definitions of twenty words from the four choices offered for each word.   *10 credits*

3. Proofread fifty words, and respell the ten that are misspelled.   *5 credits*

4. Read three passages, one of which may be a poem, and answer twenty questions testing your understanding of these passages.   *20 credits*

5. Write a 250-word essay in which you answer a question by making specific references to two literary works of your choice.   *25 credits*

6. Write a composition of 250 words in response to a specific question, or on one of several suggested topics.   *30 credits*

TOTAL....   *100 credits*

1

PART I OF THE EXAMINATION

The Listening Test [*10 credits*]

> "Friends, Romans, countrymen, lend me your ears;
> I come to bury Caesar, not to praise him."

So begins what may be regarded as one of the most famous listening tests in all literature. The time is the day of Caesar's funeral in 44 B.C. The place is the Roman forum. The speaker is Antony, in William Shakespeare's *Julius Caesar*, and the listeners are a crowd of Roman citizens.

These particular Roman citizens were poor listeners; they flunked the test. They completely missed the clear evidence in Antony's speech that he was not the honest leader he seemed to be, but a demagogue—a selfish politician scheming to gain power over them by arousing their emotions, passions, and prejudices.

Many are the benefits of becoming a good listener; let us mention just a few. You will be less likely to miss the point of a joke, or a lesson, or to misinterpret an explanation and come to a wrong conclusion, or to be taken in by a clever sales pitch, or to become a college dropout.

What Happens in a Typical Comprehensive English Listening Test?

You will see these directions on the cover of your examination booklet, and the teacher will read them to you:

DIRECTIONS FOR THE LISTENING SECTION

(1) The teacher will read a passage aloud. Listen carefully. DO NOT WRITE ANYTHING.

(2) Then the teacher will tell you to open your test booklet to page 2 and to read questions 1 through 10. At that time you may mark your tentative answers to questions 1 through 10 if you wish.

(3) Next, the teacher will read the passage aloud a second time. As you listen to the second reading, WRITE THE NUMBER of the answer to each question in the appropriate space on the answer sheet.

(4) After you have listened to the passage the second time, you will have up to 5 minutes to look over your answers.

(5) The teacher is not permitted to answer questions about the passage.

(6) After you have answered the listening questions on page 2, go right on to the rest of the examination.

STEP 1: The teacher will do the first of two readings of a listening passage. YOU WILL NOT SEE THE PASSAGE. You are to listen only and not to write anything.

Below is a typical listening passage. We have numbered the lines to facilitate reference because we plan to come back to this passage.

TYPICAL LISTENING PASSAGE

[The following passage is adapted from *The Memoirs of Chief Red Fox*, published in 1971.]

I have acted in the movies and in Wild West shows, and served as an interpreter between the Indian and the White man. I have met presidents and kings, writers, scientists, and artists. I have had much joy and received many honors, but I have never forgotten my wild, free

5　childhood when I lived in a tepee and heard the calling of the coyotes
　under the stars . . . when the night winds, the sun, and everything
　else in our primitive world reflected the wisdom and benevolence of
　the Great Spirit. I remember seeing my mother bending over an open
　fire toasting buffalo meat, and my father returning at night with an
10　antelope on his shoulder. I remember playing with the other children
　on the banks of a clean river, and I shall never forget when my grand-
　father taught me how to make a bow and arrow from hard wood and
　flint, and a fishhook from the rib of a field mouse. I am not senti-
　mental but memories haunt me as I review scenes from those days
15　before I was old enough to understand that all Indian things would
　pass away.
　　We were told that the Great Spirit looked after everything in nature;
　that he instructed the badger to burrow deep into the ground and the
　coyote to find shelter in the side of a hill when a cold winter was
20　coming; and that he protected his animals by giving them heavier fur;
　and that he even looked after the ear of corn by giving it a thicker
　husk. We were never asked to bend our knees or to bow our heads in
　prayer, but we learned to look into the sky and reach out our hands
　for a blessing, or to ask forgiveness for some deviation from the paths
25　of righteousness we were commanded to follow.
　　The Indians did not have a written language, so the older people
　had to be encyclopedias of knowledge that could be passed from one
　generation to another. They knew the chants and rituals used in the
　dances and other ceremonies, and taught them to their pupils. One of
30　the subjects they emphasized was the sign language, which was a
　universal medium of communication among the many tribes, and
　through which they could exchange commodities and hold councils
　with almost as much understanding as is achieved among the nations
　of the world today.
35　　The average American child of today would enjoy the privileges I
　had out there on the unspoiled prairie one hundred years ago. I was
　usually awake in time to see the sun rise. If the weather was warm, I
　went down to the river that flowed near our village and dipped water
　out of it with my hands for a drink, then plunged into it. The river
40　came down out of the hills, ferrying leaves, blossoms, and driftwood.
　Fish could be seen in the pools formed near the rapids over which it
　rippled. Birds nested and flew among the banks, and occasionally I
　would see a coon or a fox in the brush. Hawks circled overhead,
　searching the ground for mice or other small animals for their break-

45 fast, or to feed the young in their nests. There were never enough
    hours in a day to exhaust the pleasure of observing every living crea-
    ture—from the orb spider spinning his magic and all but invisible web
    to the bald eagles on their bulky nests atop the tallest trees, teaching
    fledglings how to eject safely.
50   The halcyon days I like to remember were not by any means con-
    tinuous. The Indians had not been completely subdued, and their lands
    were still wanted by the Whites. The Sioux were determined to keep
    the territory that was theirs by inheritance and treaty, and fierce battles
    were yet to be fought and lost while I still was a child. Our deep
55 reverence for the invisible Creator of all things—the Great Spirit—
    was a sensitive influence in our struggle for survival; and we were to
    learn, as man has learned since the dawn of time, that religion is the
    most sensitive and intense thing that men have fought over.

STEP 2: The teacher will give you a few minutes to look over the ques-
         tions about the passage. At this time, you may mark your tenta-
         tive answers to these questions, if you wish, before the teacher
         reads the passage aloud for the second time. These are the
         questions:

Listening Questions

1. At the beginning of the passage, the speaker contrasts the accomplishments of his adulthood with the
   (1) length of his life   (3) pleasures of his childhood
   (2) breadth of his experiences   (4) poverty of his ancestors

2. To the Native Americans, everything that exists reveals characteristics
   of
   (1) the earth   (3) the family
   (2) their creator   (4) their tribe

3. According to the speaker, what development had he not foreseen?
   (1) His culture would die.   (3) His religion would change.
   (2) His family would separate.   (4) His skill would diminish.

4. How does the speaker describe his people's way of communicating with the Great Spirit?
   (1) He portrays it as unrealistic.
   (2) He depicts it as rigid.
   (3) He compares it with that of other tribes.
   (4) He contrasts it with other forms of worship.

5. During the speaker's childhood, transmission of knowledge depended upon
   (1) the White man   (3) a written language
   (2) the oral tradition   (4) the Great Spirit

6. According to the speaker, sign language was necessary for
   (1) trade   (3) healing
   (2) entertainment   (4) religion

7. The speaker probably describes the prairie as "unspoiled" to highlight the
   (1) White man's later influence on the land
   (2) expanse of the prairie
   (3) discipline of his childhood
   (4) friendliness of neighboring tribes

8. In confronting their losses, the Sioux regarded their god with an attitude of
   (1) disappointment   (3) respect
   (2) anger   (4) indifference

9. The autobiographical nature of this passage has the effect of
   (1) hiding the truth   (3) exaggerating the past
   (2) objectifying memory   (4) personalizing history

10. The speaker suggests that the survival of his people can be attributed to their
    (1) military skill   (3) tribal unity
    (2) religious beliefs   (4) family ties

STEP 3: The teacher will now read the passage aloud for the second and final time. As you listen, you are to WRITE THE NUMBER of each answer in the appropriate space on the answer sheet. ANSWER ALL QUESTIONS. LEAVE NO ANSWER SPACE BLANK.

STEP 4: After the second reading, you will be allowed five minutes to finish writing your answers. The listening test will then be over.

HOW CAN YOU FIND THE CORRECT ANSWERS TO THE LISTENING TEST QUESTIONS?

IMPORTANT: No question ever was asked in a Comprehensive English Listening Test unless there was stated or implied evidence IN THE PASSAGE to guide listeners to the correct answer. The evidence needed for a perfect score will be IN THE PASSAGE. You will hear it if you listen carefully.

Here are the answers to the questions you just saw on pages 5 and 6, plus the evidence on which each of those answers is based.

QUESTION 1: ANSWER (3). EVIDENCE: In lines 1–16, the speaker contrasts the achievements of his adulthood (acted in movies, served as interpreter, met with presidents, etc.) with the PLEASURES OF HIS CHILDHOOD (lived in tepee, heard calling of coyotes under the stars, etc.).

QUESTION 2: ANSWER (2). EVIDENCE: Chief Red Fox says in lines 6–8: "the night winds, the sun, and everything else in our primitive world reflected the wisdom and benevolence of the Great Spirit." Note that wisdom and benevolence are regarded as characteristics of their creator.

QUESTION 3: ANSWER (1). EVIDENCE: In lines 14–16, the speaker says: "memories haunt me as I review scenes from those days before I was old enough to understand that all Indian things would pass away." This indicates that the development he did not foresee as a child was that HIS CULTURE WOULD DIE.

QUESTION 4: ANSWER (4). EVIDENCE: Chief Red Fox contrasts his people's way of communicating with the Great Spirit with other forms of worship: "We were never asked to bend our knees or to bow our heads in prayer (as some other religions do), but we learned to look into the sky and reach out our hands for a blessing, or to ask forgiveness . . ." (lines 22–24)

QUESTION 5: ANSWER (2). EVIDENCE: Since the Indians had no written language, their older people had to be encyclopedias of knowledge so that they could pass on knowledge from generation to generation by ORAL TRADITION (word of mouth). (lines 26–28)

QUESTION 6: ANSWER (1). EVIDENCE: The speaker suggests the sign language was necessary for trade. It was "a universal medium of communication...through which they could exchange commodities..." (lines 30–32)

QUESTION 7: ANSWER (1). EVIDENCE: Chief Red Fox states that ONE HUNDRED YEARS AGO, that is, in 1871 (his book appeared in 1971), the prairie was UNSPOILED (line 36). He also states that the Indians' lands were WANTED BY THE WHITES, and that FIERCE BATTLES WERE YET TO BE FOUGHT AND LOST (lines 52–54) by the Indians for that land. The foregoing evidence from the passage makes it probable that the Chief's purpose in describing the prairie as it was in 1871 as "unspoiled" is to highlight the White man's later influence on the land.

QUESTION 8: ANSWER (3). EVIDENCE: The chief mentions not only the FIERCE BATTLES the Indians FOUGHT AND LOST, but also their DEEP REVERENCE (respect) FOR THE INVISIBLE CREATOR in their STRUGGLE FOR SURVIVAL. (lines 54–56)

QUESTION 9: ANSWER (4). EVIDENCE: This passage is autobiographical, as we can tell from its opening words (I have acted in the movies); it is about Chief Red Fox, and it was written by him. The effect of the autobiographical style of writing about historical events is to PERSONALIZE history—to show history as it affected the life of one person.

QUESTION 10: ANSWER (2). EVIDENCE: The speaker says: "The Great Spirit was a sensitive influence in our struggle for survival," and "religion is the most sensitive and intense thing that men have fought over" (lines 55–58). By these comments, he suggests that the survival of his people can be attributed to their RELIGIOUS BELIEFS.

WHAT IS MEANT BY THE TONE OF A PASSAGE?

There was no question about TONE in the listening test about *The Memoirs of Chief Red Fox*. However, such a question may appear on the test you will take. Let us therefore define TONE now.

Tone is "the author's or speaker's attitude toward his or her subject."

Suppose our test had contained a question like this:

11. What is the tone of the passage (about *The Memoirs of Chief Red Fox*)?
    (1) pessimistic   (3) fearful
    (2) boastful   (4) nostalgic

Go back now to pages 3 through 5 to try to find evidence for an answer. Then compare your reasoning with the following:

QUESTION 11: ANSWER (4). EVIDENCE: The passage is full of NOS-TALGIA (longing for the past). See especially lines 4–16 ("I have never forgotten my wild, free childhood..."); lines 35–49 ("The average American child of today would enjoy the privileges I had out there on the unspoiled prairie..."); and line 50, where the Chief refers again to "The HALCYON (peacful, happy) days I like to remember..." The tone of the passage is therefore predominantly NOSTALGIC.

How Should You Use Past Listening Tests for Practice Purposes?

We reprint here, as practice material, several past listening tests to help you sharpen your listening skills, **but you must not read the listening passages.** Instead, use the following procedure with each of these tests:

1. Secure the cooperation of a good reader to administer the test to you. Let that person have the passage in advance of the test to become familiar with it.
2. Ask the cooperating person to begin the test by reading the passage aloud to you as you listen carefully.
3. Silently read to yourself the ten listening questions.
4. Have the person read the passage aloud to you a second time.
5. Record your answers in the next five minutes. Answer all questions; do not leave any answer space blank.
6. Finally, check your answers with the answer key provided by your teacher. Make whatever adjustments are necessary in your reasoning so that you will not repeat past mistakes.

Past Comprehensive English Listening Tests for Practice

LISTENING PASSAGE: TEST 1

[The following passage was taken from an essay by Ted Williams, "Bringing Back the Beast of Lore."]

For centuries we trapped them, poisoned them, shot them. In 1905 we even tried infecting them with mange. Ten years later Congress passed a law requiring their elimination from federal lands. We had cleansed Yellowstone Park by 1926. It hasn't been easy, but finally we have won against the wolf.

While some 6,000 wolves persist in Alaska (down from 10,000 a decade ago), all other U.S. populations are officially "threatened"—as is the case in northern Minnesota—or "endangered," as in northern Michigan, Wisconsin, and Montana's Glacier National Park.

Yet, with the Endangered Species Act, we have charged the same Federal Government that got rid of what Theodore Roosevelt called "the beast of waste and desolation" with putting it back again.

What has come over us? Wolves, after all, have been eliminated from the British Isles. Populations of wolves in the Middle East, China, Spain, Italy, and Germany are vastly diminished. In the old Soviet Union wolves had been holding their own, but the public, having been exposed to the movie *Never Cry Wolf*, was suddenly so soft on them that alarmed Communist party bosses had to triple the bounty.

What has come over us is ecology—the study of how organisms and their environments interrelate. We are beginning to grasp the basic principle of this young science: that if the whole is good, no part can be bad.

Native Americans understood it all along. They would watch attentively as early settlers sought to render wolfless the surrounding countryside by pumping dead cows full of poison and setting them out in their fields. Such behavior amazed Native Americans.

The white man's fear and loathing of the wolf dates to medieval Europe. During the Inquisition the populace was kept in hand by "werewolf" control; i.e., identifying and executing these human-look-alikes. Wolves that prowl our literature exploit the young and the innocent; the inescapable message to children is that the same fate will befall them unless they acquire sobriety and diligence.

"Vicious" was a term applied to the wolf, but it was applied also to revered predators. The difference was that while certain large cats and bears attacked humans, wolves charged in the opposite direction. Wolves have learned that *Homo sapiens* is deadly, and that attacking him never pays. In the ancient accounts of European wolves running down sleighs and picking off wandering villagers it is difficult to distill fact from fiction, but if there was a time when wolves did such things, it surely was before man was so well armed. In 1985, while humans were arguing about whether or not to restore wolves to Glacier National Park, the wolves did it themselves, slipping down from British Columbia. Wolves show up occasionally in central Idaho, and pack activity may start before the recovery team gets around to making any releases. While natural recolonization seems unlikely in Yellowstone, establishing wolves there would require no more than a simple transplant.

Yellowstone is the largest essentially intact ecosystem in Earth's temperate zones. Wolves belong there and, indeed, had been there in one form or another for 15 million years prior to 1926. They are, in fact, the major missing element. Favored prey—elk, deer and bison—are present in staggering quantity. From 1935 to 1968 the National Park Service saw fit to trim, by rifle and relocation, the northern elk herd to what it perceived as a balanced 4,000. Since 1968, when the shooting stopped, the herd has swollen to 19,000.

Perhaps subconsciously we have missed wolves. Without them our lives are a little duller and a little sadder. Even for those still frightened by fairy tales it might be thrilling to venture now and then from safe, shadeless, synthetic places into wolf country. To hear wolves singing again amid their star-washed mountains and forests. To see their passage written in fresh snow. To glimpse a silhouette backlit by the moon or a shadow flowing over a barren ridge. But, mostly, just to know they are out there as they used to be, part of the ancient equation and of big woods and of dark, beautiful, mysterious places.

Listening Questions

1. How does the speaker begin the passage?
   (1) by causing confusion   (3) by arousing fear
   (2) by creating suspense   (4) by generating suspicion

2. In the United States, official responsibility for restoring the wolf population depends on
   (1) local laws   (3) a Federal act
   (2) each state legislature   (4) private organizations

3. In which place do wolves no longer exist?
   (1) Spain   (3) England
   (2) Italy   (4) Germany

4. The speaker suggests that one principle of ecology focuses on the relationship of the
   (1) part to the whole   (3) old to the new
   (2) environment to science   (4) nation to the environment

5. The speaker feels that the reason wolves are sometimes portayed as villains in literature is to
   (1) illustrate a moral   (3) criticize authority
   (2) personify laziness   (4) exemplify impatience

6. According to the speaker, wolves have learned that humans are
   (1) cowardly   (3) careless
   (2) shrewd   (4) dangerous

7. Who finally solved the problem of restoring wolves to Glacier National Park?
   (1) the wolves   (3) the National Park Service
   (2) the Congress   (4) the recovery team

8. The speaker's term "simple transplant" refers to
   (1) expanding the park's boundaries
   (2) relocating the wolf packs
   (3) selective breeding of wolves
   (4) abandoning natural recolonization

9. According to the speaker, wolves belong in Yellowstone Park because they
   (1) have lived there since 1926
   (2) need large spaces to live in
   (3) have become too numerous in other parks
   (4) are part of the ecological community

10. What does the speaker say happens to people as a result of the absence of wolves?
   (1) We feel safer.   (3) Our fairy tales change.
   (2) Our lives are less exciting.   (4) We can hunt more easily.

LISTENING PASSAGE: TEST 2

[The following passage is taken from an essay in *Pilgrim at Tinker Creek* by Annie Dillard, a field naturalist and Pulitzer Prize-winning author.]

When I was six or seven years old, I used to take a precious penny of my own and hide it for someone else to find. It was a curious compulsion. For some reason I always "hid" the penny along the same stretch of sidewalk up the street. I'd take a piece of chalk and, starting at either end of the block, draw huge arrows leading up to the penny from both directions. I was greatly excited, during all this arrow-drawing, at the thought of the first lucky passerby who would receive in this way, regardless of merit, a free gift from the universe. I'd go straight home and not give the matter another thought, until, some months later, I would be gripped by the impulse to hide another penny.

There are a lot of things to see, unwrapped gifts and free surprises. The world is fairly studded and strewn with pennies cast broadside from a generous hand. But—and this is the point—who gets excited by a mere penny? If you follow one arrow, if you crouch motionless on a riverbank to watch a tremulous ripple thrill on the water, and are rewarded by the sight of a muskrat kit paddling from its den, will you count that sight a chip of copper only, and go your rueful way? It is very dire poverty indeed for a man to be so malnourished and fatigued that he won't stoop to pick up a penny. But if you cultivate a healthy poverty and simplicity, so that finding a penny will make your day, then, since the world is in fact planted in pennies, you have with your poverty bought a lifetime of days. What you see is what you get.

Unfortunately, nature is very much a now-you-see-it, now-you-don't affair. A fish flashes, then dissolves in the water before my eyes like so much salt. Deer apparently ascend bodily into heaven; the brightest oriole fades into leaves. These disappearances stun me into stillness and concentration; they say of nature that it conceals with a grand nonchalance.

Nature, however, does reveal as well as conceal: now-you-don't-see-it, now-you-do. For a week this September, migrating red-winged blackbirds were feeding heavily down by Tinker Creek at the back of the house. One day I went to investigate the racket; I walked up to a tree, an Osage orange, and a hundred birds flew away. They simply materialized out of the tree. I saw a tree, then a whisk of color, then a tree again. I walked closer and another hundred blackbirds took flight. Not a branch, not a twig budged: the birds were apparently weightless as well as invisible. Or, it was as if the leaves of the Osage orange had been freed from a spell in the form of red-winged blackbirds; they flew from the tree, caught my eye in the sky, and vanished. When I looked again at the tree, the leaves had reassembled as if nothing had happened. Finally I walked directly to the trunk of the tree and a final hundred, the real diehards, appeared, spread, and vanished. How could so many hide in the tree without my seeing them? The Osage orange, unruffled, looked just as it had looked from the house, when three hundred red-winged blackbirds cried from its crown. I looked upstream where they flew, and they were gone. Searching, I couldn't spot one. I wandered upstream to force them to play their hand, but they'd crossed the creek and scattered. One show to a customer. These appearances catch at my throat; they are the free gifts, the bright coppers at the roots of trees.

Listening Questions

1. The child's behavior in hiding the penny was a
   (1) saddening experience
   (2) spontaneous impulse
   (3) practical joke
   (4) constant mystery

2. The "generous hand" refers to
   (1) fate
   (2) the child
   (3) the poor
   (4) nature

3. The speaker seems to think that today most people's reaction to finding a penny is one of
   (1) indifference
   (2) amusement
   (3) surprise
   (4) exasperation

4. According to the speaker, what is the effect of "cultivating" poverty?
   (1) Others provide what you need.
   (2) You become receptive to small wonders.
   (3) Every cent becomes a source of anxiety.
   (4) You live longer.

5. The speaker suggests that opportunities to encounter the world's surprise wonders are
   (1) infrequent
   (2) controlled
   (3) endless
   (4) declining

6. The expression "dissolves...like so much salt" describes the
   (1) losing of money
   (2) passing of a glimpse of nature
   (3) fading of a childhood memory
   (4) living of a life of poverty

7. What is the effect on the speaker when the creatures vanish from her sight?
   (1) She is frightened.
   (2) She feels sad and lonely.
   (3) She is irritated.
   (4) She becomes quietly attentive.

8. The speaker believed that the sudden appearance of the birds from the orange tree could be described as
   (1) magical   (3) startling
   (2) commonplace   (4) predictable

9. The speaker implies that the reason she could not find even one of the birds she had disturbed was that
   (1) she did not search
   (2) nature hides things well
   (3) birds are too swift
   (4) the birds continued to migrate

10. The phrase "force them to play their hand" most likely means to
    (1) give the birds a chance to hide again
    (2) watch the birds enjoy themselves
    (3) cause the birds to reveal themselves
    (4) continue the hide-and-seek game

LISTENING PASSAGE: TEST 3

[The following passage was taken from "The Wilborn Temple" by Jeanne Finley.]

At first they were only a small movement on the unlit street corner, but as they turned south and came toward me I could see who they were: two old women, one white, one black, dressed on Saturday night for Sunday in flowered straw hats with veils of net over their white hair, short-sleeved flowered dresses and low-heeled summer orthopedic sandals, big handbags dangling over their arms. The white woman, nearest the curb, guided the black woman gently by her left arm, crooked the way a young girl walking with her sweetheart under the moonlight would crook her arm. I could see the gentleness, the tenderness of their holding in the lines of their bodies as they walked slowly, taking the night air. The light at the corner had frozen halfway between yellow and red, and the whole movement of the city seemed to stop as though waiting for them to take their next few steps down the uneven concrete slabs.

And then I saw that the black woman was blind. She moved under the guiding arm of her companion not with the sliding, hesitant gait of the blind who are afraid of the next step, but by sound: her head tilted slightly toward the other woman, she listened for the strike of her footstep on the ground the way you listen for lightning to precede thunder, the way a symphony conductor anticipates, by an eighth of a second, the next constellation of notes and placement of rhythm and thus constructs, for himself and for the audience, the entire score in the air just ahead of the sound. They walked, this couple, like dancers in a small but elegant choreography down the slope of South Swan Street, the white woman the lightning rod, the black woman, by instinct and grace, actually leading her, summoning her to follow.

And when they had moved exactly underneath one of the open cathedral windows, the singing started. "When Israel was in Egypt's land," it began, in moderate walking time, and the women stopped as though struck. I could see them perfectly. Slowly the white woman looked above her, straining to see the music. But the black woman did not move. Her dark glasses glinted off the streetlight, and she seemed to look directly at me, and then she smiled, as slowly as she had walked, and she kept smiling a smile that knew the words to the song, knew what was coming next, knew where it all was going and was happy to hear it come and go, as though she knew everything in the world or at least in Albany had conspired to summon this night, on her request, the singing voices, the river of rhythms and the gypsy tambourines, the words that unrolled out of the high narrow windows before the three of us and filled the deserted block with their people: "Go down, go down, go down Moses, let my people go!" She began to nod, keeping time, the streetlight reflecting on her shiny dark glasses, and her time was a little bit ahead of the music, just a hair, and then they both moved down South Swan Street that way, the sighted woman still looking up, trying to see, the blind woman leading her, urging her to hear. I watched them, eyes burning, until they turned the corner, dancing their ghost dance and walking their rounds down the long sloping sidewalk against the backdrop of voices, and then I sat in my car with my eyes closed for a long time.

Listening Questions

1. During which season does this scene take place?
   (1) winter   (3) summer
   (2) spring   (4) autumn

2. The narrator suggests that the blind woman's manner is primarily one of
   - (1) humbleness
   - (2) confidence
   - (3) hesitancy
   - (4) fatigue

3. The narrator compares the two women to
   - (1) a married couple
   - (2) an orchestra
   - (3) a church choir
   - (4) dancers

4. The most likely reason the sighted woman is described by the narrator as a "lightning rod" is that she
   - (1) would deflect danger from her companion
   - (2) has excellent posture
   - (3) is tall and thin
   - (4) is more nervous than her companion

5. According to the narrator, what is the women's first reaction to the music?
   - (1) They begin to sing.
   - (2) They are moved to tears.
   - (3) They stand still.
   - (4) They turn toward the church.

6. Which word best describes how the black woman feels as she listens to the singing?
   - (1) amused
   - (2) anxious
   - (3) saddened
   - (4) gratified

7. The narrator implies that the black woman's response to the music is most similar to that of
   - (1) a choreographer
   - (2) an orchestra conductor
   - (3) a gypsy
   - (4) an elegant queen

8. The purpose of the women's outing is to
   - (1) go for a walk
   - (2) see a movie
   - (3) visit a shop
   - (4) go to church

9. The narrator's statement that she sat in the car with her "eyes closed for a long time" is used to show that she is
   - (1) sympathetic
   - (2) tired
   - (3) moved
   - (4) patient

10. What is the predominant organizational pattern of the passage?
    (1) definition   (3) contrast
    (2) chronological order   (4) deductive reasoning

LISTENING PASSAGE: TEST 4

[The following statement of beliefs by Leo Rosten is adapted from the book *Passions and Prejudices.*]

I believe that you can understand people better if you look at them—no matter how old or important or impressive they may be—as if they are children. For most of us never mature; we simply grow taller.

I have learned that everyone—in some small, secret sanctuary of the self—is mad. If we want to stay sane we must moderate our demands—on ourselves and on others. Those who do not understand mercy cannot in the end escape the punishment which waits within ourselves.

I have learned that everyone is lonely, at bottom, and cries to be understood; but we can never entirely understand someone else, no matter how much we want to; and each of us will forever be part stranger—even to those who love us most.

I have learned that the dimensions of suffering, of anguish, resentment, despair exceed our wildest imagings. I have learned, too, that the human capacity for sacrifice, for devotion and compassion can forever hearten and surprise us.

I have learned that it is the weak who are cruel, and that kindness is to be expected only from the strong.

I have come to see that every person is subject to yearnings so deceitful, drives so destructive that even to mention them shakes the gates we have erected against the barbarian within.

Nothing in nature, not the glories of the sky nor the mysteries of the atom, is half so strange as our unconscious—that hidden, heaving sea of impulse in which the most confounding contradictions beat side by side.

I cannot believe that the purpose of life is to be "happy." I think the purpose of life is to be useful. It is, above all, to *matter*: to have it make some difference that you lived at all.

And so, before the final day of doom, let us come to terms with the fact that we live knowing that our dearest hopes may never be fulfilled, that life—so short, so long, so delicious and baffling and horrid and beautiful—holds nothing more precious than the process by which we stretch the mind and heart.

Listening Questions

1. The narrator contrasts maturity and physical growth to emphasize that most people
   - (1) do not mature
   - (2) grow slowly
   - (3) mature early
   - (4) grow differently

2. According to the narrator, we can maintain our mental balance by
   - (1) seeking pleasant goals
   - (2) demanding more of others
   - (3) expecting nothing from ourselves
   - (4) modifying our own expectations

3. The narrator suggests that for those of us who show no mercy the final judge will be
   - (1) humanity
   - (2) history
   - (3) ourselves
   - (4) fate

4. What is the narrator's belief about our capacity to understand other people?
   - (1) Our hard work leads to understanding.
   - (2) Sometimes we know strangers best.
   - (3) We can only understand those we love.
   - (4) We can never completely know another person.

5. According to the narrator, we can be encouraged by people's capacity for
   - (1) surprising others
   - (2) showing compassion
   - (3) demonstrating honesty
   - (4) overcoming pain

6. According to the narrator, acting without mercy is characteristic of people who
   - (1) are not strong
   - (2) have been hurt
   - (3) are misunderstood
   - (4) are ignorant

7. In the passage, the word "barbarian" represents
   - (1) our ancestors
   - (2) personal enemies
   - (3) our worst impulses
   - (4) social evils

8. According to the narrator, the reason for living is to
   - (1) accomplish something
   - (2) achieve perfection
   - (3) search for contentment
   - (4) ask questions

9. The narrator urges us to accept the idea that
   (1) all we have is each other
   (2) our days are numbered
   (3) everything will end peacefully
   (4) our expectations may be unfulfilled

10. According to the narrator, the most important thing life has to offer is
    (1) the ability to be happy
    (2) a means for improving ourselves
    (3) the chance to fall in love
    (4) a reason to explore our subconscious

LISTENING PASSAGE: TEST 5

[This passage is from an interview conducted in 1980 with Jamake High-water, an expert in traditional Native American culture and author of children's literature.]

In a very real sense, I am the brother of the fox. My whole life revolves around my kinship with four-legged things. I am rooted in the natural world. I'm two people joined into one body. The contradiction doesn't bother me, but people always assume the one they're talking to is the only one there is. That bothers me. There is a little of the legendary Native American in me but also a little of the modern writer. I stand in both those worlds, not between them. I'm very much a 20th-century person, and yet I'm a traditional native of the Northern Plains.

I've always had an enormous regard for the intellect. Still, I like to go home to my people who are in touch with the beginning of things. At home, people are carpenters; some are poets, painters, and teachers; some work on construction jobs. They are people who perceive the importance of small things that are easily missed by those of us who move much too quickly.

I came to terms with the solemn aspects of life very early. I was always among Native Americans, for we traveled the powwow circuit. I was always listening to some older person telling stories. They are nameless to me now, and countless, because there were so many. I was introduced to the Native American world in the same way as children in my tribe were in the 1870's when we were a nomadic people. I was rootless, yet connected to a vital tradition. The elders talked to me and gave me a sense of the meaning of my existence.

I talk and think as a poet, but I don't want to perpetuate the romantic notion of the Native American as watching chipmunks his entire life, waiting to see which side of the tree the moss grows on. For the Native American, art is not reserved for a leisure class, as it is in Anglo society. It is part of our fundamental way of thinking. We are an aesthetic people. Most primal people are. We represent a constant chord that's been resounding ever since man began. While those Cro-Magnon people in the caves of southern France (at least according to Western mentality) should have been out worrying about the great likelihood that they wouldn't survive, they were building scaffolds fifty or sixty feet high and with tiny oil lamps were painting the ceilings of their caves with marvelous magical images. These images were an implicit and important part of their lives. For us, this aesthetic reality is a continuous process. Native American murals and pottery rival the finest accomplishments of Western art. This idea of life as art is part of being a Native American. It's not quaint or curious or charming. It's fundamental, like plowing a field. There's great beauty in plowing a field.

I think Native Americans have become a metaphor for a larger idea. We are building bridges toward cultures. Some people in white society are also building bridges toward us, and they sometimes join together. That means that it's possible for each person to find the Native American in himself or herself. It's a kind of sensibility that I'm talking about.

Listening Questions

1. In his opening statement, the narrator's reference to himself as "the brother of the fox" suggests that he
   (1) is clever and crafty
   (2) feels close to nature
   (3) rejects modern civilization
   (4) believes in reincarnation

2. What disturbs the narrator about living in two different worlds?
   (1) People do not understand his dual nature.
   (2) He gets confused about his heritage.
   (3) People in both worlds make him feel uncomfortable.
   (4) He feels he must choose between the two worlds.

3. The narrator portrays the natives of the Northern Plains as people who
   (1) are more intellectual than practical
   (2) live a hectic lifestyle
   (3) are employed in lowly occupations
   (4) take time to appreciate the simple things in life

4. The narrator suggests that his childhood experiences among Native Americans gave him a
   (1) desire for the nomadic life
   (2) love of poetry
   (3) sense of identity
   (4) reason for studying his heritage

5. The narrator's reference to Cro-Magnon people indicates that
   (1) art was vital to primitive cultures
   (2) ancient societies were not well organized
   (3) primitive people worshipped the images they painted
   (4) building was a complex process in prehistoric times

6. According to the narrator, the significance of the murals and pottery of Native Americans is that both are
   (1) natural expressions of everyday life
   (2) valuable reminders of ancient religions
   (3) forerunners of Western art
   (4) unusual examples of Native American culture

7. The narrator's reference to Native Americans as a ''metaphor for a larger idea'' implies that Native Americans
   (1) represent a primitive society
   (2) use storytelling to record history
   (3) understand the importance of leisure time
   (4) are teaching us about ourselves

8. The narrator's use of the term ''sensibility'' at the end of this passage most likely refers to
   (1) an appreciation for art
   (2) an understanding of primitive cultures
   (3) an awareness of self and others
   (4) a concern for the downtrodden

9. The narrator's purpose is to persuade people to value
   (1) Native American poetry
   (2) ancient art
   (3) the nomadic lifestyle
   (4) the Native American perspective

10. The tone of the passage can best be described as
    (1) humorous   (3) ironic
    (2) reflective   (4) objective

The Vocabulary Test [*10 credits*]

THE IMPORTANCE OF VOCABULARY

Improving your vocabulary should be one of your top priorities. Words represent ideas. Words are the tools for thinking. If your knowledge of words is limited, your ability to think will be limited, keeping you from effectively receiving and communicating ideas on an advanced level. But if you follow the methods discussed in this chapter, your vocabulary will grow substantially, you will improve as a listener, speaker, reader, and writer, and you will have a better chance of getting ahead in your career or profession.

IMPORTANT: Do not assume that the Comprehensive Examination in English tests your vocabulary only in the 10-point vocabulary test. It tests your vocabulary—as we have already seen—in the 10-point listening test; and also—as we shall see—in the 20-point reading test, the 25-point literature essay test, and the 30-point composition test.

Below is a typical Comprehensive English Vocabulary Test. As you read each question, jot down your answer on a piece of scrap or in your notebook. Then compare your answers with the answer key immediately following the test.

TYPICAL VOCABULARY TEST

Directions (11–30): In the space provided on the separate answer sheet, write the *number* of the word or phrase that most nearly expresses the meaning of the word printed in heavy black type. [10]

11. **allure**
    (1) charm
    (2) secrecy
    (3) sincerity
    (4) judgment

12. **meager**
    (1) faulty
    (2) expensive
    (3) inadequate
    (4) measurable

23

13. **deflect**
    (1) do over
    (2) remove
    (3) turn aside
    (4) discuss

14. **slipshod**
    (1) rough
    (2) excessive
    (3) glossy
    (4) careless

15. **adage**
    (1) essay
    (2) poem
    (3) proverb
    (4) play

16. **avidly**
    (1) rigidly
    (2) eagerly
    (3) colorfully
    (4) impishly

17. **uncanny**
    (1) without kindness
    (2) beyond the normal
    (3) without talent
    (4) full of emotion

18. **saunter**
    (1) pause
    (2) bend
    (3) slide
    (4) stroll

19. **weather**
    (1) endure
    (2) regulate
    (3) discover
    (4) permit

20. **carnage**
    (1) extreme frustration
    (2) widespread theft
    (3) massive slaughter
    (4) deafening noise

21. The group was known for its **pacifism.**
    (1) concern for the environment
    (2) opposition to violence
    (3) interest in religion
    (4) views on education

22. The secretary **collated** the pages of the report.
    (1) arranged
    (2) typed
    (3) duplicated
    (4) proofread

23. The athlete's **tenacity** was amazing.
    (1) poise
    (3) determination
    (2) luck
    (4) strength

24. The newspaper reported that the committee's decision seemed **equitable**.
    (1) unusual
    (3) predictable
    (2) just
    (4) unavoidable

25. His chief role was that of **arbitrator**.
    (1) developer
    (3) observer
    (2) organizer
    (4) judge

26. The scouts were trained to **forage** as a survival skill.
    (1) build a shelter
    (3) search for food
    (2) identify animal tracks
    (4) interpret weather signals

27. The speaker referred **obliquely** to the problem.
    (1) objectively
    (3) indirectly
    (2) hesitantly
    (4) sympathetically

28. The lecturer used **parables** to illustrate her point.
    (1) charts
    (3) slides
    (2) stories
    (4) statistics

29. A **nimble** mind is universally admired.
    (1) logical
    (3) sound
    (2) trained
    (4) quick

30. Some people believe that astrologers are **omniscient**.
    (1) possessed of universal knowledge
    (2) controlled by unseen forces
    (3) devoted to seeking perfection
    (4) capable of interpreting nature

ANSWER KEY

11. 1	15. 3	19. 1	23. 3	27. 3
12. 3	16. 2	20. 3	24. 2	28. 2
13. 3	17. 2	21. 2	25. 4	29. 4
14. 4	18. 4	22. 1	26. 3	30. 1

HINTS FOR FINDING THE MEANING OF A TROUBLESOME TEST WORD

HINT 1. If the troublesome word, except for its ending, is like a word you are familiar with, use the familiar word as a clue. Examples:

PROBLEM: What does **allure** (word 11) mean?

CLUE: Get help from **alluring,** a word you are more familiar with. You know, for example, that an **alluring** smile is a "charming" (full of charm or fascination) smile.

SOLUTION: **Allure** probably means "charm." ANSWER (1)

PROBLEM: What does **pacifism** (word 21) mean?

CLUE: Get help from **Pacific** Ocean. You may recall that Magellan, the first to cross that vast body of water, named it the **Pacific** (peaceful) Ocean because its waters looked so calm.

SOLUTION: **Pacifism** is peacefulness, or "opposition to violence." ANSWER (2)

HINT 2. Try to remember a context in which you have seen or heard the troublesome word. Examples:

PROBLEM: What does the verb **weather** (word 19) mean?

CLUE: Get help from these lines by Walt Whitman that may have stuck in your mind:

"O Captain! My Captain! our fearful trip is done,
The ship has **weathered** every rack, the prize we sought is won."

The Captain, in these lines, is the assassinated Abraham Lincoln; the fearful trip that is done is the War Between the States; and the ship that has **weathered** every rack (torment) is, of course, our suffering country.

SOLUTION: Of the four choices offered for the meaning of the verb **weather,** the only one that fits the above context is "*endure.*" ANSWER (1)

PROBLEM: What does **nimble** (word 29) mean?

CLUE: The following nursery rhyme may come to mind:

> Jack be **nimble.**
> Jack be quick.
> Jack jump over the candlestick.

SOLUTION: **Nimble** means "quick." ANSWER (4)

HINT 3: Break down the troublesome word into its component parts.
Examples:

PROBLEM: What does **omniscient** (word 30) mean?

CLUES: **Omniscient** contains the roots **omni-,** meaning "all," and **sci-,** meaning "know."

SOLUTION: **Omniscient** means "knowing all," or "possessed of universal knowledge." ANSWER (1)

PROBLEM: What does **deflect** (word 13) mean?

CLUES: **Deflect** consists of the prefix **de-,** meaning "down" or "away," and the root **flect-,** meaning "bend" or "turn."

SOLUTION: **Deflect** means "turn away" or "turn aside." ANSWER (3)

HOW TO BUILD A SUPERIOR VOCABULARY

1. Develop the habit of reading widely for pleasure and information in newspapers, magazines, and books.

Just by regularly reading a good newspaper, you could have learned practically all the words that appeared in the vocabulary test we just discussed. There have been numerous stories in the press, for example, about the **carnage** (word 20) that drunken drivers cause on the highways; the **meager** (word 12) diets of people in famine-stricken lands; the reluctance of union and management to submit disputes to an **arbitrator** (word 25) because of fears that the outcome may not be **equitable** (word 24); and the **uncanny** (word 17) ability of some goalies to **deflect** (word 13) puck shots.

2. Purchase a recent edition of a good desk dictionary and develop the habit of consulting it. The following desk dictionaries are listed alphabetically, without indication as to relative merit. Examine them at a bookstore and choose the one that appeals to you most.

American Heritage Dictionary. Houghton Mifflin.
Merriam-Webster's Collegiate Dictionary. Merriam-Webster, Inc.
Random House College Dictionary. Random House.
Webster's New World Dictionary. Simon & Schuster.

Here are a couple of interesting ways to begin getting returns from your dictionary.

a. Differentiate between commonly confused words. In the following pairs of words, one is frequently mistaken for the other. Eliminate the confusion by looking up the meaning of each word and using it in a complete (written) sentence:

1. stationary, stationery	6. hypercritical, hypocritical
2. allusion, illusion	7. ingenious, ingenuous
3. continual, continuous	8. ancestor, descendant
4. disinterested, uninterested	9. respectfully, respectively
5. effect, affect	10. translucent, transparent

b. Trace word histories. This can be one of the most fascinating ways of building your vocabulary. Do you know, for example, that "boycott" was actually the name of a land agent in Ireland, Captain Charles C. Boycott? Because he refused to lower the rents and evicted many tenants, the inhabitants organized a campaign of retaliation. They would have no dealings with him, and they prevented him from dealing with anyone, even to purchase food. Since that time (1880), to "boycott" has meant to follow a policy of refusing to deal in any way (with a person, group, or nation) as a punitive measure.

After consulting your dictionary, record in your notebook the origin and meaning of each of the following words:

1. Adonis	8. hector	15. philippic
2. atlas	9. iridescent	16. Pyrrhic victory
3. chauvinist	10. laconic	17. quisling
4. congregation	11. Machiavellian	18. quixotic
5. curfew	12. mentor	19. solon
6. Damoclean	13. mesmerize	20. stentorian
7. gargantuan	14. odyssey	

3. Use the context. Often you can tell the meaning of an unfamiliar word from its *context*—the other words with which it is used. The context may help by providing a synonym, an antonym, or a commonsense clue.

a. CONTEXT WITH A SYNONYM:

Now that you have heard his *version* of the accident, listen to my account.

(The context reveals that *version* means ''account.'')

b. CONTEXT WITH AN ANTONYM:

Are the inhabitants *hostile* or friendly?

(The context tells us that *hostile* means ''unfriendly.'')

c. CONTEXT WITH A COMMONSENSE CLUE:

Were you fired, or did you leave of you own *volition*?

(The context indicates that *volition* means ''will.'')

Caution: Whenever you learn the meaning of a word from its context, check with your dictionary as soon as possible to make sure you are right.

4. Listen. If someone you respect uses a word you do not know—for example, *genial* or *glib*—make a note of it so that you may look it up in your dictionary and add it to your vocabulary.

5. Keep a vocabulary notebook. Look up any of the following words that are unfamiliar. Record them, together with a definition and illustrative sentence, in your notebook. Use the entries for *impartial* and *import*, below, as models. In the same way, record other new words as you meet them.

WORD	DEFINITION	ILLUSTRATIVE SENTENCE
impartial	just	A judge should be *impartial*.
import	meaning	I did not get the *import* of your remark.

1. fictitious	13. prerogative	25. insurgent	37. posterity
2. proximity	14. pensive	26. tremulous	38. arrogance
3. siphon	15. allot	27. celerity	39. enmesh
4. placid	16. impeach	28. facade	40. vivacious
5. intern	17. glib	29. scrutinize	41. deft
6. fluctuate	18. prevaricate	30. dexterous	42. coalition
7. dilemma	19. utilitarian	31. cardiac	43. prudent
8. writhe	20. jargon	32. instigate	44. garrulous
9. rudiment	21. condole	33. rescind	45. genial
10. invariable	22. chaotic	34. maudlin	46. evasive
11. consensus	23. irate	35. volition	47. pomp
12. annals	24. appraisal	36. immunity	48. jostle

Review your vocabulary notebook entries from time to time, and try to use each new word in an appropriate situation in your speaking and writing as soon as possible. Only by using your new words can you make them a part of your vocabulary.

6. Learn the common prefixes, roots, and suffixes.

You should memorize the meanings of common prefixes, roots, and suffixes because they form countless words in our language. Notice how a knowledge of prefixes, roots, and suffixes can help you to answer these vocabulary questions:

QUESTION:

adhere
(1) argue forcefully
(2) hold tightly
(3) understand completely
(4) answer clearly

ANSWER: (2) hold tightly

EXPLANATION:

adhere contains the following:

ad—a prefix meaning "to"
here—a root meaning "stick" or "cling"

Therefore, **adhere** means "stick to," "cling to," or "hold tightly."
A postage stamp, for example, **adheres** to an envelope if properly affixed.

QUESTION:

immutable
(1) unified
(2) questionable
(3) structured
(4) unchanging

ANSWER: (4) unchanging

EXPLANATION:

immutable contains the following:

im—a prefix meaning "not"
mut—a root meaning "change"
able—a suffix meaning "capable of being"

Therefore, **immutable** means "not capable of being changed"; "unchanging."

LATIN PREFIXES

PREFIX	MEANING	SAMPLE DERIVATIVES
a, ab	away, from	*avert* (turn away), *abhor* (shrink from)
ad	to	*adhere* (stick to), *adjoin* (be next to)
ante	before	*anteroom* (room before), *antedate* (come before in date)
bene	good, well	*benefactor* (one who does some good for another), *benevolent* (well-wishing)
bi	two	*bilateral* (having two sides), *bisect* (cut in two)
circum	around	*circumnavigate* (sail around), *circumvent* (go around)
co (com, con, col)	together	*coherent* (sticking together), *compatible* (able to exist together), *convoke* (call together), *collaborate* (work together)
contra, contro	against	*contravene* (go against; violate), *controversy* (a "turning against"; quarrel)
de	down, away	*demote* (move down), *deduct* (take away; subtract)
dis	apart, differently	*dissect* (cut apart), *dissent* (feel differently)
e, ex	out	*emit* (send out), *exclusive* (shutting out others)
extra	outside	*extracurricular* (outside the curriculum), *extravagant* (outside the bounds of reason)
in (il, im, ir)	not	*inflexible* (not easily bent), *illegible* (not able to be read), *immaculate* (not spotted), *irrelevant* (not pertinent)
in, im	in, on	*inhibit* (hold in), *immerse* (dip in)
inter	between	*intercede* (go between), *interurban* (between cities)
intra	within	*intraparty* (within a party), *intravenous* (within the veins)

mal, male	evil, badly	*malefactor* (evildoer), *maladjusted* (badly adjusted)
ob	in the way	*obstacle* (something standing in the way), *obstruct* (be in the way)
per	through	*perennial* (continuing through the years), *permeate* (pass through)
post	after	*posterity* (generations that will come after), *posthumous* (occurring after one's death)
pre	before	*preclude* (put a barrier before), *premature* (before the proper time)
pro	forward, forth	*propel* (drive forward), *provoke* (call forth)
re	again, back	*renovate* (make new again), *repel* (drive back)
retro	backward	*retrogress* (move backward), *retrospect* (backward look)
se	apart	*secede* (go apart; withdraw), *segregate* (set apart)
semi	half	*semicircle* (half circle), *semiconscious* (half-conscious)
sub	under	*submerge* (put under water), *subterranean* (underground)
super	above	*superlative* (above all others), *supersonic* (above the speed of sound)
trans	across, over	*transgress* (step across; violate), *transcribe* (write over; copy)
ultra	exceedingly	*ultraconservative* (exceedingly conservative)

LATIN ROOTS

ROOT	MEANING	SAMPLE DERIVATIVES
ag, act	act	*agent* (one who acts for another), *react* (act back; respond to a stimulus)
am(i), amor	like, love	*amiable* (likable; good-natured), *amorous* (loving)

cad, cas	fall	*cadaver* (body of one who has fallen; corpse), *casualty* (one who has fallen victim to accidental injury or death)
cap, cept	take, hold	*captor* (one who takes or captures), *receptacle* (something that holds smaller objects; container)
ced, cess	go	*secede* (go apart; withdraw), *recessive* (tending to go back)
cid, cis	kill, cut	*suicide* (killing of oneself), *incision* (act of cutting into)
clud, clus	shut	*exclude* (shut out), *recluse* (one who lives shut off from the world)
cred, credit	believe	*credible* (believable), *discredit* (refuse to believe)
cur(r), curs	run	*concurrent* (running together; happening simultaneously), *precursor* (forerunner)
dict	tell	*predict* (tell beforehand; prophesy)
duc, duct	lead, conduct	*induce* (lead on), *aqueduct* (artificial channel for conducting water)
fact	make	*artifact* (thing made by human skill)
fer	bear	*odoriferous* (bearing an odor; fragrant)
flect, flex	bend, turn	*genuflect* (bend the knee), *flexible* (bendable), *deflect* (turn away)
grad, gress	step, go	*gradual* (by steps), *progressive* (going forward to something better)
here, hes	stick	*adhere* (stick to; cling), *cohesion* (act of sticking together)
ject	throw	*projectile* (anything thrown forward)
junct	join	*junction* (place where things join)
leg, lect	read, choose	*legible* (easy to read), *select* (chosen as the best; superior)
loqu, locut	talk, speak	*loquacious* (talkative), *elocution* (art of speaking)
mit(t), miss	send	*emit* (send out; give off), *emissary* (person sent on a mission)

mov, mot, mob	move	*immovable* (incapable of being moved), *remote* (moved back in place or time), *mobile* (movable)
mut	change	*mutable* (changeable), *mutation* (change)
omni	all	*omnipotent* (all-powerful), *omnipresent* (present in all places)
ped	foot	*pedestrian* (foot traveler)
pel(l), puls	drive	*expel* (drive out), *repulse* (drive back)
pend, pens	hang	*pendant* (hanging ornament), *suspense* (condition of being left "hanging" or in doubt)
pon, posit	put	*postpone* (put off), *imposition* (a "putting on"; burdensome demand)
port	carry	*portable* (able to be carried)
press	press, hold	*depress* (press down; discourage), *repress* (hold back)
rupt	break	*abrupt* (broken off; sudden)
sci	know	*science* (knowledge), *conscious* (knowing what one is doing)
scrib, script	write	*scribe* (person who writes), *inscription* (something written on a monument, coin, etc.)
sect	cut	*dissection* (act of cutting apart)
sent, sens	feel	*sentiment* (feeling), *sensitive* (having a capacity for feeling)
sequ, secut	follow	*sequel* (something that follows), *consecutive* (following in regular order)
spect	look	*prospect* (thing looked forward to)
sta, stat	stand	*stable* (able to stand; not changing; enduring), *status* (standing)
tang, tact	touch	*intangible* (incapable of being touched), *tactile* (pertaining to the sense of touch)
termin	end	*terminate* (bring to an end)
tract	draw, pull	*tractor* (vehicle used for drawing or pulling)

ven, vent	come	*convene* (come together; meet), *advent* (coming; arrival)
vert, vers	turn	*invert* (turn upside down), *versatile* (able to turn with ease from one thing to another)
vid, vis	see	*provident* (foreseeing; making provision for the future), *invisible* (not able to be seen)
vinc, vict	conquer	*invincible* (not conquerable), *victor* (conqueror)
voc (voke), vocat	call	*vocal* (pertaining to the voice), *revoke* (call back; annul), *vocation* (calling)
vol	wish, will	*benevolent* (well-wishing), *involuntary* (done or occurring against one's will)
volv, volut	roll, turn	*evolve* (unroll or work out; develop gradually), *revolution* (a turning around)

EXERCISE 1. Each of the italicized words below is made up of a prefix and a root discussed previously. Define each word and then check your definitions with the dictionary.

1. a *circumspect* person
2. Don't *involve* me.
3. an *abject* beggar
4. *Repel* the attack.
5. a *disruptive* force
6. to *intercede* in a quarrel
7. an *eloquent* speaker
8. *Eject* that rowdy.
9. an *incisive* reply
10. a vicious *obloquy*

EXERCISE 2. Construct word families (at least five words to a family) with each of the following italicized roots. Then check your results with the dictionary. Example:

ag, act (do): agent, actor, inactive, agency, transaction

1. *cap, cept* (take)
2. *cur(r), curs* (run)
3. *duc, duct* (lead)
4. *mit(t), miss* (send)
5. *mov, mot, mob* (move)
6. *ped* (foot)
7. *pel(l), puls* (drive)
8. *port* (carry)
9. *scrib, script* (write)
10. *vid, vis* (see)

GREEK PREFIXES AND ROOTS

PREFIX OR ROOT	MEANING	SAMPLE DERIVATIVES
a, an	not, without	*atypical* (not typical), *anonymous* (without a name)
anthropo	man	*anthropology* (science dealing with man)
anti	against	*antipathy* (feeling against; repugnance)
aster, astro	star	*asterisk* (star-shaped mark), *astronaut* ("star sailor"; traveler in space)
auto	self	*autonomous* (self-governing)
baro	pressure	*barometer* (instrument for measuring atmospheric pressure)
biblio	book	*bibliophile* (lover of books; book collector)
bio	life	*biography* (story of a person's life written by another person)
chrom	color	*polychromatic* (showing a variety of colors)
chron, chrono	time	*synchronize* (cause to agree in time), *chronological* (arranged in order of time)
cosmo	world	*cosmopolitan* (composed of persons from many parts of the world)
cracy	government	*bureaucracy* (government by bureaus)
dem	people	*epidemic* ("among the people"; widespread)
eu	good, well	*euphonious* ("good" or pleasing in sound), *eulogize* (speak "well" or in praise of someone)
geo, gee	earth	*geophysics* (science of forces that modify the earth), *apogee* (farthest point from earth in orbit of a satellite)
gram, graph	write	*cryptogram* (something written in secret code), *graphic* (vividly written or told)
hydr	water	*dehydrate* (remove the water from)
hyper	over	*hypercritical* (overcritical)

hypo	under	*hypodermic* (injected under the skin)
log	speech	*monolog* (long monopolizing speech by one person)
logy	science, study	*bacteriology* (science dealing with bacteria)
meter	measure	*odometer* (instrument for measuring distance traveled)
micro	small	*microfilm* (film of very small size)
mis	hate	*misanthropy* (hatred of mankind)
mono	one	*monosyllabic* (having but one syllable)
onym	name, word	*pseudonym* (fictitious name; pen name), *synonym* (word having same meaning as another word)
pan	all	*panacea* (cure-all)
path	feeling	*apathy* (lack of feeling; indifference)
peri	around	*perimeter* ("around" or outer measurement of a closed plane figure)
phil	love	*philanthropy* (love of mankind)
phob	fear	*claustrophobia* (fear of confined spaces)
phon	sound	*cacophony* (harsh or clashing sound)
poly	many	*polyphonic* (having many sounds or voices)
pseudo	false	*pseudoscience* (something falsely or erroneously considered as a science)
psycho	mind	*psychology* (study of the mind)
scope	see	*fluoroscope* (instrument for seeing objects exposed to X rays)
soph	wisdom	*philosopher* (lover of wisdom)
syn, sym	together	*synthetic* (put together), *symbiosis* (living together of two dissimilar organisms)
tele	at a distance	*telecommunication* (communication at a distance)
theo	God	*theology* (study of God or religion)
therm, thermo	heat	*diathermy* (generation of heat in body tissues for medical purposes), *thermostat* (device for regulating temperature)

EXERCISE 3. Test your skill. First define each word below, using your knowledge of Greek prefixes and roots. (Each of the words has two such components.) Then check your definitions with the dictionary.

1.	monolog	6.	bibliophile
2.	psychology	7.	hydrophobia
3.	perimeter	8.	monotheism
4.	democracy	9.	geology
5.	anonymous	10.	philanthropy

SUFFIXES

SUFFIX	MEANING	SAMPLE WORDS
-able, -ible	capable of being	lovable, reversible
-ance, -ence, -cy, -ty	act of or state of being	appearance, independence, infancy, novelty
-ary, -ic, -ical	having to do with	revolutionary, democratic, musical
-ate, -ize, -fy	to make	liberate (make free), pauperize (make poor), magnify (make big)
-en	made of, like	earthen (made of earth), ashen (like ashes)
-er, -or, -ant, -ent, -ian, -ist	one who	teacher, editor, servant, resident, comedian, pianist
-ion, -age, -(a)tion, -ment	act or result of	rebellion, marriage, conversation, judgment
-ish, -like	resembling a	clownish, childlike
-itis	inflammation of	sinusitis, tonsilitis
-less	without	senseless
-ly	in a (specified) manner	eagerly, anxiously
-ous, -y	full of	perilous, risky
-ship	office, skill	kingship, penmanship

EXERCISE 4. In this final exercise, make use of your knowledge of suffixes, as well as of prefixes and roots. Define each of the following words by giving the meaning of each of its component parts. Then check your results with the dictionary.

Example: The word "eruption" is made up of "e" (out), "rupt" (break), and "ion" (act of). It means "the act of breaking out."

1. incredible	4. terminate	7. inscription
2. convocation	5. psychologist	8. psychopathic
3. porter	6. victor	9. visualize

Matching Tests in Vocabulary

Match the words in column A with the definitions in column B.

Test 1

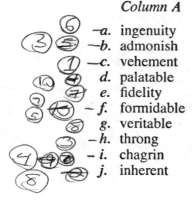

Column A	Column B
a. ingenuity	1. violent C
b. admonish	2. actual J
c. vehement	3. warn h
d. palatable	4. embarrassment D
e. fidelity	5. awe-inspiring B
f. formidable	6. inventiveness A
g. veritable	7. loyalty Q
h. throng	8. inborn G
i. chagrin	9. crowd i
j. inherent	10. appetizing f

Test 2

Column A	Column B
a. conception	1. horrible e
b. plausible	2. matchless f
c. inimitable	3. tan i
d. viable	4. reasonable B
e. grisly	5. shrewd G
f. amorphous	6. idea A
g. astute	7. confusion h
h. perplexity	8. workable D
i. tawny	9. contradict J
j. refute	10. shapeless G

Test 3

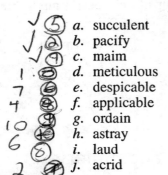

✓ ⑤	*a.* succulent	1. careful ⑤
✓ ②	*b.* pacify	2. calm ⑤
✓ ⑨	*c.* maim	3. sharp D
1 ③	*d.* meticulous	4. suitable
7 ⑥	*e.* despicable	5. juicy A
4 ⑧	*f.* applicable	6. wrong e
10 ④	*g.* ordain	7. hateful J
6 ⑧	*h.* astray	8. praise f
2 ⑩	*i.* laud	9. disfigure c
	j. acrid	10. decree h

Test 4

7 ⑦	*a.* tantalize	1. destruction D
✓ ⑤	*b.* proximity	2. external e
✓ ⑥	*c.* perceptible	3. unite A
✓ ①	*d.* havoc	4. persistence h
✓ ②	*e.* consolidate	5. nearness B
✓ ⑨	*f.* discrepancy	6. aware J
2 ⑩ -*g.*	superficial	7. tease g
6 ④	*h.* cognizant	8. energy i
4 ⑧	*i.* tenacity	9. difference f
8 ③	*j.* vitality	10. observable c

Test 5

6 ⑧	*a.* defame	1. one-sided D
✓ ③	*b.* retaliation	2. laziness c
9 ②	*c.* zeal	3. revenge B
✓ ①	*d.* unilateral	4. intolerance G
8 ⑥	*e.* bewitch	5. strange e
✓ ⑩	*f.* desist	6. slander J
✓ ④	*g.* bigotry	7. gloomy h
✓ ⑦	*h.* somber	8. fascinate a
5 ⑨	*i.* eccentric	9. enthusiasm i
2 ⑤	*j.* inertia	10. stop f

Past Comprehensive English Vocabulary Tests for Practice

Directions (11–30): In the space provided on the separate answer sheet, write the *number* of the word or phrase that most nearly expresses the meaning of the word printed in heavy black type.

VOCABULARY TEST 1

11. **inadvertently**   (1) infrequently   (2) unintentionally   (3) unfeelingly   (4) incapably

12. **roster**   (1) description   (2) outline   (3) format   (4) list

13. **charisma**   (1) personal appeal   (2) fair play   (3) social etiquette   (4) self-control

14. **elude**   (1) delay   (2) escape   (3) reverse   (4) annoy

15. **infringe**   (1) decorate   (2) subdue   (3) trespass   (4) criticize

16. **endow**   (1) enrich through a gift   (2) feel sorrow for   (3) predict the outcome   (4) form an opinion

17. **immutable**   (1) unified   (2) questionable   (3) structured   (4) unchanging

18. **agrarian**   (1) industrial   (2) primitive   (3) agricultural   (4) pagan

19. **warily**   (1) sleepily   (2) cleverly   (3) sympathetically   (4) cautiously

20. **frugal**   (1) not wasteful   (2) very greedy   (3) very thoughtful   (4) not hasty

21. By the time the detectives arrived, evidence of the crime had been **obliterated.**   (1) scattered   (2) labeled   (3) examined   (4) erased

22. **Discord** between the neighboring countries has increased in recent years.   (1) trade   (2) conflict   (3) respect   (4) communication

23. Congress was called into session in an attempt to **override** the veto.   (1) debate   (2) postpone   (3) reverse   (4) defend

24. The solution suggested by the committee is **unpalatable.**   (1) unconditional   (2) insignificant   (3) impossible   (4) unacceptable

25. The neighborhood bully was easily recognized by his **swagger.**
(1) voice   (2) strut   (3) clothing   (4) gestures

26. Ignoring safety rules is **imprudent.**   (1) unwise   (2) thoughtless
(3) improper   (4) undesirable

27. The presence of computers in the movie was considered **anachronistic.**   (1) symbolically significant   (2) essential to the plot
(3) chronologically out of place   (4) artistically bold

28. The teacher and the students shared a strong **rapport.**   (1) sense of
integrity   (2) love of learning   (3) harmonious relationship
(4) respect for discipline

29. He was **prodigiously** talented.   (1) enormously   (2) undoubtedly
(3) naturally   (4) relatively

30. The mother **harangued** her son because of the messiness of his room.
(1) punished   (2) lectured   (3) threatened   (4) teased

VOCABULARY TEST 2

11. **induce**   (1) deceive   (2) scare   (3) ridicule   (4) cause

12. **encore**   (1) additional performance   (2) standing ovation   (3) dramatic ending   (4) favorable review

13. **plausible**   (1) believable   (2) circumstantial   (3) intricate
(4) unemotional

14. **fiasco**   (1) serious undertaking   (2) complete failure   (3) long delay
(4) important observation

15. **enhance**   (1) influence   (2) cultivate   (3) intensify   (4) establish

16. **arrogantly**   (1) expertly   (2) cleverly   (3) overbearingly
(4) recklessly

17. **tainted**   (1) contaminated   (2) deflated   (3) softened   (4) adapted

18. **delve**   (1) prepare for   (2) apply to   (3) bring up   (4) dig into

19. **maim**   (1) mutilate   (2) misuse   (3) betray   (4) prevent

20. **jocular**   (1) manly   (2) lucky   (3) comical   (4) slippery

21. Many people with physical disabilities have learned to **transcend** their
limitations.   (1) forget about   (2) rise above   (3) accept   (4) exploit

22. According to the review, the leading actress gave a **lackluster** performance. (1) powerful (2) sensitive (3) shocking (4) dull

23. She wondered if her employer would **sanction** her actions. (1) discover (2) permit (3) remember (4) understand

24. Do you know if she is Jane's **ally**? (1) supervisor (2) supporter (3) substitute (4) beneficiary

25. The woman spoke **imperiously** to the young boy. (1) in a domineering manner (2) persuasively (3) politely (4) with gentle patience

26. The executive behaved in an **omnipotent** manner. (1) dignified (2) optimistic (3) all-powerful (4) supportive

27. The lawyer's questions **unnerved** the witness. (1) upset (2) misled (3) challenged (4) embarrassed

28. She was **scrupulous** in the care of her garden. (1) imaginative (2) precise (3) inconsistent (4) unsurpassed

29. His job was to **expedite** the manufacturing process. (1) check on (2) design (3) oversee (4) speed up

30. The announcement was delivered in a **guttural** voice. (1) clear (2) loud (3) authoritative (4) harsh

VOCABULARY TEST 3

11. **laxity** (1) carelessness (2) bitterness (3) sarcasm (4) conviction

12. **nurture** (1) rescue (2) arrange (3) plow (4) foster

13. **barrage** (1) betrayal (2) attack (3) expression (4) absence

14. **optimum** (1) dynamic (2) enjoyable (3) most favorable (4) very sincere

15. **hinder** (1) disperse (2) quit (3) throw away (4) interfere with

16. **surcease** (1) end (2) trouble (3) laughter (4) doubt

17. **sporadically** (1) previously (2) occasionally (3) chronologically (4) presently

18. **feasible** (1) mechanical (2) hesitant (3) likely (4) tolerant

19. **wily** (1) quick (2) crafty (3) skilled (4) shy

20. **defunct** (1) extinct (2) balanced (3) saddened (4) degraded

21. She **brazenly** presented her opinion to the group.   (1) nervously (2) cautiously   (3) honestly   (4) boldly

22. Several **irate** parents attended the school board meeting. (1) influential   (2) angry   (4) distressed   (4) noisy

23. The prisoner was judged to be **incorrigible.**   (1) incapable of being reformed   (2) unlikely to cause trouble   (3) unable to understand the charges   (4) ineligible for parole

24. Most people are happy with their **niche** in life.   (1) goals   (2) position (3) recognition   (4) accomplishments

25. The attorney stood up to **illuminate** the points of the argument. (1) list   (2) repeat   (3) clarify   (4) deny

26. The swimmer **flailed away** in the swift current.   (1) plunged forward (2) thrashed about   (3) shouted for help   (4) gasped for air

27. He was noted for his **philanthropic** interests.   (1) religious (2) athletic   (3) intellectual   (4) humanitarian

28. In some cultures, kings were **deified.**   (1) selected for life (2) believed to be infallible   (3) buried with their possessions (4) worshiped as gods

29. The criminal's **guise** surprised the police.   (1) skill   (2) intelligence (3) appearance   (4) attitude

30. The climbers knew they could **traverse** the glacier.   (1) go across (2) encounter   (3) explore   (4) tunnel through

VOCABULARY TEST 4

11. **rouse**   (1) rescue   (2) misinform   (3) awaken   (4) eliminate

12. **ravenously**   (1) hungrily   (2) fearfully   (3) carelessly   (4) angrily

13. **decrepit**   (1) poor   (2) humble   (3) complaining   (4) weak

14. **quandary**   (1) dilemma   (2) journey   (3) accident   (4) contest

15. **trauma**   (1) crime   (2) injury   (3) failure   (4) invasion

16. **fortitude**   (1) strength of mind   (2) generosity of spirit   (3) grace of movement   (4) ease of understanding

17. **stark**   (1) remote   (2) closed   (3) barren   (4) foreign

18. **pinnacle**   (1) convenient shelter   (2) wooded area   (3) secluded beach   (4) lofty peak

19. **allot**   (1) scheme   (2) distribute   (3) review   (4) multiply
20. **convivial**   (1) sociable   (2) important   (3) wealthy   (4) lucky
21. As a result of illness, he lost his **equilibrium.**   (1) balance   (2) memory   (3) strength   (4) vitality
22. The publicity about the politician was **demeaning.**   (1) unreliable   (2) degrading   (3) incriminating   (4) contradictory
23. The resort was known for its **ambience.**   (1) convenient location   (2) recreational facilities   (3) healthful climate   (4) distinct atmosphere
24. The student felt like a **nonentity** in the new school.   (1) an inexperienced person   (2) an insignificant person   (3) an incompetent person   (4) an unpopular person
25. When the scientist switched on the machine, it began to **oscillate.**   (1) hum   (2) glow   (3) vibrate   (4) spark
26. In ancient times, people **invoked** their gods in elaborate ceremonies.   (1) called upon   (2) sacrificed to   (3) thanked   (4) pacified
27. At the **commencement** of the festivities, the mayor spoke to the crowd.   (1) close   (2) midpoint   (3) climax   (4) beginning
28. The student had a reputation for telling **blatant** lies.   (1) harmless   (2) obvious   (3) imaginative   (4) elaborate
29. The child's **astute** answer surprised his father.   (1) rude   (2) unfeeling   (3) humorous   (4) shrewd
30. The tiger lay **languorously** in the shadow of a large boulder.   (1) sluggishly   (2) patiently   (3) expectantly   (4) silently

VOCABULARY TEST 5

11. **detest**   (1) deny   (2) specify   (3) examine   (4) loathe
12. **fracas**   (1) feast   (2) brawl   (3) search   (4) fracture
13. **juncture**   (1) decision   (2) climax   (3) connection   (4) emergency
14. **constrict**   (1) make smooth   (2) make narrow   (3) make flexible   (4) make flat
15. **meticulous**   (1) careful of details   (2) considerate of others   (3) worthy of honor   (4) taken for granted
16. **absolve**   (1) engage   (2) relate   (3) suggest   (4) pardon

17. **wrath**   (1) intense fear   (2) deep despair   (3) bitter resentment
(4) fierce anger

18. **zenith**   (1) summit   (2) path   (3) flight   (4) goal

19. **clandestine**   (1) secret   (2) silent   (3) strange   (4) sacred

20. **genial**   (1) desirable   (2) generous   (3) friendly   (4) happy

21. He was **grievously** ill.   (1) seriously   (2) frequently   (3) constantly
(4) fatally

22. She was able to devise a **viable** solution to the plan.   (1) unique
(2) workable   (3) novel   (4) simple

23. The newspaper reported the Senate's **nullification** of the treaty.
(1) postponement   (2) revision   (3) invalidation   (4) confirmation

24. One reason gold is used for jewelry is that it is very **malleable.**
(1) delicate   (2) shiny   (3) beautiful   (4) pliable

25. The President listened to the news with **equanimity.**   (1) disbelief
(2) composure   (3) amazement   (4) annoyance

26. The child **recoiled** when the lightning flashed.   (1) trembled   (2) fled
(3) flinched   (4) cried

27. The scientist hoped to **eradicate** the bacteria that caused the disease.
(1) destroy   (2) identify   (3) study   (4) alter

28. The offender received a hearing that was **impartial.**   (1) speedy
(2) private   (3) preliminary   (4) fair

29. The judge directed the jury to ignore the witness's **scathing** remarks.
(1) obviously rehearsed   (2) totally irrelevant   (3) bitterly severe
(4) highly opinionated

30. The **russet** leaves were piled by the roadway.   (1) newly fallen
(2) wet   (3) decaying   (4) reddish-brown

VOCABULARY TEST 6

11. **variance**   (1) authority   (2) nuisance   (3) regulation   (4) difference

12. **entail**   (1) produce   (2) involve   (3) emphasize   (4) forbid

13. **trudge**   (1) retreat   (2) slouch   (3) plod   (4) scurry

14. **acme**   (1) highest point   (2) final proposal   (3) detailed explanation
(4) preliminary investigation

15. **vanquish** (1) clean (2) criticize (3) comfort (4) conquer
16. **salve** (1) gauge (2) ointment (3) scar (4) bandage
17. **repress** (1) insult (2) disturb (3) subdue (4) refuse
18. **trifling** (1) useless (2) insignificant (3) grotesque (4) dull
19. **profoundly** (1) deeply (2) anxiously (3) pleasantly (4) loudly
20. **insatiable** (1) envious (2) coarse (3) disgusting (4) greedy
21. The young man had a **debonair** attitude toward life. (1) lighthearted (2) pessimistic (3) childlike (4) cautious
22. After so many years of war, the people held little hope for any **armistice.** (1) victory (2) election (3) independence (4) truce
23. The judge decided to **mitigate** the criminal's sentence. (1) review (2) overrule (3) lessen (4) postpone
24. The teacher asked the **recalcitrant** students to sit down. (1) tardy (2) unruly (3) unhappy (4) eager
25. The teacher presented a **synopsis** of the play to the class. (1) critique (2) history (3) summary (4) segment
26. **Dissidence** is not usually tolerated by dictators. (1) disagreement (2) disorganization (3) desertion (4) democracy
27. No one could **mollify** the lost child. (1) identify (2) understand (3) approach (4) soothe
28. The writing was poetic as well as **utilitarian.** (1) creative (2) entertaining (3) witty (4) useful
29. She was **inundated** by the work that had been assigned to her. (1) overwhelmed (2) discouraged (3) astounded (4) inspired
30. The ex-convicts were engaged in a number of **nefarious** actions. (1) pessimistic (2) wholesome (3) wicked (4) regrettable

The Spelling Test [5 *credits*]

THE IMPORTANCE OF SPELLING

Just as you check your personal appearance before going out in public, so you should proofread what you have written before submitting it, especially if it is a composition, or term paper, or letter of application for employment or admission to a college. The sad truth is that the world regards errors in spelling as signs of ignorance, although some of the most intelligent people have been poor spellers. Of course, if you do your writing on a word processor, you can use a spelling-checker program to help you do your proofreading; yet even such a program requires you to know how to spell. Word processors, by the way, are not yet available to students taking the Comprehensive Examination in English.

This chapter presents a thorough review of spelling. Use it selectively. For each specific weakness you have, study the applicable rule or hint in the section beginning on page 51, and do the accompanying remedial exercise. If you are an excellent speller, you should be able to skim most of this chapter.

CAUTION: Do not assume that this examination tests your spelling only in the 5-point spelling test. There will be further tests of your spelling in the 25-point literature essay test and the 30-point composition test. In rating these tests, your teachers are required by the Board of Regents to consider whether you have "followed the conventions of standard written English." One of these conventions, of course, is spelling.

TYPICAL SPELLING TEST

Take this sample test, jotting down your answers on a piece of scrap or in your notebook. Then compare your answers with those in the **Answers and Explanation** section that follows the test.

Directions (31–40): In each of the following groups of words, only one of the words is misspelled. In *each* group, select the misspelled word and spell it correctly in the space provided on the separate answer sheet.   [5]

31. adjustible
    calendar
    technique
    transmitted
    quadrant

32. cynical
    geology
    pennant
    naturaly
    expiration

33. applicant
    enviroment
    suppress
    mortgage
    novelist

34. piece
    sincerely
    official
    immature
    truthfullness

35. forecast
    ministry
    keenness
    poison
    defendent

36. misrule
    maxamize
    consultant
    referred
    absorb

37. mamoth
    recycle
    panorama
    mutineer
    mournful

38. laughable
    horrifying
    ernestly
    vegetable
    shaving

39. illegally
    forfeit
    sterile
    unrelieved
    labratory

40. stagnent
    roommate
    article
    remedy
    urban

Answers and Explanations

QUESTION 31:   **adjustible   calendar   technique   transmitted   quadrant**

ANSWER: **adjustable**

EXPLANATION: See p. 60, Rule 15, "Adding the Suffix **ABLE** or **IBLE**."

QUESTION 32:   **cynical   geology   pennant   naturaly   expiration**

ANSWER: **naturally**

EXPLANATION: See p. 57, Rule 11, "Attaching the Suffix **LY**."

QUESTION 33:   **applicant enviroment suppress mortgage novelist**

ANSWER: **environment**

EXPLANATION: See 3, p. 68, "Do not carelessly omit a required consonant."

QUESTION 34:   **piece sincerely official immature truthfullness**

ANSWER: **truthfulness**

EXPLANATION: See 1, p. 51, "The **-ful** rule."

QUESTION 35:   **forecast ministry keenness poison defendent**

ANSWER: **defendant**

EXPLANATION: There is no easy way to explain why nouns like **defendant, assailant, descendant, commandant,** and **lieutenant** end in **ant.** Call this your **ant** list of nouns, and review it once in a while.

QUESTION 36:   **misrule maxamize consultant referred absorb**

ANSWER: **maximize**

EXPLANATION: **Maximize** comes from **maximum,** whose root is **maxi,** not **maxa.**

QUESTION 37:   **mamoth recycle panorama mutineer mournful**

ANSWER: **mammoth**

EXPLANATION: There is no easy explanation. Suggested mnemonic to remember the **mm:** "A ma**mm**oth is an elephantlike ma**mm**al." See pp. 75, 76.

QUESTION 38:   **laughable horrifying ernestly vegetable shaving**

ANSWER: **earnestly**

EXPLANATION: The first syllable begins with **ea.** Suggested mnemonic: "Those who **ea**rnestly try to help us **ea**rn our gratitude."

QUESTION 39:	**illegally forfeit sterile unrelieved labratory**
ANSWER:	**laboratory**
EXPLANATION:	Do not carelessly omit the unstressed **o.** See p. 68, section 1.

QUESTION 40:	**stagnent roommate article remedy urban**
ANSWER:	**stagnant**
EXPLANATION:	There is a noun **stagnation,** ending in **ation.** Therefore adjective **stagnant** should end in **ant,** rather than **ent.** See Rule 17, p. 61.

How to Improve Your Spelling

To help you to do your best not only in the spelling test but also in the literary essay test and the composition test, this chapter will provide a thorough review of spelling under headings A through G below.

A. KNOW YOUR SPELLING RULES

Spelling Certain Sounds

1. The -*ful* rule: The sound *full* added to a word is spelled with only one *l*. Examples: careful, graceful, healthful, truthful, teaspoonful, etc.
   Exception: the word *full* itself.

2. The *-ceed* or *-cede* rule: There are only three verbs in the English language ending in *-ceed*. All other verbs with that sound end in *-cede*.

> *-ceed:* succeed, proceed, exceed
> *-cede:* secede, recede, intercede, concede, accede,
> cede, precede, antecede

Exception: super*sede*. This is the only verb ending in *-sede*.

EXERCISE 1. Rewrite each word, inserting *ceed*, *cede*, or *sede*.

1. ante_____nt	6. ex_____ed
2. super_____d	7. re_____s
3. inter_____s	8. pro_____s
4. suc_____ing	9. con_____d
5. pre_____nt	10. ex_____ingly

3. The *ie* and *ei* rules: In some words, the sound of *e* as in *eve* is spelled *ie* (achi*e*ve, beli*e*ve). In certain other words, the same sound is spelled *ei* (c*ei*ling, rec*ei*ve).

To help yourself to recognize when *i* comes before *e* (believe, relief, grief) and when *e* comes before *i* (receive, deceit, receipt), master the following rule and its exceptions:

Write *i* before *e*

(Examples: achieve, belief, brief, chief, fiend, fierce, grief, piece, shriek, siege, yield, etc.)

Except after *c*

(After *c*, the rule is reversed; we write *e* before *i*. Examples: ceiling, conceit, conceive, deceit, deceive, perceive, receipt, receive, etc.)

Or when sounded like *ay*
As in *neighbor* or *weigh*.

(In such cases, too, we write *e* before *i*. Examples: freight, reign, sleigh, vein, weight, etc.)

Master these seven common exceptions, each of which has *e* before *i*: either, neither, foreigner, height, leisure, seize, weird.

EXERCISE 2. Rewrite each word, inserting *ie* or *ei*.

1. bes____ged
2. misch____f
3. gr____vance
4. conc____ted
5. n____ther
6. rel____f
7. fr____ndly
8. sl____gh
9. inconc____vable
10. hyg____ne
11. p____ce
12. h____ght
13. dec____tful
14. r____gned
15. unperc____ved
16. cash____r
17. s____zure
18. n____ghborly
19. f____ndish
20. v____l
21. n____ce
22. ach____vement
23. bel____f
24. rec____pt
25. w____rd
26. c____ling
27. retr____ve
28. fr____ght
29. ____ther
30. sh____lding
31. rel____ve
32. v____n
33. br____f
34. p____rcing
35. unw____ldy
36. l____surely

Attaching Prefixes

Rule 4: Do not omit or add a letter when attaching a prefix to a word. Keep *all* the letters of the prefix and *all* the letters of the word.

PREFIX		WORD		NEW WORD
dis	+	satisfied	=	dissatisfied
dis	+	organized	=	disorganized
mis	+	spell	=	misspell
un	+	natural	=	unnatural
un	+	acceptable	=	unacceptable

EXERCISE 3. Write the new words formed by adding the prefixes.

1. dis + similar
2. inter + related
3. extra + ordinary
4. un + necessary
5. dis + service
6. re + election
7. with + hold
8. de + emphasize
9. mis + understand
10. pre + arrangement

Attaching Suffixes

Rule 5: Do not omit or add a letter when attaching a suffix to a word—unless the word ends in *y* or silent *e*. Keep *all* the letters of the word and *all* the letters of the suffix.

WORD		SUFFIX		NEW WORD
accidental	+	ly	=	accidentally
drunken	+	ness	=	drunkenness
ski	+	ing	=	skiing
foresee	+	able	=	foreseeable

EXERCISE 4. Write the new words formed by adding the suffixes.

1. possess + ing
2. govern + ment
3. book + keeper
4. radio + ed
5. sudden + ness
6. Hindu + ism
7. room + mate
8. embarrass + ment
9. total + ly
10. disagree + able

Attaching Suffixes to Words Ending in Y

Rule 6: If the letter before final *y* is a *consonant*, change the *y* to *i* before attaching a suffix.

WORD		SUFFIX		NEW WORD
hurry	+	ed	=	hurried
sturdy	+	er	=	sturdier
costly	+	ness	=	costliness
greedy	+	ly	=	greedily

Exception A. Except before *ing:* hurry + ing = hurrying.

Exception B. Learn these special exceptions: dryly, dryness, shyly, shyness, babyish, ladylike.

Rule 7: If the letter before final *y* is a *vowel*, do not change the *y* before attaching a suffix.

WORD		SUFFIX		NEW WORD
destroy	+	ed	=	destroyed
play	+	ing	=	playing

Exceptions: laid, paid, said, and their compounds (mislaid, underpaid, unsaid, etc.); daily.

EXERCISE 5. Add the suffixes *er*, *est*, *ly*, and *ness* to each word below.

EXAMPLE: happy—happier, happiest, happily, happiness

1. lazy	6. weary
2. heavy	7. stealthy
3. sly	8. hearty
4. clumsy	9. ugly
5. icy	10. busy

EXERCISE 6. Add the suffixes *ing* and *ed* to each of the words below.

EXAMPLE: occupy—occupying, occupied

1. deny	6. rely
2. stay	7. convey
3. fortify	8. supply
4. repay	9. say
5. delay	10. satisfy

EXERCISE 7. Write the new words formed by adding the suffixes.

1. accompany + ment	11. deny + al
2. mercy + ful	12. ceremony + ous
3. decay + ed	13. shy + ness
4. fancy + er	14. oversupply + ing
5. foolhardy + ness	15. contrary + wise
6. pacify + ed	16. disqualify + ed
7. magnify + ing	17. bury + al
8. overpay + ed	18. harmony + ous
9. momentary + ly	19. worry + some
10. controversy + al	20. lucky + est

Attaching Suffixes to Words Ending in Silent E

Rule 8: Drop the silent *e* if the suffix begins with a *vowel*.

WORD		SUFFIX		NEW WORD
write	+	ing	=	writing
love	+	able	=	lovable
use	+	age	=	usage
produce	+	er	=	producer

Exception A. When the word ends in *ce* or *ge*, keep the *e* if the suffix begins with *a* or *o*.

notice	+	able	=	noticeable
manage	+	able	=	manageable
advantage	+	ous	=	advantageous

Exception B. Learn these additional exceptions: acreage, mileage, singeing, canoeing, hoeing, shoeing.

Rule 9: Keep the silent *e* if the suffix begins with a *consonant*.

excite	+	ment	=	excitement
care	+	ful	=	careful
fierce	+	ly	=	fiercely
complete	+	ness	=	completeness

Exceptions: argument, awful, duly, truly, wholly, ninth.

Attaching Suffixes to Words Ending in IE

Rule 10: If the word ends in *ie*, drop the *e* and change the *i* to *y* before adding *ing*.

WORD		SUFFIX		NEW WORD
die	+	ing	=	dying
lie	+	ing	=	lying
tie	+	ing	=	tying
vie	+	ing	=	vying

EXERCISE 8. Write the new words formed by adding the suffixes.

1. disadvantage + ous
2. excite + able
3. untie + ing
4. encourage + ment
5. true + ly
6. pursue + ing
7. mile + age
8. believe + able
9. avenge + ing
10. hope + less
11. peace + able
12. singe + ing
13. desire + ous
14. service + able
15. discourage + ing
16. argue + ment
17. sense + ible
18. whole + ly
19. outrage + ous
20. die + ing

Attaching the Suffix LY

Rule 11: To change an adjective to an adverb, we usually add *ly*.

ADJECTIVE		SUFFIX		ADVERB
brave	+	ly	=	bravely
calm	+	ly	=	calmly
usual	+	ly	=	usually

Exception A. If the adjective ends in *ic*, add *al* before attaching *ly*.

drastic	+	al	+	ly	=	drastically
scientific	+	al	+	ly	=	scientifically

Exception B. If the adjective ends in *ble*, simply change *ble* to *bly*.

ADJECTIVE	ADVERB
able	ably
noble	nobly
probable	probably

Reminders:

1. Remember: duly, truly, wholly.

2. If the adjective ends in *y* preceded by a *consonant*, remember to change *y* to *i* before adding *ly* (easy + ly = easily).

EXERCISE 9. Change the following adjectives to adverbs:

1. normal	6. possible	11. quiet	16. respectful
2. hasty	7. frantic	12. economic	17. specific
3. democratic	8. definite	13. annual	18. steady
4. final	9. partial	14. surprising	19. favorable
5. due	10. heroic	15. horrible	20. general

Doubling Final Consonants Before Suffixes

Why is the *r* in *defer* doubled (defe*r*red) when *ed* is added, whereas the *r* in *differ* is not (differed)? Why is the *n* in *plan* doubled (plan*n*ing) before *ing*, whereas the *n* in *burn* is not (bur*n*ing)? To clear up these matters, review Rules 12 and 13 for doubling final consonants.

Rule 12: In a one-syllable word, double the final consonant before a suffix beginning with a vowel.

WORD		SUFFIXES		NEW WORDS
plan	+	ing, er	=	planning, planner
stop	+	ed, age	=	stopped, stoppage
big	+	er, est	=	bigger, biggest

Exception A. If the final consonant comes right after two vowels, do not double it.

fail	+	ed, ing	=	failed, failing
stoop	+	ed, ing	=	stooped, stooping

Exception B. If the final consonant comes right after another consonant, do not double it.

warm	+	er, est	=	warmer, warmest
last	+	ed, ing	=	lasted, lasting

Rule 13: In a word of two or more syllables, double the final consonant only if it is in an *accented* syllable before a suffix beginning with a vowel.

deFER′	+	ed, ing, al	=	deferred, deferring, deferral
resubMIT′	+	ed, ing	=	resubmitted, resubmitting

Note carefully that the rule does not apply if the final consonant is an *unaccented* syllable.

DIF′fer	+	ed, ing, ent	=	differed, differing, different
BEN′efit	+	ed, ing	=	benefited, benefiting

Exception A. The rule does not apply if the final consonant comes right after two vowels.

obTAIN′	+	ed, ing	=	obtained, obtaining
conCEAL′	+	ed, ing	=	concealed, concealing

Exeption B. The rule does not apply if the final consonant comes right after another consonant.

abDUCT′	+	ed, ing, or	=	abducted, abducting, abductor
comMEND′	+	ed, ing, able	=	commended, commending, commendable

Exception C. The rule does not apply if the accent shifts back to the first syllable.

conFER′	+ ence	=	CON′ference
preFER′	+ ence	=	PREF′erence
reFER′	+ ence	=	REF′erence

However: exCEL′ + ence = EX′cellence.

EXERCISE 10. Write the new words formed by adding the suffixes.

1. concur + ing	9. occur + ed	17. append + age
2. entail + ed	10. drum + er	18. regret + able
3. abhor + ent	11. elicit + ing	19. discredit + ed
4. flat + er	12. imperil + ed	20. adapt + able
5. retract + able	13. absorb + ent	21. bar + ed
6. refer + al	14. defer + ence	22. rebel + ion
7. dispel + ed	15. propel + ant	23. slim + est
8. deter + ent	16. infer + ing	24. excel + ent

EXCERCISE 11. Add the indicated suffixes to each word below.

1. regret + ing + ed + ful	9. defer + ing + ed + ment
2. sin + ing + ed + er	10. dissent + ing + ed + er
3. patrol + ing + ed + er	11. protract + ing + ed + or
4. confer + ing + ed + ence	12. spot + ing + ed + er
5. remit + ing + ed + ance	13. commit + ing + ed + ment
6. flip + ing + ed + ant	14. excel + ing + ed + ence
7. transmit + ing + ed + er	15. recur + ing + ed + ent
8. profit + ing + ed + able	

Attaching Suffixes to Words Ending in IC

Rule 14: Insert a *k* after the *c* before adding *ed*, *er*, *ing*, or *y*. (The *k* keeps the *c* from being pronounced as *s*.)

picnic—picnicked, picnicker, picknicking

Reminder: When adding *ly* to an *ic* word, first add *al*, and then *ly*.

magic + al + ly = magically

EXERCISE 12. Write the new words formed by adding the suffixes.

1. panic + ed
2. frolic + ing
3. mimic + ed
4. hectic + ly
5. traffic + ing
6. frolic + ed
7. mimic + ing
8. panic + y
9. romantic + ly

Adding the Suffix ABLE or IBLE

Rule 15: An adjective usually ends in *able*, rather than *ible*, if you can trace it to a noun ending in *ation*.

NOUN	ADJECTIVE
adaptation	adaptable
alteration	alterable
commendation	commendable

Exception: sensation—sensible.

Aside from the above rule, there is no easy way to tell whether an adjective ends in *able* or *ible*. Study each word separately and consult your dictionary when in doubt. Here are some words to review:

ABLE		*IBLE*	
acceptable	excusable	accessible	indelible
adjustable	favorable	audible	inexhaustible
believable	formidable	collapsible	intelligible
changeable	incurable	contemptible	invincible
charitable	indefatigable	credible	legible
comfortable	laughable	edible	negligible
comparable	manageable	eligible	permissible
debatable	memorable	feasible	reversible
dependable	perishable	flexible	sensible
desirable	preferable	forcible	tangible
despicable	profitable	illegible	visible

EXERCISE 13. Write the words formed by adding the suffixes *able* or *ible*.

1. uncomfort_____
2. imagin_____
3. inflex_____
4. forc_____
5. unchange_____
6. illeg_____
7. present_____
8. unaccept_____
9. inflamm_____
10. invis_____
11. unprofit_____
12. cur_____
13. irrit_____
14. sens_____
15. communic_____

Rule 16: Verbs ending in *ate* usually become nouns ending in *or*, rather than *er*.

VERB	NOUN
create	creator
demonstrate	demonstrator
indicate	indicator

Exception: debate—debater.

Aside from the above rule, there is no easy way to tell whether a noun ends in *or* or *er*. Study each word separately and consult your dictionary when in doubt. Here are some words to review:

OR		*ER*	
aggressor	negotiator	consumer	organizer
ambassador	possessor	coroner	philosopher
censor	professor	defender	pretender
contributor	prosecutor	dissenter	purchaser
creditor	sculptor	interpreter	subscriber
debtor	tailor	invader	supporter
governor	traitor	laborer	sympathizer
monitor	vendor	manufacturer	treasurer

EXERCISE 14. From each verb below, form a noun ending in *or* or *er*.

1. own	6. liberate	11. legislate
2. regulate	7. possess	12. manufacture
3. report	8. debate	13. send
4. generate	9. buy	14. elevate
5. advertise	10. originate	15. labor

Adding the Suffix ANT or ENT

Rule 17: Spell an adjective with *ant*, rather than *ent*, if you can trace it to a noun ending in *ation*, *ance*, or *ancy*.

NOUN	ADJECTIVE
stagnation	stagnant
brilliance	brilliant
vacancy	vacant

Rule 18: Spell an adjective with *ent*, rather than *ant*, if you can trace it to a noun ending in *ence* or *ency*.

independence   independent
decency   decent

Study the following:

ANCE, ANCY		ENCE, ENCY	
abundance	nonchalance	adherence	frequency
assistance	observance	adolescence	imminence
attendance	poignancy	coherence	incompetence
compliance	relevance	convalescence	negligence
defiance	reliance	correspondence	permanence
extravagance	repentance	currency	pertinence
fragrance	resistance	decadence	potency
hesitancy	truancy	eloquence	recurrence
ignorance	vagrancy	eminence	urgency
inconstancy	vigilance	fluency	vehemence

EXERCISE 15. Rewrite each word, supplying the missing letter.

1. perman____nt
2. ignor____nt
3. adolesc____nt
4. impot____nt
5. tru____nt
6. irrelev____nt
7. unobserv____nt
8. decad____nt
9. vagr____nt
10. inconst____nt
11. adher____nt
12. impertin____nt
13. correspond____nt
14. hesit____nt
15. poign____nt
16. urg____nt
17. nonchal____nt
18. extravag____nt
19. resist____nt
20. infrequ____nt
21. repent____nt
22. eloqu____nt
23. self-reli____nt
24. vigil____nt

Forming Contractions

Rule 19: When contracting two words, insert an apostrophe in the space where a letter (or letters) has been lost.

does	+	not	=	doesn't	I	+	am	=	I'm
it	+	is	=	it's	we	+	are	=	we're
they	+	will	=	they'll	she	+	would	=	she'd
you	+	have	=	you've	can	+	not	=	can't

Notice this special contraction: will + not = won't.

EXERCISE 16. Write each of the following as a contraction:

1. we would	8. it is	15. you are
2. has not	9. must not	16. will not
3. let us	10. they are	17. she will
4. would not	11. I have	18. they would
5. he will	12. could not	19. was not
6. were not	13. it will	20. we will
7. there is	14. who is	

Forming Plurals

Rule 20: (*a*) Add *s* to form the plural of most nouns.

> bird—birds   lamp—lamps
> tree—trees   desk—desks

(*b*) Add *es* if the noun ends in *s*, *sh*, *ch*, or *x*.

> class—classes   inch—inches   Jones—Joneses
> dish—dishes   box—boxes

Rule 21: (*a*) If the noun ends in *y* preceded by a *consonant*, change the *y* to *i* and add *es*.

> city—cities   lady—ladies
> liberty—liberties   melody—melodies

(*b*) If the noun ends in *y* preceded by a *vowel*, add *s*.

> essay—essays   journey—journeys
> monkey—monkeys   survey—surveys

Exception: words ending in -*quy*, as soliloquy—soliloquies.

Rule 22: (*a*) If the noun ends in *o* preceded by a *vowel*, add *s*.

> cameo—cameos   studio—studios
> radio—radios   ratio—ratios
> folio—folios   patio—patios

(*b*) If the noun ends in *o* preceded by a *consonant*, the situation is as follows:

(1) Some nouns take *es*.

potato—potatoes	echo—echoes
tomato—tomatoes	veto—vetoes

(2) Some nouns take *s* only.

piano—pianos	silo—silos	soprano—sopranos
dynamo—dynamos	solo—solos	alto—altos

(3) Some nouns take either *s* or *es*.

cargo—cargos, cargoes	domino—dominos, dominoes
motto—mottos, mottoes	tornado—tornados, tornadoes
buffalo—buffalos, buffaloes	zero—zeros, zeroes

Rule 23: Add *s* to most nouns ending in *f*.

brief—briefs	belief—beliefs	sheriff—sheriffs
proof—proofs	staff—staffs	chief—chiefs

Exceptions: Change *f* or *fe* to *v* and add *es* in the following:

leaf—leaves	wife—wives	wolf—wolves
knife—knives	half—halves	self—selves
life—lives	thief—thieves	

But not in the case of a name: Mr. Wolf—the Wolfs.

EXERCISE 17. Write the plural of each word below.

1. spy	8. turkey	15. potato
2. wife	9. convoy	16. shelf
3. eyelash	10. yourself	17. birch
4. portfolio	11. hostess	18. fox
5. attorney	12. rodeo	19. tariff
6. handkerchief	13. Burns	20. alley
7. tomato	14. ally	21. piano

Rule 24: In compound words, make the principal word plural.

        mother-in-law   mothers-in-law
        passerby   passersby

Exception A. If there is no noun in the compound word, add *s* to the end of the word.

        takeoff   takeoffs
        mix-up   mix-ups

Exception B. If the compound ends in *ful*, add *s* to the end of the word.

        cupful   cupfuls

Rule 25: (*a*) In the following, form the plural by changing the spelling, rather than by adding *s* or *es*.

foot—feet	mouse—mice	man—men
tooth—teeth	goose—geese	woman—women
louse—lice	child—children	ox—oxen

(*b*) In the following, use the same spelling for the plural as for the singular: deer, swine, series, sheep, moose, species.

Also, Portuguese (and other nationalities ending in *ese*)

(*c*) Study these foreign plurals:

        alumnus—alumni   criterion—criteria
        alumna—alumnae   stimulus—stimuli
        bacterium—bacteria

EXERCISE 18. Write the plural of each word below.

1. sister-in-law	6. criterion	11. louse
2. fireman	7. Vietnamese	12. frame-up
3. mouthful	8. Commander in Chief	13. attorney-at-law
4. sheep	9. hanger-on	14. alumnus
5. series	10. spoonful	15. moose

Forming Possessives

Rule 26: To form the possessive of singular nouns, add an apostrophe and *s*.

SINGULAR NOUNS	POSSESSIVE
boy	boy's hat
friend	friend's book
child	child's toy
James	James's mother

Rule 27: To form the possessive of plural nouns ending in *s*, add the apostrophe alone after the *s*.

PLURAL NOUNS	POSSESSIVE CASE
girls	girls' lockers
ladies	ladies' dresses
students	students' projects
players	players' averages

Rule 28: To form the possessive of plural nouns that do not end in *s*, add the apostrophe and *s*.

PLURAL NOUNS	POSSESSIVE CASE
men	men's clothes
women	women's handbags
mice	mice's tails
sheep	sheep's wool

Rule 29: To form the possessive of (*a*) a compound noun, (*b*) a business name, or (*c*) a joint owner, put the apostrophe and *s* after the last word.

(*a*) brother-in-law	brother-in-law's age
(*b*) Lord and Taylor	Lord and Taylor's prices
(*c*) Gilbert and Sullivan	Gilbert and Sullivan's operettas

Note: Possessive pronouns (*yours, his, hers, its, ours, theirs,* and *whose*) do *not* require an apostrophe.

That boat is *ours* (not *our's*).
That dog is *hers* (not *her's*).
Her hair lost *its* (not *it's*) gloss.

But:

It's all over. (Here *it's* is correct because it means *it is*, the apostrophe standing for the missing *i*.)

EXERCISE 19. Reduce each of the following to fewer words by using a possessive form.

Example: the work done by Gerald: *Gerald's work*

1. the cats belonging to our neighbor
2. the mark Phyllis received
3. an experiment done by Frank and George
4. novels written by Dickens
5. the troops of the enemy
6. styles for teenagers
7. a pen belonging to somebody
8. the competitors of Barnes and Noble
9. duties of police officers
10. the business owned by her father-in-law
11. entertainment for an hour
12. the reputation of the class
13. fees charged by physicians
14. the rights that belong to everyone
15. the nest where the mice lived
16. the importance of it
17. the desk of the editor in chief
18. a trip lasting a day
19. wages earned by a laborer
20. the speech given by Charles
21. food for the babies
22. the garage owned by the Smiths
23. supplies for a week
24. the responsibilities of the pupils
25. the flight of the Wright brothers

B. WATCH YOUR PRONUNCIATION

Careless pronunciation often results in careless spelling. If you have been misspelling any of the words below, it is most likely the result of your leaving out a sound or inserting one that doesn't belong. Form the habit of pronouncing these words correctly (check with the dictionary) and you will have no trouble in spelling them correctly.

1. Do not carelessly omit an unstressed vowel.

bound*a*ry	lab*o*ratory	temp*e*rature
choc*o*late	min*i*ature	veg*e*table
di*a*mond	monot*o*nous	veter*i*narian
int*e*resting	orig*i*nal	visu*a*lize

2. Do not carelessly omit an unstressed syllable.

accident*a*lly   incident*a*lly   super*in*tendent

3. Do not carelessly omit a required consonant.

Arc*t*ic	enviro*n*ment	quan*t*ity
can*d*idate	Feb*r*uary	recog*n*ize
dip*h*theria	gover*n*ment	represen*t*ative
dip*h*thong	lib*r*ary	su*r*prise
eig*h*th	proba*b*ly	sym*p*tom

4. Do not carelessly insert an unnecessary vowel between the two letters in italics.

at*hl*etics	*for*ty	pro*nun*ciation
bur*gl*ar	hin*dr*ance	remem*br*ance
chi*mn*ey	jewe*lr*y	sche*du*le
disas*tr*ous	ligh*tn*ing	um*br*ella
encum*br*ance	mischie*v*ous	won*dr*ous

EXERCISE 20. Write correctly the misspelled word in each group.

1. unnoticeable, bigger, pronounciation, superseded, height
2. original, cupsful, differed, besieging, overpaid
3. benefited, pursuing, library, withheld, specificly
4. proceeded, ninety, clumsiest, government, probaly
5. fourty-four, sleigh, unforeseeable, preference, management
6. leisure, disasterous, tying, unpaid, excellence
7. skiing, barrenness, supprised, canoeing, remittance
8. eigth, ladylike, de-emphasized, pianos, boundary
9. lonelier, monkeys, argument, bacterias, disbelieved
10. candidate, awful, does'nt, denial, exceedingly

C. STUDY UNPHONETIC WORDS

An unphonetic word is one that is spelled differently from the way it sounds.

1. Silent letters. The following words have a letter that is not pronounced. Be sure to include that letter in your spelling.

silent *b:* clim*b*, com*b*, crum*b*, de*b*t, dou*b*t, dum*b*, plum*b*er, redou*b*table, su*b*poena, su*b*tle, thum*b*, undou*b*tedly

silent *c:* a*c*quaint, a*c*quire, a*c*quit, as*c*ertain, corpus*c*le, *c*zar, des*c*end, fas*c*inate, indi*c*t, mis*c*ellaneous, mus*c*le, s*c*ent, s*c*issors

silent *d:* a*d*join, a*d*just (and all other *adj-* words), han*d*kerchief

silent *g:* ali*g*n, desi*g*n, diaphra*g*m, *g*narled, *g*naw, *g*nome

silent *h:* ex*h*aust, ex*h*ibit, ex*h*ilaration, fore*h*ead, *g*hastly, *g*hetto, *g*host, ging*h*am, *h*eir, *h*erb, r*h*etoric, r*h*eumatism, r*h*yme, r*h*ythm, shep*h*erd, spag*h*etti, ve*h*icle

silent *k:* ac*k*nowledge, *k*nack, *k*nob, (and all other *kn-* words)

silent *l:* a*l*mond, ba*l*m, ca*l*m, fo*l*k, ha*l*f, sa*l*mon, ta*l*k, wa*l*k

silent *m:* *m*nemonic

silent *n:* autum*n*, colum*n*, condem*n*, hym*n*, solem*n*

silent *p:* corp*s* (the *s* is silent too), cu*p*board, em*p*ty, *p*neumatic, *p*neumonia, *p*salm, *p*seudonym, *p*sychology

silent *s:* ai*s*le, corp*s* (the *p* is silent too), debri*s*, i*s*land, li*s*le, Loui*s*ville, rendezvou*s*, vi*s*count

silent *t:* bankrup*t*cy, Chris*t*mas, lis*t*en, mor*t*gage, mus*t*n't, stre*t*ch, whis*t*le, wres*t*le

silent *u:* body*g*uard, ga*u*ge, g*u*arantee, g*u*ardian, g*u*ess, g*u*est, g*u*ide, lifeg*u*ard

silent *w:* ans*w*er, play*w*right, s*w*ord, t*w*o, *w*hole, *w*rap, *w*rite (and all other *wr-* words)

2. *-ain* words. Review these words, in which the sound *-in* is spelled *-ain:*

Brit*ain*	cert*ain*	curt*ain*	porcel*ain*
capt*ain*	chieft*ain*	mount*ain*	vill*ain*

3. *e*, not *i*. Observe that in these words there is an *e* where you might expect an *i*:

beaut*e*ous	extemporan*e*ous	met*e*or
Caribb*e*an	hid*e*ous	naus*e*ate
court*e*ous	liqu*e*fy	pit*e*ous
delin*e*ate	mall*e*able	simultan*e*ous

4. *-cian* words. End the word with *-cian* (not *-tian*) if you can trace it to an *-ic* word:

electri*cian* (from electr*ic*)	opti*cian* (from opt*ic*)
logi*cian* (from log*ic*)	pediatri*cian* (from pediatr*ic*)
magi*cian* (from mag*ic*)	physi*cian* (from phys*ic*)
mathemati*cian* (from mathemat*ic*s)	politi*cian* (from polit*ic*)
musi*cian* (from mus*ic*)	statisti*cian* (from statist*ic*)

5. *y*, not *i*.

ab*y*ss	h*y*pocrisy	s*y*mphony
anal*y*ze	paral*y*sis	s*y*nonym
anon*y*mous	s*y*llable	s*y*nopsis
c*y*linder	s*y*mmetry	s*y*nthesis
c*y*nical	s*y*mpathy	t*y*ranny

6. *-ar*, not *-er*.

begg*ar*	burs*ar*	cell*ar*
burgl*ar*	calend*ar*	li*ar*

7. Additional unphonetic words for study. If you are in doubt about the pronunciation of these words, look them up in a dictionary.

biscuit	forfeit	sergeant
bouquet	furlough	sieve
brooch	hiccough	sovereign
buoy	lieutenant	suite
bureau	naïve	surgeon
chamois	naphtha	thorough
colonel	parliament	Wednesday
Connecticut	pigeon	yacht
draught	quay	

EXERCISE 21. Rewrite each word, supplying the missing letter or letters.

1. porcel____n
2. W____day
3. statisti____an
4. s____non____m
5. naus____ting
6. s____geant
7. Carib____an

8. parl____ment
9. l____tenant
10. hic____gh
11. erron____us
12. burgl____r
13. col____nel
14. pediatri____an

15. Conne____cut
16. surg____n
17. politi____ian
18. furl____gh
19. anon____mous
20. delin____te

D. KNOW YOUR HOMONYMS

Homonyms are words that are pronounced alike but are different in meaning and spelling. Be careful to use the spelling required by the context. Review the following:

already, before, previously   The train had *already* left.
all ready, everyone prepared   We are *all ready.*

all together, everyone at one time   We sang the hymn *all together.*
altogether, completely   This is *altogether* wrong.

altar, table-like structure in a place of worship   The bride was led to the *altar.*
(to) alter, (to) change   The captain had to *alter* the ship's course.

ascent, act of rising or mounting   The *ascent* to the 64th floor took a few seconds.
assent, act of agreeing   Indicate your *assent* by saying "aye."

bare, without any covering   They fought with *bare* fists.
(to) bear, 1. (to) endure   Can you *bear* the pain?
   2. large shaggy animal   The zoo has a new polar *bear.*

born, brought into life   When were you *born?*
borne, endured, suffered   These burdens can no longer be *borne.*

brake, device for stopping   The driver stepped on the *brake.*
(to) break, (to) shatter   Don't *break* the dishes!

capital, seat of government   Washington, D.C., is our nation's *capital.*
Capitol, building where the U.S. legislature meets   Congress meets in the *Capitol.*

coarse, rough   The overalls were made of *coarse* cloth.
course, way, path   The Mississippi has often altered its *course*.

complement, full quantity   He has his *complement* of troubles.
compliment, praise   Your work deserves the highest *compliment*.

council, group that advises   Who are the members of the executive's inner *council?*
counsel, advice   Thank you for your good *counsel*.

(to) desert, (to) abandon   Rats *desert* a sinking ship.
dessert, last course of a meal   She had watermelon for *dessert*.

dual, double   Driver-training cars have *dual* controls.
duel, combat between two persons   The rivals fought a *duel*.

(to) hear, (to) perceive by ear   Did you *hear* that noise?
here, in or to this place   Please come *here*.

its, belonging to *it*.   The bird hurt *its* wing.
it's, it is   *It's* too late.

lead, marking substance   I need *lead* for my mechanical pencil.
led, conducted   Firefighters *led* the tenants to safety.

miner, worker in a mine   How much does a coal *miner* earn?
minor, 1. Person under the age of legal responsibility   You are a *minor* if you are under 21.
   2. less important   The composition had one serious fault and several *minor* ones.

passed, went by   We *passed* your house.
past, 1. gone by   You helped us on *past* occasions.
   2. time gone by   You helped us in the *past*.
   3. close to and then beyond   We went *past* your house.

peace, opposite of war   The warring nations were urged to make *peace*.
piece, fragment   Don't step on that *piece* of glass.

principal, 1. main   Broadway is our city's *principal* street.
   2. head of a school   Mr. Brown is our new *principal*.
principle, rule of conduct   He made it a *principle* never to buy what he could not afford.

shone, shined   The moon *shone* brightly.
shown (used after a helping verb), taught   We were *shown* how to add fractions.

their, belonging to *them*   They returned to *their* homes.
there, in or at that place   Have you ever been *there?*
they're, they are   *They're* coming.

to, in the direction of and reaching   Joe walks *to* school.
too, 1. also   I agree and Fred does *too.*
  2. excessively   The room is *too* cold.
two (the number)   It's *two* o'clock.

who's who is   *Who's* there?
whose, belonging to *whom*   *Whose* book is this?

your, belonging to *you*   You must do *your* work.
you're, you are   *You're* altogether right.

The following pairs, though not precisely homonyms, are similar enough to cause confusion:

(to) **accept,** (to) receive with approval   He *accepted* my apology.
(to) **except,** (to) leave out   In granting raises, he *excepted* the newest employees.

advice, recommendation; counsel   What is your *advice?*
(to) **advise,** (to) give advice to   What do you *advise* me to do?

(to) **affect,** (to) influence   Absence may *affect* your mark.
effect, result, outcome   One possible *effect* of absence is a lower mark.

formally, following established custom; conventionally   Certain restaurants insist that their guests be *formally* attired.
formerly, previously   Our principal was *formerly* the dean of boys.

have (helping verb)   He might *have* become rich.
of (preposition)   The rest *of* us went home.

loose, free; not fastened   Who turned the dog *loose?*
(to) **lose,** (to) part with accidentally   How did you *lose* your wallet?

quiet, silent   When the teacher spoke, the room became *quiet.*
quite, completely   By bedtime, the children were *quite* exhausted.

than (conjunction used in comparisons)   My sister is younger *than* I.
then, at that time   Chicago was *then* a small frontier town.

weather, condition of the atmosphere   The *weather* is cloudy.
whether, if it is or was true that   Find out *whether* he agrees or disagrees.

EXERCISE 22. Write the correct choice, and state the reason for your choice.

1. John and Mary wish to go because (their, there, they're) eager to visit the museum.
2. Is that (your, you're) jacket on the floor?
3. Have you successfully (passed, past) all your final examinations?
4. The article describes the (principal, principle) (affects, effects) of the new drug.
5. I expected a (complement, compliment)—not criticism.
6. If you drop this vase, it will (brake, break).
7. Had you listened to my (counsel, council), you would have passed.
8. (Who's Whose) at the door?
9. In the violent storm, the boat broke (loose, lose) from its moorings.
10. We did not realize that the boys' father had forbidden them to keep (there, their, they're) puppy.
11. We want to go to the movies (to, too, two).
12. In the (passed, past) we have always held our commencement exercises in the evening.
13. A true friend will never (desert, dessert) you.
14. It's (already, all ready) past the deadline.
15. The tiny bulb (shown, shone) weakly in the dim hallway.
16. A (minor, miner) cannot vote in public elections.
17. He is taller (then, than) his brother by several inches.
18. She is the girl (who's, whose) poster was chosen for the contest.
19. I was advised to review the (principals, principles) of correct usage.
20. They have (borne, born) these hardships without complaint.
21. The weather forced us to (altar, alter) our plans.
22. (Formally, Formerly), an elderly couple lived here.
23. From the base of the mountain to the halfway point, the (assent, ascent) is not too difficult.
24. She was (quite, quiet) breathless from running upstairs.
25. Macbeth was afraid he would (loose, lose) his crown to one of Banquo's descendants.
26. There were fewer candidates (then, than) we had been (led, lead) to expect.
27. Your interpretation of the results of the test is (all together, altogether) inaccurate.
28. The (peace, piece) of string is too short.

29. Albany is the (Capitol, capital) of New York State.
30. Unfortunately, I am unable to (accept, except) your kind invitation.
31. The (dual, duel) was to have taken place at dawn.
32. How will the new tax (effect, affect) your business?
33. The reward must (have, of) pleased them very much.
34. The horse lifted (its, it's) head and snorted.
35. My English teacher gave me ample opportunity to make up for (passed, past) mistakes.
36. You have been (led, lead) astray by your own carelessness.
37. Homeowners say they are already (baring, bearing) very heavy tax burdens.
38. What (course, coarse) of action do you suggest?
39. We could not learn (weather, whether) they had arrived or not.
40. I (advice, advise) you not to do it.
41. The reply was loud enough for everyone to (hear, here).
42. Doing a task promptly is better (than, then) worrying about it.
43. It's (your, you're) turn to drive now, if you're ready.
44. The alumni have announced that (their, there, they're) sending a representative to our graduation.
45. You should (of, have) been in the assembly yesterday.
46. What is the (effect, affect) of sunlight on plants?
47. Tell me (who's, whose) on third base; I don't recognize him.
48. On her doctor's (advice, advise), she resumed a full program of physical activities.
49. The dog wagged (its, it's) tail and barked happily.
50. The merchant promised to refund my money if I were not (all together, altogether) satisfied.

E. INVENT MNEMONICS

A *mnemonic* (the first *m* is silent) is a trick of association that helps you to remember. The following mnemonics may help you remember when the correct spelling is *principle* and when it is *principal*. (The associated or similar elements have been italicized.)

1. A princip*le* is a ru*le*.
2. A princi*pal* (the head of a school) ought to be a *pal*.
3. A princip*al* street is a m*ain* street.

When you have unusual difficulty in spelling a word, try to invent a mnemonic. No matter how farfetched or ridiculous the association may be, if it can help you spell correctly, it is a good mnemonic. Here are some additional mnemonics that have proved helpful:

WORD	MNEMONIC DEVICE
beginning	the beg*inning* of the *inning*
believe	Don't be*lie*ve that *lie!*
calendar	Janu*ar*y and Febru*ar*y are in the calend*ar*.
friend	a fri*end* to the *end*
parallel	*All* rails are par*all*el.
piece	a *piece* of *pie*
privilege	It is a pr*i*v*i*l*e*ge to have two eyes (*i*'s) and a *leg*.
pronunciation	The *nun*'s pro*nun*ciation is excellent.
stationary	Station*a*ry means st*a*nding still.
stationery	Station*e*ry is writing pap*e*r.
there	*There*, *here*, *where* all refer to place.

F. FOLLOW RECOMMENDED STUDY PROCEDURES

When you study a new word, carefully follow this step-by-step method:

1. Pronounce the word. Use it correctly in a sentence.
2. See the word. Say it by syllables. Say the letters in order.
3. Close your eyes and spell the word mentally. Check your spelling to be sure that it is correct.
4. Write the word correctly. Form every letter carefully, especially *i*'s and *e*'s, *a*'s, and *o*'s.
5. Cover the word and write it once more. If the spelling is correct, cover the word and write it again.
6. If you make a mistake during step 5, repeat the previous steps before repeating step 5.

G. STUDY COMMONLY MISSPELLED WORDS

1. One Hundred Spelling Demons

ache	done	making	they
again	don't	many	though
always	early	meant	through
among	easy	minute	tired
answer	enough	much	tonight
any	every	none	too
been	February	often	trouble
beginning	forty	once	truly
believe	friend	piece	Tuesday
blue	grammar	raise	two
break	guess	read	used
built	half	ready	very
business	having	said	wear
busy	hear	says	Wednesday
buy	heard	seems	week
can't	here	separate	where
choose	hoarse	shoes	whether
color	hour	since	which
coming	instead	some	whole
cough	just	straight	women
could	knew	sugar	won't
country	know	sure	would
dear	laid	tear	write
doctor	loose	their	writing
does	lose	there	wrote

2. Words With Troublesome Consonants

Doubled Consonant Followed by Single Consonant

a*cc*e*l*erate	ci*nn*a*m*on	i*nn*o*c*uous
a*cc*u*m*ulate	co*ll*a*t*eral	i*rr*e*l*evant
a*ll*i*t*eration	co*mm*e*m*orate	mo*cc*a*s*in
a*ll*o*t*ment	co*rr*e*l*ation	o*cc*a*s*ion
a*pp*are*l*	co*rr*i*d*or	para*ll*e*l*
a*ss*i*m*ilate	co*rr*o*b*orate	pi*cc*o*l*o
bro*cc*o*l*i	gui*ll*o*t*ine	scu*rr*i*l*ous
bu*ll*e*t*in	i*mm*a*c*ulate	va*cc*i*n*ate

Single Consonant Followed by Doubled Consonant

beginning	necessary	recurrent
Caribbean	omitted	Renaissance
dilemma	penicillin	sheriff
dilettante	Philippine	tariff
harass	professional	tomorrow
Mediterranean	rebellion	tyranny
metallic	recommend	vacillate

Doubled Consonant Followed by Another Doubled Consonant

accessible	assessment	misspell
accommodate	committee	possession
aggression	connoisseur	reconnaissance
assassinate	embarrass	Tennessee

3. Words from Past Examinations for Study or Review

abbreviate	adversely	anesthetic	arbitrary
abominable	advisable	anniversary	architecture
abscess	affirmative	announcement	arguing
absence	aggravate	annual	argument
absolutely	aggregate	anonymous	arouse
abyss	agitation	anthology	article
academic	allocated	anticipate	artificial
acceptable	allotted	antique	ascending
accidentally	allowance	antonym	ascertain
accompanying	alphabetical	anxious	assailant
accuracy	amateur	apartment	assassination
achievement	ambassador	apologetic	assistance
acknowledge	ambiguous	apology	assurance
acquaintance	amendment	apparatus	athletic
acquisition	ammunition	apparently	attendant
adage	amplify	appetite	audience
adequate	analysis	appraisal	auspicious
adjacent	anatomy	apprehension	authentic
adjournment	ancestor	appropriation	auxiliary
adjustment	ancestry	approximately	average
admittance	anchored	aquarium	aversion
advantageous	anecdote	aquatic	awkward

bachelor
balloon
banana
bankruptcy
barbecue
bargain
beautifully
belief
beneficial
benefit
besieged
betrayal
biased
bibliography
bicycle
bigamy
bituminous
blizzard
bolster
bookkeeping
boulevard
boundary
boycotted
brilliance
budget
bureau
burglaries

cafeteria
calendar
callous
callus
campaign
candidacy
capacity
capsule
carburetor
career
carnival

carriage
casualty
category
cathedral
caucus
cauliflower
cavalry
ceiling
celebration
celebrity
cellar
cellophane
cemetery
certainly
challenge
champagne
chancellor
changeable
charitable
chauffeur
cholera
choosing
civilian
clearance
collegiate
combustible
comedy
commandant
commercial
commitment
committing
comparative
comparison
competent
competition
competitor
compulsory
computer
concentrate
concerning

conclusively
condemned
confectionery
conferring
confidential
congratulate
congressional
conscientious
conscious
consequently
conservatory
consonant
conspicuous
constant
contemptuous
continuous
controversial
convenience
conveyance
copyright
cordial
coronation
coroner
corporal
corpuscle
corrugated
countenance
courageous
criminal
criticism
criticize
cruelty
curiosity
cylinder

debtor
deceitful
decided

defendant
defense
deferred
definite
delegate
deliberate
delicacy
delicious
delinquent
delirious
deluge
descendant
description
desirous
despise
destruction
deteriorate
detrimental
diagnosis
dilapidated
dimension
dirigible
disagreeable
disappeared
disappoint
disapprove
discernible
disciplinary
discouragement
disease
disillusioned
disintegrate
dispatch
disperse
dissatisfied
dissolve
distinguished
dormitory
dramatize
duped

earnest	extracurricular	grammar	immovable
ecstasy	extraordinary	graphics	implement
eighth	extravagant	grateful	inadequate
elaborate	extricate	grease	inaugural
eligible		greenness	inconceivable
eliminate		guarantee	incredible
elliptical	familiarize	guardian	indebtedness
embarrass	fascinate		indefinite
embassies	fatiguing		independence
emperor	feasible	handicapped	indifferent
emphasis	feminine	handkerchief	individual
encourage	feminist	handwriting	inefficient
encyclopedia	fertile	heaviness	influential
engagement	fervent	height	information
enormous	fickle	hemorrhage	ingenuity
entertaining	fictitious	hereditary	ingredients
enthusiastic	fiendish	heritage	initiative
entitled	fierce	heroes	inquiry
entrance	filial	hoping	institute
envelope	finally	humiliate	instrumental
environment	fiscal	humorous	insurance
epidemic	flexible	hundredth	integrity
equipment	forecast	hurricane	intelligence
equipping	forehead	hybrid	intelligible
escapade	foreign	hypnotize	intensified
essentially	foremost	hypocrisy	intercede
evaporate	foreshadow		interchangeable
exaggerate	foresight		interfered
exceedingly	forfeit	icing	interpretation
excellent	fortunately	icy	interrogative
excitement	forty-fourth	identity	interrupt
exercise	frostbitten	illegally	interview
exhausted		illegible	intimate
exhaustion		illiterate	intriguing
exhibition	gadget	illness	irresistible
existence	gallery	illogical	irresponsible
expedition	gardener	imagination	
expense	gaseous	imitate	
explanation	ghetto	immature	jealousy
exquisite	gracefulness	immediately	jeopardy

journal	mattress	nonsense	parachute
journeying	maximize	notary	paradise
juvenile	meanness	noticeable	paradoxical
	medallion	notoriety	parallel
	medicine	nourishment	paralysis
keenness	medieval	nuclear	parliament
kindergarten	memorandum	nucleus	partially
kindliness	merchandise	nuisance	peaceable
	merely		peculiarity
	metaphor		pedigree
laboratory	metropolitan	obliterate	peninsula
larceny	microphone	oblivious	pennant
lavender	millimeter	obnoxious	perforated
legend	millionaire	obstacle	performance
legendary	minimum	obstinate	permanent
legitimate	misappropriate	occasional	permissible
leisure	mischievous	occupancy	persevere
liability	misdemeanor	occurrence	personnel
librarian	misinterpreted	offense	perspire
license	missile	offering	physical
lieutenant	missionary	official	physician
literally	Mississippi	omitted	pianos
loneliness	misunderstood	onomatopoeia	picnicking
loyalty	monkeys	opponents	piercing
lubricant	mortified	opportunity	pleasant
luxury	municipal	oppression	poise
	murderer	optimistic	poisonous
	murmuring	orbit	politician
magnificent	musical	ordinarily	porcelain
maintain	mystery	organization	postponed
maintenance		original	poultice
management		ornament	poultry
maneuver	narrative	orphaned	practical
manually	negative	outrageous	prairie
marmalade	negligible	overrule	preceding
marriage	neither		precious
masquerade	neutral		precipice
massacre	niece	pageant	predecessor
masterpiece	nineteenth	pamphlet	predominant
mathematics	ninety	papal	prefabricate

preface
preference
preferred
prejudice
preliminary
preparation
pretense
prevalent
primarily
prisoner
privacy
privilege
proceedings
proclamation
professor
proficiency
projectile
prominent
promissory
promptness
propaganda
proprietor
prosperous
psychology
publicity
purchase

quandary
quizzes

rabid
rearmament
rearrangement
rebelled
rebuttal
reciprocate
recognize
recommendation

reconciliation
recruit
recurring
referee
refrigerator
regardless
regretting
rehabilitate
rehearsal
relieve
religious
relinquish
renewal
repetitious
replacement
resemblance
reservoir
resistance
responsible
restaurant
revival
rewriting
rheumatism
rhythm
ridiculous
righteous
routine

sacrifice
safety
salaries
sandwich
satellite
saucy
scandal
scarcity
scenery
schedule
scissors

séance
secretarial
seize
seizure
seldom
senatorial
sequence
session
settlement
severity
sieges
sieve
similar
simile
simultaneous
sincerity
softening
soliciting
solos
soluble
sophisticated
sophomore
specific
spectacle
spectacular
spiral
sponsor
standard
standardize
statistics
strategy
stretcher
stubborn
stunning
submitting
subsidy
substantial
successful
suffrage
superb

superintendent
supremacy
surgeon
surgery
surprising
suspense
syllable
symbolize
symptom
synonym

telegram
television
temperature
temporary
tendency
testimony
tomatoes
tragedy
tragic
transferred
transition
transparent
treachery
tremendous
trophies
troupe
truthfulness
turkeys
twelfth

umbrella
unbearable
unconscious
uncontrollable
undecided
unmanageable

unrelieved	vegetable	villain	warrior
unscheduled	vegetarian	vinegar	weird
unveiling	vehicle	virtue	whistle
utensil	vengeance	visibility	wield
	vertical	visualize	windshield
	vicinity	volume	witnessed
vacant	victim	voluble	wrestling
vacuum	viewpoint	volunteer	
valuable	village	vulgar	yield

Former Comprehensive English Spelling Tests

Directions (31–40): In each of the following groups of words, only one of the words is misspelled. In *each* group, select the misspelled word and spell it correctly in the space provided on the separate answer sheet. [5]

Test 1

31. changeable   monarch   mortifyed   legislator   genetics
32. schedule   recruit   heir   parachute   temperture
33. grammer   truly   ceiling   bargain   physician
34. argument   recesive   belief   submission   convenient
35. edition   ninth   guarantee   utterence   urban
36. delagate   fluent   inferiority   maximum   perilous
37. glorious   fatallity   efficiency   reluctance   capable
38. innocence   calendar   abdominible   harassment   deceitful
39. biscuit   forbidden   spectacular   apologies   femenist
40. obnoxous   whistle   volunteer   yacht   villain

Test 2

31. cafeteria   patron   amateur   perceive   pledgeing
32. requirement   financial   accesory   government   college

33. approxamate mirror destroy disregard promising
34. sincerely discern wrangle truely audiovisual
35. tomatoes purity negligent dramatize plentifull
36. theoretical seige volcano innocence dexterity
37. tommorrow reluctant shady unveil lightning
38. auction lenient prejudice sculpter originally
39. rhapsody perplex obtuse mortgage quandery
40. friendless hundreth singular channel attitude

Test 3

31. missile propelled beautefy spirited spectacles
32. spaghetti missionery twelfth vegetable stifle
33. corrode hygiene irrelevant asociate maintenance
34. monogram minister criticle frequency genuine
35. introduce thematic economy valuable laboror
36. precede defalt heathen attain conscious
37. greivance chivalry scary obscure pastime
38. assurance immoderate patriotism combustible stressfull
39. inginuity legitimate schedule accompanying substantial
40. grafics merger global sensitive exhibit

Test 4

31. pierce irritible ceiling portfolio hereditary
32. meanness anxious challange grief priority
33. anouncement politeness routine dependable bashful
34. scold pigeon transistor stomach decietful
35. antibiotic exagerate anticipation heavily essential
36. embarrass friendly diameter quite anguler
37. suffix persuade morgage exclusive pertinent

38. prologue gaseous stallion indevisible erroneous
39. acquarium tireless starred fried porous
40. innocent automatic reign primative substitute

Test 5

31. satisfactory deceived existence anceint resolving
32. scandalize conferred aptitude spirited assurred
33. convenient already savage acheivement schedule
34. intercede cashier leisurely barameter interrelated
35. brittle freight rigidity tobacco excellance
36. ballet biscuit whimsecal inertia endeavor
37. intentionally mysterious nickel indicisive guarantee
38. occurred calendar sophmore extension prevail
39. truant syllabus justifyable peasant library
40. recomendation unanimous symmetrical manageable necessity

Test 6

31. artillery patriotism fiery avalanche lieing
32. glossery omitted noticeable gaseous loveless
33. convocation particularly prevailing recollect impressonable
34. incompetent hereditery medicinal sustained turmoil
35. forgetting argument apparantly secrecy monopoly
36. against furthermore brief explore unanamous
37. suspision formerly opportunity concentrate intelligent
38. league analyze bribery usully straighten
39. rediculous recommend vengeance cemetery library
40. mountain percentage manageable unisen truly

The Reading Comprehension Test
[20 credits]

A Battle of Wits

The reading comprehension test is a battle of wits between the Board of Regents and you, and—believe it or not—it is a battle that they want you to win. They will never ask you a reading comprehension question without providing evidence in the reading passage, stated or implied, that can guide you to the correct answer. The evidence is always there; they challenge you to find it and to use it intelligently.

SUGGESTION: Jot down your answers to questions 41–60 of the following sample test. We will be going into these questions thoroughly, one by one, to help you learn some things you may not know about how to find the right answers.

TYPICAL READING COMPREHENSION TEST

Directions (41–60): Below each of the following passages, there are several incomplete statements or questions about the passage. For *each*, select the word or expression that best completes the statement or answers the question *in accordance with the meaning of the passage*, and write its *number* in the space provided on the separate answer sheet.   [20]

Passage A

On weekdays, when Mrs. Willoughby and her daughter, Miss Joanne, were alone, they took their lunch on trays in the drawing room, and after my mother had cleared up and washed the kitchen, the hour and a half till teatime was her own. My mother tells me that all morning she would plan what she
5   might do with it. She wanted to write to me; she wanted to write to her parents, and she must get a letter off to the Refugee Committee in London

to find a sponsor for them; she wanted to take a bath; she wanted to walk in the fresh air; she wanted to study her English, for she found herself too exhausted at night after cooking, serving, and clearing up from dinner; she
10 needed to sleep an hour, but my father had gone to lie down upstairs and what she needed above all was to be alone. She sat at the kitchen table, aware of her leisure slipping away. She kept looking at the clock, calculating how much time she still had before preparing the tea tray. One afternoon, the door opened and Miss Joanne came through the kitchen, trailing grass and
15 hay from the stables. She dropped a dirty blouse into the sink and went out again, leaving both doors open. This caused a draft where my mother sat, and my mother got up and slammed the door behind the girl. Then she was sorry. She remembered how she had disliked the ill-natured maids in her mother's house, who fussed over their clean floors. She remembered that she
20 owed these people her life. She went to the sink and washed Miss Joanne's blouse and starched it; then, angry at herself for this servile act, she went to the china closet, took out Mrs. Willoughby's best Minton, and made herself some powerful Viennese coffee. She tasted the delicate fluted china between her lips, half afraid that Mrs. Willoughby might come in and catch her, half
25 wishing that she would. My mother wanted to make herself known to the other woman.

—Lore Segal

41. According to the narrator, what did her mother wish most to do in the afternoon?   (1) read a book   (2) plan for the future   (3) have her tea   (4) enjoy some privacy

42. From the description in lines 1 through 12, the mother could best be described as feeling   (1) anxious   (2) enthusiastic   (3) incompetent   (4) important

43. Miss Joanne's actions reveal behavior that could be described as   (1) thoughtless   (2) foolish   (3) stubborn   (4) impulsive

44. The passage implies that the mother's family had once been   (1) famous   (2) influential   (3) charitable   (4) well-to-do

45. The phrase "servile act" in line 21 refers to   (1) disliking the maids   (2) slamming the door   (3) laundering the blouse   (4) making the coffee

46. The narrator develops the mother's character and personality by   (1) quoting her conversations   (2) describing her work habits   (3) revealing her thoughts   (4) explaining her daydreams

47. The tone of this passage could best be described as   (1) sympathetic   (2) critical   (3) resigned   (4) tolerant

Passage B

Thermometer Wine

Always hung on its plaque
on the porch like a mounted
icicle, but was so old
already the painted numbers
5   were peeling and hard to read.
Only Daddy could tell
the measurements—he'd known
the instrument since a boy.
At ten below it really
10   meant twenty, being slow
with age, he said. At
ten above it was roughly
accurate, but on a hot day
he added twenty to its reading.
15   I watched the red needle
rise in the dog days and
marveled how the tiny
hair was both sensitive
and significant.
20   The blood rose in that stem
just a capillary of
bright, as though the day
were sipping through its ice
straw that special wine,
25   and about to taste the
color from the drop at
the bottom that never clotted
or dulled no matter how
far up or down it wrote,
30   always chilled as snake or worm.

—Robert Morgan

48. Which aspect of the thermometer is alluded to in the phrase "Always
. . . icicle" (lines 1 through 3)? (1) its size (2) its permanence
(3) its worth (4) its accuracy

49. In line 16, the phrase "dog days" refers to a time when the temperature is (1) steady (2) unmeasurable (3) high (4) erratic

50. Which lines contain an example of personification? (1) lines 6 and 7 (2) lines 2 and 3 (3) lines 15 and 16 (4) lines 22 through 24

51. The mercury in the thermometer is compared to each of the following *except* (1) a hair (2) an icicle (3) a capillary (4) wine

52. The narrator suggests that the "color from the drop at the bottom" (lines 26 and 27) might be tasted by the (1) narrator (2) father (3) day (4) needle

53. In which form is the poem written? (1) blank verse (2) free verse (3) couplets (4) quatrains

Passage C

The Big Tree (*Sequoia gigantea*) is nature's forest masterpiece and, as far as I know, the greatest of living things. It belongs to an ancient stock, as its remains in old rocks show, and has a strange air of other days about it, a thoroughbred look inherited from the long ago, the *auld lang syne* of trees.
5 Once the genus was common, and with many species flourished in the now-desolate Arctic regions, in the interior of North America, and in Europe; but in long eventful wanderings from climate to climate only two species have survived the hardships they had to encounter, the *gigantea* and *sempervirens*: the former now restricted to the western slope of the Sierra, the other to the
10 Coast Mountains, and both to California, excepting a few groves of redwood which extend into Oregon.

The Pacific coast in general is the paradise of conifers. Here nearly all of them are giants and display a beauty and magnificence unknown elsewhere. The climate is mild, the ground never freezes, and moisture and sunshine
15 abound all the year. Nevertheless, it is not easy to account for the colossal size of the sequoias. The largest are about three hundred feet high and thirty feet in diameter. Who of all the dwellers of the plains and prairies and fertile home forests of round-headed oak and maple, hickory and elm, ever dreamed that earth could bear such growths? Sequoias are trees that the familiar pines
20 and firs seem to know nothing about, lonely, silent, serene, with an appearance almost godlike, and so old that thousands of them still living had already counted their years by tens of centuries when Columbus set sail from Spain, and were in the vigor of youth or middle age at the time of the birth of Jesus of Nazareth. As far as humanity is concerned, they are the same
25 yesterday, today, and forever, emblems of permanence.

—John Muir

54. The use of the phrase "ancient stock" in line 2 suggests that sequoias (1) have a firmly established heritage   (2) had no natural enemies (3) were originally imported   (4) were probably planted by Native Americans

55. The author suggests that the suvival of sequoias was greatly affected by   (1) environmental   difficulties   (2) industrial   expansion (3) cosmic forces   (4) human settlements

56. The author characterizes the Pacific coast as being   (1) rich in history (2) varied in climate   (3) abundant in animal life   (4) nurturing to some plants

57. The author characterizes the sequoias' exceptional growth as (1) mysterious   (2) seasonal   (3) completed   (4) uncontrollable

58. The author suggests that the most probable reaction to seeing a giant sequoia   would   be   (1) fear   (2) disbelief   (3) indifference (4) envy

59. In lines 17 through 19, the narrator makes his point through the use of (1) order of importance   (2) an extended metaphor   (3) a rhetorical question   (4) cause and effect

60. In lines 24 and 25, the author suggests that people consider sequoias to be   (1) vulnerable   (2) endearing   (3) beneficial   (4) eternal

HOW YOU COULD HAVE FOUND THE CORRECT ANSWERS TO THE TYPICAL READING TEST

The purpose of the following is to give you a model of reasoning for finding answers to reading questions. Next to each question below is the correct answer to each question on our sample test, together with supporting evidence.

Passage A (Questions 41–47)

QUESTION 41:   ANSWER 4 (enjoy some privacy)

EVIDENCE: The narrator states, "and what she (the mother) needed above all was **to be alone**" (line 11).

QUESTION 42: ANSWER 1 (anxious)

EVIDENCE: Lines 4–11 reveal the overworked mother's feeling of anxiety over not being able to take care of her numerous personal concerns in the little time she has for herself. Note, too, that nothing in the passage suggests that she feels **enthusiastic, incompetent,** or **important.**

QUESTION 43: ANSWER 1 (thoughtless)

EVIDENCE: Line 17, which describes Miss Joanne as "the girl," suggests that she is just a child. Her actions—coming into the clean kitchen trailing grass and hay, and creating a draft by leaving without closing the doors—are the actions of a thoughtless child. In an adult, such behavior could be described as **foolish,** but she is not an adult. There is nothing in the passage to suggest that Miss Joanne did these things because she was **stubborn** or **impulsive.**

QUESTION 44: ANSWER 4 (well-to-do)

EVIDENCE: Note the statement "she (the mother) remembered how she had disliked the ill-natured maids in her mother's house" (lines 18–19). It implies that the mother's family was prosperous enough to employ more than one servant.

QUESTION 45: ANSWER 3 (laundering the blouse)

EVIDENCE: The phrase **servile** (demeaningly subservient) **act** (line 21) refers to the mother's going to the sink and washing and starching Miss Joanne's blouse (line 20).

QUESTION 46: ANSWER 3 (revealing her thoughts)

EVIDENCE: Nowhere in the passage does the narrator quote the mother's conversations or explain her daydreams. She does describe some of the work the mother does, but she does not describe her work habits. What she does do throughout the passage, and especially in lines 4–13 and 17–26, is reveal the mother's thoughts.

QUESTION 47: ANSWER 1 (sympathetic)

EVIDENCE: **Tone** is the author's attitude toward his or her subject. In this passage, the author's mother is the subject. By focusing on the mother's numerous problems (lines 4–13) and her exhausting job (lines 3, 8–9, 13, 20), the author shows sympathy for the mother. The hints of a tragic upheaval in the mother's life in lines 5–8 and 18–21 are further evidence of the author's sympathetic attitude.

Passage B (Questions 48–53)

QUESTION 48: ANSWER 2 (its permanence)

EVIDENCE: **Permanence** is the condition of being **always** in existence.

QUESTION 49: ANSWER 3 (high)

EVIDENCE: "I watched the needle **rise** (go high) in the dog days" (lines 15–16).

QUESTION 50: ANSWER 4 (lines 22 through 24)

EVIDENCE: **Personification** is a poetic device which attributes human characteristics to nonhuman objects or ideas. In the lines 22–24, the **day,** which is nonhuman, is personified when it is portrayed as **sipping** something through a straw.

QUESTION 51: ANSWER 2 (an icicle)

EVIDENCE: The mercury in the thermometer is compared to a "hair" (line 18), a "capillary" (line 21), and "wine" (line 24), but not to an icicle. What, then, is it that is compared to an icicle? The answer is the thing that "always hung on its plaque on the porch," namely, the thermometer itself.

QUESTION 52: ANSWER 3 (day)

EVIDENCE: "...as though the **day** were sipping through its ice straw...and about to taste the color from the drop at the bottom..." (lines 22–27).

QUESTION 53:   ANSWER 2 (free verse)

EVIDENCE: Note the following characteristics of this poem: First, there is no rhyme. Second, the lines are irregular in length. For example, there are six syllables in line 1, seven in line 2, eight in line 4, nine in line 14, and only five in line 19. Obviously, there is no regular meter. A poem that is free of the restrictions imposed by rhyme and meter is said to be written in **free verse.**

Passage C (Questions 54–60)

QUESTION 54:   ANSWER 1 (have a firmly established heritage)

EVIDENCE: The fact that there are remains (fossils) of the Big Tree in old rocks (lines 3–4) proves that it comes from an "ancient stock."

QUESTION 55:   ANSWER 1 (environmental difficulties)

EVIDENCE: ". . . but in long eventful wanderings from **climate to climate** (this suggests environmental difficulties) two species have survived the **hardships** they had to encounter" (lines 7–8).

QUESTION 56:   ANSWER 4 (nurturing to some plants)

EVIDENCE: In lines 12–15, the author characterizes the Pacific Coast as "the paradise of conifers (sequoias are conifers). Here nearly all of them are giants . . . The climate is mild, the ground never freezes, and moisture and sunshine abound all the year . . ." These conditions are apparently ideal for the **nurturing** (nourishing) of conifers.

QUESTION 57:   ANWSER 1 (mysterious)

EVIDENCE: A **mystery** is something beyond understanding. In line 15, the author states: "Nevertheless (in spite of the ideal nurturing conditions in the Pacific coast region), it is not easy to account for the colossal size of the sequoias."

QUESTION 58: ANSWER 2 (disbelief)

EVIDENCE: "Who . . . ever dreamed that earth could bear such growths?" (lines 17–19)

QUESTION 59: ANSWER 3 (a rhetorical question)

EVIDENCE: A **rhetorical question** is not really a question, but a statement in the form of a question. It is used to emphasize a point.

QUESTION 60: ANSWER 4 (eternal)

EVIDENCE: In lines 24–25, the author says: "As far as humanity is concerned, they (sequoias) are the same yesterday, today, and forever, emblems of **permanence**" (eternal existence).

LITERARY TERMS YOU ARE EXPECTED TO BE FAMILIAR WITH

Surely you must have noticed that the above reading test required the student to know the meaning of terms like *tone, personification, free verse,* and *rhetorical question.* Let us therefore review these and other literary terms you are likely to encounter in the reading test you are going to take.

1. Figurative Language. Words may be used *literally* or *figuratively.*

a. The structure is supported by concrete *pillars* (long, slender upright columns).

Here *pillars* is used in its **literal** (ordinary) sense.

b. Bill and Vera are the *pillars* (main supports) of our organization; without them it would collapse.

Here *pillars* is used in a **figurative** (unusual, nonliteral) sense.

Figurative language adds beauty and vitality to expression.

2. Figures of Speech (also known as **Literary Devices**). Figures of speech are ways in which words are used figuratively. Here are some figures you should know:

a. **Alliteration** is the repetition of initial consonant sounds. Note the repetition of the consonant "f" in the following line from *The Rime of the Ancient Mariner* by Samuel T. Coleridge:

The *f*urrow *f*ollowed *f*ree.

b. **Exaggeration,** also known as **hyperbole,** is overstatement for the purpose of emphasizing something that the author considers important, as in the following description of the folk hero Jesse James by William Rose Benét:

He could put six shots through a woodpecker's eye...

c. **Irony** describes (1) the use of words to express the *opposite* of the intended meaning, as when we refer to a latecomer as being "too early"; also (2) a situation which is the *reverse* of what was expected, as the killing of the giant Goliath by the boy David.

d. A **metaphor** is an implied comparison, without the use of "like" or "as." A good example is the second line of "The Highwayman" by Alfred Noyes:

The moon was a ghostly galleon tossed upon cloudy seas,

in which the poet compares the moon to a storm-tossed galleon.

e. **Onomatopoeia** is the use of words whose sounds suggest their meaning, as in the following lines by Alfred, Lord Tennyson:

The moan of doves in immemorial elms
And the murmuring of innumerable bees.

f. A **paradox** is a seemingly contradictory statement which is nevertheless true, as in these lines from *Macbeth*:

And you all know security
Is mortals' chiefest enemy.

Normally, we consider *security* our friend. Yet, by causing us to relax our vigilance, it may turn out to be our worst *enemy*.

g. **Personification** is the giving of human characteristics to objects, ideas, animals, or plants.

The mountain sat upon the plain
In his eternal chair.

—Emily Dickinson

h. **A pun** is a play on words. It almost always involves homonyms (words alike in pronunciation but different in meaning), as in *Board* of Education and *bored* of education. In William Shakespeare's *Julius Caesar*, a cobbler (shoemaker) puns when he says, humorously, that he is "a mender of bad *soles*," knowing that *soles* can be interpreted also as *souls* (people).

i. **Satire** is writing that holds up abuses, stupidities, and vices to ridicule. Joseph Heller's novel *Catch-22* is a satire on Army life in World War II.

j. **Simile** is a comparison that makes use of "like" or "as."

> My heart is like a singing bird...
> —Christina Georgina Rossetti

EXERCISE 1. Which figure of speech is used in the following lines? Enter your answers in your notebook.

    (*a*) "like a mounted icicle"

        lines 2–3, **Thermometer Wine,** page 88.

    (*b*) "deaf heaven"

        line 3, **When in Disgrace with Fortune and Men's Eyes,** page 179

    (*c*) "lonely as a cloud"

        line 1, **The Daffodils,** page 172

    (*d*) "And Richard Cory one calm summer night,
        Went home and put a bullet through his head."

        lines 15–16, **Richard Cory,** page 177

    (*e*) "Sorrow never scorned to speak
        To any who
        Were false or true."

        lines 23–24, **Any Human to Another,** page 178

   3. Point of View. Point of view in a narrative passage is determined by the person through whose eyes we see the events of the story. There are three principal points of view.

In a *First-Person Point of View*, the narrator refers to himself or herself by a pronoun like *I, me, my,* or *we, us, our.* These are known as *first-person* pronouns.

In a *Third-Person Point of View*, the narrator is referred to by a pronoun like *he, him, she, her, it, they,* or *them.* These are known as *third-person* pronouns.

In an *Omniscient Point of View* (the view of an all-knowing observer), the narrator uses not only *first-person* pronouns, but also— if necessary—*third-person* pronouns to convey the feelings and thoughts of others, including animals, who enter the story.

EXERCISE 2. In your notebook, write the point of view used in the following passages.

  (*a*) Listening Passage on page 10
  (*b*) first paragraph of "The Little Cask" on page 167.
  (*c*) Listening Passage adapted from *The Memoirs of Chief Red Fox* on page 3.

4. Tone. The tone of a passage is the author's attitude toward his or her subject—serious, indifferent, satiric, objective, etc.

EXAMPLE: See discussion of QUESTION 47 on page 92.

5. Mood. The mood of a passage is its predominant emotion.

QUESTION: What is the mood of **"The Gettysburg Address"** (page 182)—anger, despair, dedication, or joy?

6. Setting. The setting of a passage is the time and place of its action, plus the customs and attitudes of people of that time and place.

QUESTION: What is the setting of **"After Blenheim"** on page 175?

7. Rhetorical Question. This is not really a question but a statement in the form of a question. It is used to emphasize a point.

EXAMPLE: See discussion of QUESTION 59 on page 94.

8. Free Verse. Poetry that has no rhyme and no regular meter is known as **free verse.**

> EXAMPLE: See **"Thermometer Wine"** on page 88, and the discussion of QUESTION 53 on page 93.

> For another example of a poem in free verse, see **"When I Heard the Learn'd Astronomer"** (page 180).

9. Sonnet. A sonnet is a poem of fourteen rhyming lines. The lines are about of even length because they are written in a meter known as *iambic pentameter.*

> EXAMPLE: William Shakespeare's **"When in Disgrace with Fortune and Men's Eyes"** (page 179) is a **sonnet.**

10. Internal Rhyme. This is rhyme within a line, as in the third line of the following stanza from Edgar Allan Poe's "Annabel Lee."

> And neither the angels in heaven above,
> Nor the demons down under the sea,
> Can *ever dissever* my soul from the soul
> Of the beautiful Annabel Lee.

11. Sense Impressions (also known as **Sensory Images** or **Sensory Impressions**). These are words or expressions that make a description more vivid by appealing to the reader's senses. Note how Guy de Maupassant used sense impressions in this passage from "A Piece of String."

> Just opposite to where the diners were at the table, the huge fireplace, full of clear flame, threw a lively heat on the backs of those who sat along the right. Three spits were turning, loaded with chickens, with pigeons, and with joints of mutton; and a delectable odor of roast meat, and of gravy gushing over crisp brown skin, took wing from the hearth, kindled merriment, caused mouths to water.

EXERCISE 3. To which senses—sight, hearing, taste, touch, or smell— did de Maupassant appeal in the following details? In some cases, more than one sense is involved. Enter your answers in your notebook. Hint: The answers to question (*a*) below are *sight* and *touch.*

(*a*) huge fireplace, full of clear flame
(*b*) threw a lively heat on the backs of those who sat along the right

(*c*) Three spits were turning, loaded with chickens, with pigeons, and with joints of mutton

(*d*) a delectable odor of roast meat

(*e*) gravy gushing over crisp brown skin

(*f*) caused mouths to water

12. Main Idea (also known as **Theme**). To find the main idea of a passage, calculate the amount of support in the passage for each of the four suggested choices. The choice with the greatest support is the main idea. For an example of a *main idea* question, read Passage A of Test 3 (page 108) and answer question 46.

13. Method of Development. Past examinations have asked students to state the method that an author used to develop a particular piece of writing. Here are some commonly used methods of development:

a. **Chronological Development** (Presenting events or incidents in the order of time.)

> EXAMPLE: See Abraham Lincoln's **"Gettysburg Address,"** page 182.

b. **Contrast**

> EXAMPLE: See Edwin A. Robinson's **"Richard Cory,"** page 177.

c. **Description**

> EXAMPLE: See second paragraph of Passage C on page 89.

d. **Relevant Details**

> EXAMPLE: See first paragraph of Maureen Daly's **"Sixteen,"** page 163.

e. **Reporting the Actions of the Characters**

> EXAMPLE: See first paragraph of Langston Hughes' **"Early Autumn,"** page 161.

FORMER READING COMPREHENSION TESTS

You are now at the stage of preparation in which you should do complete reading comprehension tests for additional practice. The following tests are from past Comprehensive Examinations. Take these tests, writing your answers in your notebook. Then compare them with the answer key that your teacher will provide.

Directions (41–60): Below each of the following passages, there are several incomplete statements or questions about the passage. For *each*, select the word or expression that best completes the statement or answers the question *in accordance with the meaning of the passage*, and write its *number* in the space provided on the separate answer sheet.   [20]

READING COMPREHENSION TEST 1

Passage A

The early Europeans imagined that the natives of the New World were rovers, who lived and hunted at random wherever they pleased. They were mistaken: the tribes had their separate tracts that were marked off by definite boundaries. But the fundamental difference between the European concep-
5   tion of property and that of the Native Americans was that the Native Americans' property was held in common. The Native Americans had no idea of legal title, of the individual ownership of land, and the Europeans were incapable of thinking in any other terms. In 1879, a General Allotment Act was introduced in Congress. The object, or ostensible object, was to en-
10 courage the Native Americans to engage in farming by breaking up the reservations. The fragments were to be allotted, a hundred and sixty acres to heads of families and eighty to single persons. The remainder could be bought by the government, and the individual owners, after twenty-five years, were authorized to sell their land.
15   The bill encountered opposition, but the act was passed in 1887 and had the effect of depriving the Native Americans of ninety million of their hundred and forty million acres. Few of them had taken to farming. Even if they had been eager to farm, they had no money to invest in equipment or livestock, and since their allotments were held in trust, they were unable to get com-
20 mercial credit. If they did not dispose of their property, and it was divided among their descendants, there was soon very little left for anybody.
It should be noted that the result of the first great attempt on the part of the Native Americans to assimilate themselves was not such as to encourage them further. Toward the end of the eighteenth century, the Iroquois' able
25 cousins, the Cherokees, who inhabited the Alleghenies and other regions further south, set out to master European techniques and to live as the Europeans did. They exchanged their tribal lands for farm implements, spinning wheels, looms, and other tools of civilization. In the twenties of the follow-

30   ing century, the Cherokee leader Sequoya invented a syllabary for their language, and the Cherokees began getting out a newspaper called the *Cherokee Phoenix*. The reward for this effort of adaptation was Andrew Jackson's Indian Removal Act of 1830—as a result of which the literate Cherokees, along with less adaptable tribes, were moved to the primitive wilderness beyond the Mississippi. Some of them took to their hills; but most of them—driven

35   out at the point of the gun—made the journey in winter on foot, and a quarter of their number perished.

—adapted from Edmund Wilson

41. According to the passage, early Europeans believed natives of the New World to be   (1) agrarian   (2) uncivilized   (3) nomadic   (4) disorganized

42. According to the passage, the essential difference between the Native American and European concepts of property is that Europeans believed in   (1) individual ownership of the land   (2) governmental control of the land   (3) breaking up large tracts of land   (4) farming the land instead of hunting on it

43. The official purpose of the General Allotment Act of 1879 was to   (1) introduce new methods of hunting   (2) encourage Native Americans to pursue a different way of life   (3) allow the Native Americans to move about more freely   (4) sell large tracts of land

44. Why were Native Americans unable to obtain credit?   (1) They could not read or write.   (2) They were not completely assimilated.   (3) They did not demonstrate an eagerness to farm.   (4) They did not technically own land.

45. According to the passage, what would have happened if the Native Americans had been successful in handing down their allotted land to their offspring?   (1) The plots would have been too small to be usable.   (2) The Native Americans would have become wealthy.   (3) Other acts of Congress would have been necessary.   (4) The Native Americans would have had to move beyond the Mississippi.

46. One result of Andrew Jackson's Indian Removal Act of 1830 was that   (1) the Cherokees were able to become more literate   (2) less adaptable Native Americans became settled   (3) the number of Native Americans was further reduced   (4) all Native Americans returned to their reservations

Passage B

The Burning of Books

When the Regime ordered that books with dangerous teachings
Should be publicly burnt and everywhere
Oxen were forced to draw carts full of books
To the funeral pyre, an exiled poet,
5   One of the best, discovered with fury, when he studied the list
Of the burned, that his books
Had been forgotten. He rushed to his writing table
On wings of anger and wrote a letter to those in power.
Burn me, he wrote with hurrying pen, burn me!
10   Do not treat me in this fashion. Don't leave me out. Have I not
Always spoken the truth in my books? And now
You treat me like a liar! I order you:
Burn me!

—Bertolt Brecht

47. The "Regime" mentioned in line 1 most likely represents (1) only traditional monarchies   (2) all political leaders   (3) the narrator's homeland   (4) any repressive government

48. In the poem, who considers the exiled poet "One of the best" (line 5)?   (1) the Regime   (2) the narrator   (3) the exiled poet himself   (4) the public

49. Why might the poet have studied the list of the burned books?   (1) to plan an act of retaliation   (2) to determine his status   (3) to defy authority   (4) to understand the public's reaction

50. In line 10, when the poet says, "Don't leave me out," he is asking to be included (1) among those writers considered opponents of the Regime   (2) in the Regime's hierarchy   (3) among those writers whose works should be preserved   (4) in the list of famous writers whose works have been forgotten

51. The poet's insistence that his works be burned is an example of   (1) exaggeration   (2) personification   (3) irony   (4) imagery

52. The poem criticizes those who would   (1) limit access to ideas   (2) question authority   (3) resist change   (4) seek liberty

53. In which form is the poem written?   (1) sonnet   (2) blank verse   (3) couplets   (4) free verse

Passage C

After living nearly two years in Cairo, I had brought my son Guy to enter the University of Ghana in Accra. Guy was seventeen and quick. I was thirty-three and determined. We were Black Americans in West Africa, where for the first time in our lives the color of our skin was accepted as correct and
5 normal. The future was plump with promise. For two days Guy and I laughed. On the third day, Guy, on a pleasure outing, was injured in an automobile accident. One arm and one leg were fractured and his neck was broken.

July and August stretched out like fat men yawning after a sumptuous
10 dinner. They had every right to gloat, for they had eaten me up. Gobbled me down. Consumed my spirit, not in a wild rush, but slowly, with the obscene patience of certain victors. I became a shadow walking in the white hot streets, and a dark spectre in the hospital.

Trying utterly, I could not match Guy's stoicism. He lay calm, in a prison
15 of plaster from which only his face and one leg and arm were visible. His assurances that he would heal and be better than new drove me into a faithless silence.

Admittedly, Guy lived with the knowledge that an unexpected sneeze could force the fractured vertebrae against his spinal cord, and he would be para-
20 lyzed or die immediately, but he had only an infatuation with life. He hadn't lived long enough to fall in love with this brutally delicious experience. He could lightly waft away to another place, if there really was another place, where his youthful innocence would assure him wings, a harp, and an absence of nostalgic yearning. My wretchedness reminded me that, on the other
25 hand, I would be rudderless. We had been each other's home and center for seventeen years. He could die if he wanted to and go off to wherever dead folks go, but I, I would be left without a home.

—Maya Angelou

54. The narrator notes that there are differences between herself and Guy in both age and   (1) education   (2) temperament   (3) intelligence (4) agility

55. Which literary device is used in line 9?   (1) understatement (2) hyperbole   (3) simile   (4) onomatopoeia

56. The word "they," as used in line 10, is intended to mean the (1) certain victors   (2) days of July and August   (3) fat men (4) narrator's thoughts

57. The narrator portrays the delicate nature of her son's life with the words (1) "seventeen and quick" (line 2)   (2) "dark spectre" (line 13) (3) "hadn't lived long" (line 21)   (4) "lightly waft away" (line 22)

58. What does the imagery in lines 11 and 12 convey about the narrator's situation?   (1) Her sudden helplessness seemed unreal.   (2) Her physical health had deteriorated.   (3) She was a Black American walking freely in a once white-only area.   (4) She was undefeated by the adversity of life.

59. According to the narrator, why did Guy not fear immediate death? (1) He was young and inexperienced.   (2) He was infatuated with the afterlife.   (3) He loved his family.   (4) He had accepted his fate.

60. Which words best describe the narrator's overall view of life? (1) "plump with promise" (line 5)   (2) "only an infatuation" (line 20)   (3) "brutally delicious" (line 21)   (4) "nostalgic yearning" (line 24)

READING COMPREHENSION TEST 2

Passage A

Actually, I love to talk. Words express feelings and provide images, and images give an understanding of people that creates philosophy. Unfortunately, you can also lie with words. In mime you cannot lie. You have to go to the action directly, deliberately. You see quicker—the eye perceives
5   better—because mime is beyond words. Mime is like smelling a flower, a moment of silently breathing in the perfumes of life—the best and worst. And the audience has to create in its minds the words that it heard in silence.

A writer can be political, comical, epical, satirical. But every nonverbal stage discipline also has its strength and power. Dance gives a sense of the
10   rhythm of man. Music conveys moods and images. Even in opera, where plots deal with the structure of destiny, it's music, not words, that provides power. Mime has to create all these things—but in silence. My sequence "Birth, Youth, Old Age and Death" must give the life of a man in 4 minutes. How can you do it except through the symbol of the flower that blooms
15   and decays? This is what's important about the renaissance of mime: it is the fragility and essence of life. The completely silent theater is the suspension of the body on stage that allows the invisible to become visible.

—Marcel Marceau

41. The overall tone of this passage is best described as   (1) inquiring (2) nostalgic   (3) philosophical   (4) conversational

42. In line 7, the narrator implies that   (1) silence and words negate one another   (2) words are comprehended best in silence   (3) audiences of mime need to listen carefully   (4) mime requires creativity on the part of the observer

43. In lines 9 and 10, the narrator indicates that dance and music are art forms that   (1) do not rely on words   (2) are often criticized   (3) are opposite in nature   (4) do not convey strength

44. In lines 10 and 11, the narrator implies that the success of an opera depends most on its   (1) audience   (2) setting   (3) director (4) composer

45. In line 16, the use of the word "suspension" suggests that the body (1) is almost inconsequential   (2) becomes the object of focus (3) halts all movement   (4) blends in with its surroundings

46. In lines 16 and 17, the narrator suggests that mime has the power to (1) make the abstract concrete   (2) make the unusual commonplace (3) strengthen the weak   (4) silence the outspoken

Passage B

On Lake Budi some years ago, they were hunting down the swans without mercy. The procedure was to approach them stealthily in little boats and then rapidly—very rapidly—row into their midst. Swans have difficulty in flying; they must skim the surface of the water at a run. In the first phase of their
5 flight they raise their big wings with great effort. It is then that they can be seized; a few blows with a bludgeon finish them off.

Someone made me a present of a swan: more dead than alive. It was of a marvelous species I have never seen anywhere else in the world: a black-throated swan—a snow boat with a neck packed, as it were, into a tight
10 stocking of black silk. Orange-beaked, red-eyed.

They brought it to me half-dead. I bathed its wounds and pressed little pellets of bread and fish into its throat; but nothing stayed down. Nevertheless the wounds slowly healed, and the swan came to regard me as a friend. At the same time, it was apparent to me that the bird was wasting away with
15 nostalgia. So, cradling the heavy burden in my arms through the streets, I carried it to the river. It paddled a few strokes, very close to me. I had hoped it might learn how to fish for itself, and pointed to some pebbles far below, where they flashed in the sand like silvery fish. The swan looked at them remotely, sad-eyed.
20 For the next 20 days I carried the bird to the river and toiled back with it

to my house. One afternoon it seemed more abstracted than usual, swimming very close and ignoring the lure of insects with which I tried vainly to tempt it to fish again. It became very quiet; so I lifted it into my arms to carry it home again. It was breast high, when I suddenly felt a great ribbon unfurl,
25   like a black arm encircling my face: it was the big coil of the neck, dropping down.

    It was then that I learned swans do not sing at their death, if they die of grief.

—Pablo Neruda

47. Which description of the swan contains a metaphor? (1) "more dead than alive" (line 7) (2) "marvelous species" (line 8) (3) "snow boat" (line 9) (4) "red-eyed" (line 10)

48. The swan's wounds healed in spite of its lack of (1) courage (2) nourishment (3) intelligence (4) shelter

49. The narrator implies that the swan's feeling toward him was one of (1) apprehension (2) trust (3) indifference (4) compassion

50. The narrator realized that the swan was (1) eager to recover its strength (2) suspicious of human contact (3) angry at its imprisonment (4) homesick for its former life

51. What was the swan's reaction to the narrator's attempts to teach it to fish? (1) fear (2) antagonism (3) apathy (4) stubbornness

52. According to the narrator, the swan songs of legends do not apply to death caused by (1) bludgeoning (2) starvation (3) heartbreak (4) neglect

53. The events in the passage convey a sense of (1) annoyance (2) futility (3) resignation (4) terror

Passage C

A Father's Gift

The oddest objects sum up a life,
or a moment, like the steel punch
carpenters use in countersinking,
or shoemakers expert at the trade.

5   So the stone-brick stairway down
to the cellar comes into focus,
the wide gray door with the latch,
a hook and eye to keep it locked.

Beyond these: a mud-rock floor,
10   forever damp, the 60-watt bulb
above that makeshift workbench,
and on top, the amateur's anvil.

Long thick fingers come to view,
a pair of Cat's Paw rubber heels,
15   glued first, fixed into position,
then allowed to dry for an hour.

Tiny tacks sit on a lip like cigs,
then one by one fit into pre-made
holes in the rubber, driven deeper
20   by the punch, blunted on the anvil.

The work shoes quit with retirement,
replaced by stiff oxfords. The anvil
was left in the cellar at No. 35,
the tacks and glue thrown out or lost.

25   But the punch is safe, secure, almost
immortal, conjuring up a bronze casket
now lowered, countersunk one might say,
into the town's sacred cemetery ground.

High on a hallowed shelf, it monuments
30   the past, what this child of the Grand
Depression remembers: someone hammering
down below, finding life in old leather.

—Gus Pelletier

54. In stanza 1, the narrator says that a life may be represented by (1) the work one did (2) moments spent with others (3) simple objects (4) familiar places

55. Stanzas 2 through 5 are developed by the use of (1) an extended metaphor (2) visual details (3) comparison and contrast (4) chronological events

56. The shoes mentioned in stanza 6 most likely represent (1) the narrator's maturity (2) new prosperity (3) items needing repair (4) the father's aging

57. In line 29, the word "it" refers to (1) a memory (2) the grain (3) the cemetery (4) the punch

58. The expression "Grand Depression" (lines 30 and 31) is an example of (1) irony (2) alliteration (3) assonance (4) hyperbole

59. In line 31, the word "someone" refers to (1) the narrator (2) a neighbor (3) the father (4) a carpenter

60. The use of the present tense throughout most of the poem suggests that the narrator (1) vividly recalls these events (2) is quite elderly now (3) has lost track of time (4) resists the passage of time

READING COMPREHENSION TEST 3

Passage A

Something will have gone out of us as a people if we ever let the remaining wilderness be destroyed; if we permit the last virgin forests to be turned into comic books and plastic cigarette cases; if we drive the few remaining members of the wild species into zoos or to extinction; if we pollute the last clear
5   air and dirty the last clean streams and push our paved roads through the last of the silence, so that never again will Americans be free in their own country from the noise, the exhausts, the stinks of human and automotive waste. And so that never again can we have the chance to see ourselves single, separate, vertical, and individual in the world, part of the environment of trees and
10 rocks and soil, brother to the other animals, part of the natural world and competent to belong in it. Without any remaining wilderness we are committed wholly, without chance for even momentary reflection and rest, to a headlong drive into our technological termite-life, the Brave New World of a completely man-controlled environment. We need wilderness preserved—
15 as much of it as is still left, and as many kinds—because it was the challenge against which our character as a people was formed. The reminder and the reassurance that it is still there is good for our spiritual health even if we never once in ten years set foot in it. It is good for us when we are young, because of the incomparable sanity it can bring briefly, as vacation and rest,
20 into our insane lives. It is important to us when we are old simply because it is there—important, that is, simply as idea.

—Wallace Stegner

41. The author equates the destruction of the wilderness with (1) diminished human character (2) greater domestication of wild animals (3) conflicting national interests (4) confused political priorities

42. The author develops lines 4 through 7 by using (1) paradox (2) sensory detail (3) analogy (4) rhetorical questions

43. According to the passage, the loss of wilderness will affect the (1) amount of rainfall (2) type of industrial growth (3) nation's security (4) ecological system

44. To what historical contribution of the wilderness does the passage point? (1) encouragement of territorial expansion (2) formation of our national character (3) provision of our material wealth (4) preservation of an agricultural economy

45. In the passage, the author warns that complete wilderness destruction will lead to (1) social conflicts (2) international upheaval (3) an artificial environment (4) weakened health standards

46. Which statement best expresses the main idea of this passage? (1) If the wilderness is depleted, so is human life (2) Our spiritual and physical health depend on each other. (3) The forest is essential to our economic survival. (4) Wilderness vacations should be available to all.

Passage B

When I Was a Child I Bought the Beach

> When I was a child I bought the beach,
> I blessed the boats and tamed the sand.
> Toy castles tried spires for my hand.
> I owned the creatures, two of each:
> 5   When I was a child I bought the beach.
>
> I caught the gulls and guessed their speech,
> Legs planted tall as spars I spanned
> The space and flash of waves; a band
> Of boys and beasts was mine to teach,
> 10   I caught the gulls and guessed their speech.
>
> The blown boats rock now out of reach,
> Children are hard to understand,
> Castles grew prouder than I planned,
> The gulls' small words swelled to a screech,
> 15   The blown boats rock now out of reach.
>
> I blessed the boats and tamed the sand,
> I owned the creatures, two of each,
> The space and flash of waves, a band
> Of boys and beasts, all mine to teach:
> 20   Children are slow to understand.
>
> —Carol Hall

47. Which literary device is contained in lines 1 and 2? (1) simile (2) irony (3) alliteration (4) onomatopoeia
48. Which adjective best describes the narrator as a child? (1) spoiled (2) wealthy (3) imaginative (4) educated
49. The third and fourth stanzas differ from the first and second stanzas in (1) tone (2) imagery (3) setting (4) audience
50. Which word in stanza three serves as a transition? (1) "now" (line 11) (2) "grew" (line 13) (3) "planned" (line 13) (4) "out" (line 15)
51. What do the two halves of the poem represent? (1) two conflicts the narrator experienced (2) the world at peace and the world at war (3) the world of nature and the world of civilization (4) two stages in the narrator's life
52. One function of lines 16 through 19 is to (1) summarize the first two stanzas (2) repeat the message from the third stanza (3) provide a transition in the poem (4) contradict the narrator's earlier statements
53. Which two elements are the subject of the poem? (1) faith and despair (2) innocence and experience (3) life and death (4) love and hate

Passage C

I grew up near the Atlantic Ocean among marshes and estuaries, only a few miles back from a low-lying coast. I remember the month of August with a special kind of pleasure. At this time of year, mainland, marshland, and ocean would blend together into a grey, hot, humid haze. My mother
5 would open all the windows, pull all the blinds, and hope to catch a sea breeze, but no breeze stirred. The dogs lay under the tables and panted; the cats lurked in the cool tunnels of the earth cellar. August was a time to do nothing and be proud of it.

But I also remember August with a bit of anxiety. August was the time
10 of hurricanes and polio. Hurricanes and polio were different in many ways but were alike in that both were very bad things that usually happened to other people. During my childhood, I was lucky enough never to get polio. But we had bad hurricanes three times.

The hurricanes were pretty scary for the adults, but for a child, they were
15 mostly a lot of fun. First, there was all the getting ready: buying candles and flashlight batteries and food, filling the car with gasoline, helping neighbors board up the only plate-glass window in the neighborhood, and making sure the buildings were closed up snug and everything loose was stashed away.

Then there was watching for the storm. I remember my father pointing
20 out to me the eerie sky with its banners of cirrus clouds radiating out of the
south, and I remember the strange feel of the air. The first breezes of the
hurricane were so mild, so moist, so soft as to be barely distinguishable from
the feel of one's own skin.

The storm itself wasn't so bad, except I had to stay indoors. I remember
25 peering through the windows watching the water sheet down outside, the
ocean tide creep up in the back marsh, and the trees lash back and forth.
Every time the wind let up I would say, "Is this the eye of the hurricane?
Can I go outside and see the eye?"

—Calvin Simonds

54. The mood in lines 3 through 8 is chiefly expressed through the use of
(1) descriptive details   (2) sequential order   (3) figurative language
(4) simple sentences

55. Why was the narrator "proud" (line 8) to do nothing in August?
(1) He was lazy.   (2) It was easier to keep cool.   (3) He was observing animals' actions.   (4) It was proper August behavior.

56. The narrator characterizes hurricanes and polio as reasons for
(1) fearing   the   weather   (2) being   concerned   in   August
(3) discussing misfortunes   (4) helping the neighbors

57. In the fourth paragraph, the narrator suggests that the early stages of
a hurricane are   (1) unpredictable   (2) obvious to the eye only
(3) apparent in the atmosphere   (4) felt before they are seen

58. Which words best describe the narrator's memories of August?
(1) confusing events   (2) conflict and danger   (3) contrasting feelings   (4) freedom and relaxation

59. The primary technique used to develop the third, fourth, and fifth paragraphs is   (1) cause and effect   (2) comparison and contrast
(3) chronological order   (4) definition and classification

60. The passage implies that a memorable relationship existed between the
narrator and his   (1) pets   (2) neighbors   (3) children   (4) father

READING COMPREHENSION TEST 4

Passage A

The mirror is your conscience. You've rehearsed with its definitive image
in front of you for weeks. Then the choreographer turns you around, away

from the mirror. You are on your own. You're not sure where you are. Your
image is no longer there to ratify your existence. Your orientation to space
5   is altered. You become aware of the meaning of movement and your need
to communicate to the audience because you can no longer communicate
with your own image. The music sounds different. Your spacing is off. You
are unable to check out your line, not only in relation to yourself, but also
in relation to whomever else you may be dancing with.
10   Then come the lights, lovingly painted from the front of the theater. You
realize that every nuance of your face and body will be visible. The pink
jells leave your skin with a silky glow. The spotlight following you burns
through your eyes. The bumper lights stage right and left add dimensional
color to your arms and legs. You can see absolutely no one in the audience.
15   It is alienatingly black. Then you realize it is all up to you. You are a performer. You forget everything you ever learned. You forget the intricate
processes of technique. You forget your anxieties and your pain. You even
forget who you are. You become one with the music, the lights, and the
collective spirit of the audience. You know you are there to help uplift them.
20   They want to feel better about themselves and each other.
      Then they react. Their generously communal applause means they like
you—love you even. They send you energy and you send it back. You participate with each other. And the cycle continues.

—Shirley MacLaine

41. The metaphor in the opening line implies that   (1) the mirror helps
you know yourself   (2) you cannot see your values   (3) the mirror
gives you comfort   (4) you can change the mirror

42. The author implies that one of the functions of the mirror is to
(1) provide a setting for the performance   (2) help the performer understand the audience   (3) record a great performance   (4) confirm
the dancer's existence

43. What is a consequence of turning from the mirror?   (1) joining your
fellow dancers   (2) wanting new music for the performance
(3) questioning the choreography   (4) needing to communicate with
the audience

44. According to the passage, which element flatters the performer?
(1) the mirrors   (2) the lights   (3) the stage   (4) the music

45. What is one of the results of theatrical lighting?   (1) It gives life to
the scenery.   (2) It makes the performers larger than life.   (3) It
blocks out the audience.   (4) It controls the movements of the dancers.

46. What is the performer's initial feeling in facing the audience?
(1) affection (2) disdain (3) wonder (4) isolation

47. At the end of the performance, the performer experiences a feeling of
(1) unity with the other dancers (2) respect for the choreographer
(3) accord with the audience (4) compassion for the audience

Passage B

The Victim

The hummingbird that darts and hovers
Made one fatal dart—alas!—
Against a counterfeit of flowers
Reflected in the window glass.
5   When four-o'clocks had sunk in shadow,
The window caught an extra glint
Of color, like the sudden rainbow
Arching the purple firmament.
Transcendent are the traceries
10   Illusion weaves to set a snare;
The quick competitor of bees,
Trusting his universe of air
For flight and honey, dazzled so
In quest of sweetness, was waylaid
15   By something hard that had a glow
Brighter than that the garden made.
Illusion shatters; the ideal
Is much more ruthless than the real.
The visionary hummingbird
20   Hit nothingness, and hit it hard.

—Robert Hillyer

48. Which word suggests the result of the "fatal dart" (line 2)?
(1) "sunk" (line 5) (2) "weaves" (line 10) (3) "glow" (line 15)
(4) "shatters" (line 17)

49. The function of the simile in line 7 is to (1) emphasize the imme-
diacy of the reflection (2) contrast the colors within the rainbow
(3) compare the bird to the flowers (4) change the mood within the
poem

50. In line 11, the word "competitor" refers to (1) illusion (2) another
bee (3) a flower (4) the hummingbird

51. What does the narrator state about "the ideal" mentioned in line 17? (1) It needs followers. (2) It can die.   (3) It is cruel.   (4) It hates "the real."

52. The last line of the poem is best described as   (1) humorous (2) understated   (3) optimistic   (4) paradoxical

53. To what does the title refer?   (1) a window   (2) a hummingbird (3) a flower   (4) a bee

Passage C

Leventhal's apartment was spacious. In a better neighborhood, or three stories lower, it would have rented for twice the amount he paid. But the staircase was narrow and stifling and full of turns. Though he went up slowly, he was out of breath when he reached the fourth floor, and his heart beat
5   thickly. He rested before unlocking the door. Entering, he threw down his raincoat and flung himself on the bed in the front room. Mary had moved some of the chairs into the corners and covered them with sheets. She could not depend on him to keep the windows shut and the shades and curtains drawn during the day. He got up and opened a window. The curtains waved
10   once and then were as motionless as before. There was a movie house strung with lights across the street; on its roof a water tank sat heavily uneven on its timbers; the cowls of the chimneys, which rattled in the slightest stir of air, were still.

The motor of the refrigerator began to run. There was nothing inside ex-
15   cept a few lemons and some milk. He drank a glass of milk and it refreshed him. He had already taken off his shirt and was sitting on the bed unlacing his shoes when there was a short ring of the bell. Eagerly he pulled open the door and shouted, "Who is it?" The flat was unbearably empty. He hoped someone had remembered that Mary was away and had come to keep him
20   company. There was no response below. He called out again, impatiently. It was very probable that someone had pushed the wrong button, but he heard no other doors opening. Could it be a prank? This was not the season for it. Nothing moved in the stairwell, and it only added to his depression to discover how he longed for a visitor. He stretched out on the bed. He thought
25   he would doze off. But a little later he found himself standing at the window, holding the curtains with both hands. He was under the impression that he had slept. It was only eight-thirty by the whirring electric clock on the night table, however. Only five minutes had passed.

—Saul Bellow

54. What does the author suggest about Leventhal's apartment? (1) Its location is excellent. (2) Its security is admirable. (3) Its cost is attractive. (4) Its convenience is evident.

55. What does the author suggest by the statement "The curtains waved once and then were as motionless as before" (lines 9 and 10)? (1) the stagnation of the surroundings (2) the emptiness of the flat (3) the depth of Leventhal's emotions (4) the carefulness of Mary's house-keeping

56. The contents of the refrigerator (lines 14 and 15) suggest that (1) Leventhal could not afford food (2) Mary had been in charge of the groceries (3) Leventhal could not eat because Mary was away (4) Mary and Leventhal had just moved in

57. What does the statement "This was not the season for it" (line 22) seem to reveal about Leventhal? (1) He expected things to occur at their proper times. (2) He had forgotten that it was April Fool's Day. (3) He would be angry if someone tried to trick him. (4) He was quite affected by seasonal changes.

58. What effect did the lack of movement in the stairwell (line 23) have upon Leventhal? (1) He became very frightened. (2) He gained a better understanding of his state of mind. (3) He became bitter because he had been tricked. (4) He suddenly became very tired.

59. In which lines does the author most directly give the reader insight into Leventhal's emotional state? (1) lines 7–9 (2) lines 14 and 15 (3) lines 17 through 20 (4) lines 24 through 27

60. This passage could best be described as a (1) biographical sketch (2) character study (3) personal memoir (4) dramatic monologue

READING COMPREHENSION TEST 5

Passage A

"You don't have to tell me what the temperature is!" he said in a high voice. "I'm old enough to know when I want to take my coat off!" The train glided silently away behind him, leaving a view of the twin blocks of dilapidated stores. He gazed after the aluminum speck disappearing into the woods. It seemed to him that his last connection with a larger world was vanishing forever. Then he turned and faced his mother grimly, irked that he had allowed himself, even for an instant, to see an imaginary temple in

this collapsing country junction. He had become entirely accustomed to the thought of death, but he had not become accustomed to the thought of death
10 *here.*

He had felt the end coming on for nearly four months. Alone in his freezing flat, huddled under his two blankets and his overcoat and with three thicknesses of the *New York Times* between, he had had a chill one night, followed by a violent sweat that left the sheets soaking and removed all doubt
15 from his mind about his true condition. Before this there had been a gradual slackening of his energy and vague inconsistent aches and headaches. He had been absent so many days from his part-time job in the bookstore that he had lost it. Since then he had been living, or just barely so, on his savings and these, diminishing day by day, had been all he had between him and
20 home. Now there was nothing. He was here.

"Where's the car?" he muttered.

"It's over yonder," his mother said. "And your sister is asleep in the back because I don't like to come out this early by myself. There's no need to wake her up."

25 "No," he said, "let sleeping dogs lie," and he picked up his two bulging suitcases and started across the road with them.

—Flannery O'Connor

41. The main character most likely refused to take off his coat because
(1) he is sick from a chill   (2) he would have something else to carry
(3) he has very little energy   (4) his clothes are in poor condition

42. In line 5, "last connection" refers to   (1) his job   (2) the train
(3) his flat   (4) the stores

43. The main character's physical condition is comparable to the
(1) dilapidated stores   (2) silent train   (3) aluminum speck
(4) imaginary temple

44. In line 20, the statement "Now there was nothing" refers to the fact that the main character   (1) has lost hope of living   (2) has no love for his family   (3) does not have any money   (4) was fired from his job

45. The purpose of the second paragraph is to   (1) give background information   (2) provide the setting   (3) change the author's tone
(4) establish the conflict

46. The main character has returned home to die because he   (1) wants to be near his family   (2) has nowhere else to go   (3) loves his hometown   (4) lost his job

Passage B

Trees

To be a giant and keep quiet about it,
To stay in one's own place;
To stand for the constant presence of process
And always to seem the same;
5   To be steady as a rock and always trembling,
Having the hard appearance of death
With the soft, fluent nature of growth,
One's Being deceptively armored,
One's Becoming deceptively vulnerable;
10   To be so tough, and take the light so well,
Freely providing forbidden knowledge
Of so many things about heaven and earth
For which we should otherwise have no word—
Poems or people are rarely so lovely,
15   And even when they have great qualities
They tend to tell you rather than exemplify
What they believe themselves to be about,
While from the moving silence of trees,
Whether in storm or calm, in leaf and naked,
20   Night or day, we draw conclusions of our own,
Sustaining and unnoticed as our breath,
And perilous also—though there has never been
A critical tree—about the nature of things.

—Howard Nemerov

47. In line 3, the phrase "constant presence of process" refers to
(1) monotony of life (2) approach of death (3) inevitability of change (4) pressure of society

48. Which human conditions are contrasted in lines 6 and 7? (1) love and hate (2) life and death (3) power and dependency (4) wealth and poverty

49. The poet implies that trees provide knowledge that would otherwise be (1) inaccurate (2) unbelievable (3) unimportant (4) inaccessible

50. The narrator implies that the "silence of trees" (line 18) is
(1) expressive (2) changing (3) frightening (4) excessive

51. The narrator states that by observing trees "we draw conclusions of our own" (line 20) about (1) dangers around us (2) poetry and people (3) the nature of things (4) time and its implications

52. In describing the various aspects of trees, the poet relies mainly on (1) definition (2) contrast (3) example (4) elaboration

53. The characteristic of trees that most impresses the poet is their (1) relative size (2) inner strength (3) quick growth (4) nurturing comfort

Passage C

Discoveries in science and technology are thought by "untaught minds" to come in blinding flashes or as the result of dramatic accidents. Sir Alexander Fleming did not, as legend would have it, look at the mould on a piece of cheese and get the idea for penicillin there and then. He experimented
5   with antibacterial substances for nine years before he made his discovery. Inventions and innovations almost always come out of laborious trial and error. Innovation is like hockey: Even the best players miss the net and have their shots blocked much more frequently than they score.

The point is that the players who score most are the ones who take the
10 most shots on the net—and so it goes with innovation in any field of activity. The prime difference between innovators and others is one of approach. Everybody gets ideas, but innovators work consciously on theirs, and they follow them through until they prove practicable or otherwise. They never reject any thought that comes into their heads as outlandish. What ordinary
15 people see as fanciful abstractions, professional innovators see as solid possibilities.

"Creative thinking may mean simply the realization that there's no particular virtue in doing things the way they have always been done," wrote Rudolph Flesch, the language guru. This accounts for our reaction to decep-
20 tively simple innovations like plastic garbage bags and suitcases on wheels that make life more convenient: "How come nobody thought of that before?"

Creativity does not demand absolute originality. It often takes the form of throwing an old ball with a new twist.
25 The creative approach begins with the proposition that nothing is as it appears. Innovators will not accept that there is only one way to do anything. Faced with getting from A to B, the average person will automatically set out on the best-known and apparently simplest routing. The innovator will search for alternate courses which may prove easier in the long run and are
30 bound to be more interesting and challenging even if they lead to dead ends. Highly creative individuals really do march to a different drummer.

54. Which person would the author probably consider to have an "untaught mind" (line 1)? (1) a high school dropout (2) a citizen of a society that restricts personal freedoms (3) a superstitious person (4) a person ignorant of the method of laboratory experimentation

55. According to the author, what separates innovators from noninnovators? (1) the variety of ideas they have (2) the number of successes they achieve (3) the way they approach problems (4) the manner in which they present their findings

56. According to the author, what is the common response to a new invention? (1) surprise at its simplicity (2) acceptance of its utility (3) questioning of its necessity (4) dependence on its convenience

57. In lines 23 and 24, the author uses the imagery of throwing the ball to explain the (1) significance of form (2) importance of a fresh perspective (3) importance of practice (4) relationship between science and athletics

58. In keeping with the context of the passage, what would the innovator probably state about going from point A to point B? (1) A straight line is the most direct and proven approach. (2) The shortest route is the most advantageous. (3) The most challenging route will eventually prove to be the easiest. (4) The advantages of several routes must be carefully considered.

59. The phrase "march to a different drummer" (line 31) suggests that highly creative individuals are (1) diligent in pursuing their goals (2) committed to perfection (3) motivated by their own perceptions of life (4) unconcerned about society's needs

60. What is the tone of this passage? (1) jovial (2) arrogant (3) instructive (4) argumentative

READING COMPREHENSION TEST 6

Passage A

    In the film *Frankenstein*, the monster could not speak; he was an artificial living creature, made from bits and pieces of human bodies by the scientist Dr. Frankenstein. Boris Karloff regarded the role as a challenge, and he portrayed in masterly fashion the subhuman creature of little intelligence,
5   able only to utter a few gutteral and animal noises; "he talked with his eyes." Yet he still got across the sympathetic qualities in the role. The monster appeared to be trying to grow a soul. His eyes begged for understanding.

Relatively well-behaved at first, he was goaded by cruelty and, without knowledge of right and wrong, became a killer and so he had to be destroyed.
10 No one, it has been said, who saw the film *Frankenstein* has ever been able to forget the monster's half-closed eyes: liquid, pleading, half-intelligent, peering through the outlandish makeup.

One of the odd effects of Karloff's brilliant playing of the role was that while children everywhere loved the film and felt an instinctive sympathy
15 for the monster, their parents, though fascinated, hated the picture. Karloff received hundreds of letters from children expressing pity for the poor creature. "The children have never fallen for my nonsense," said Karloff. "They sit in the cinema with their eyes glued on the screen. They watch the monster parading his stuff, and now and then give hoots of mock terror or shiver with
20 suppressed excitement, but the moment the word END flashes on the screen, they begin to laugh and chatter away about Karloff and his antics."

—Peter Underwood

41. The phrase "artificial living creature" (lines 1 and 2) is an example of   (1) a metaphor   (2) a simile   (3) a paradox   (4) an exaggeration

42. Boris Karloff considered the role of Frankenstein to be   (1) outlandish   (2) difficult   (3) unique   (4) childish

43. According to the author, Karloff's success in the role was primarily the result of his   (1) animal noises   (2) expert makeup   (3) awkward gestures   (4) facial expressions

44. According to this passage, which word best describes the monster?   (1) crafty   (2) destructive   (3) pitiable   (4) animalistic

45. What does this passage imply about the creature?   (1) He behaved knowledgeably.   (2) He was an innocent victim.   (3) He was cruel.   (4) He begged for forgiveness.

46. According to this passage, children's reactions to the monster were the result of   (1) Karloff's acting   (2) Karloff's makeup   (3) the film's plot   (4) their parents' reactions

47. The purpose of this passage is primarily to   (1) inform   (2) persuade   (3) shock   (4) defend

Passage B

There was the huge tree asleep yet in the paling moonlight, and small and hopeful Sylvia began with utmost bravery to mount to the top of it, with tingling, eager blood coursing the channels of her whole frame, with her

5   bare feet and fingers that pinched and held like bird's claws to the monstrous ladder reaching up, up, almost to the sky itself. First she must mount the white oak tree that grew alongside, where she was almost lost among the dark branches and the green leaves heavy and wet with dew; a bird fluttered off its nest, and a red squirrel ran to and fro and scolded pettishly at the harmless housebreaker. Sylvia felt her way easily. She had often climbed

10   there and knew that higher still one of the oak's upper branches chafed against the pine trunk, just where its lower boughs were set close together. There, when she made the dangerous pass from one tree to the other, the great enterprise would really begin.

    She crept out along the swaying oak limb at last and took the daring step

15   across into the old pine tree. The way was harder than she thought; she must reach far and hold fast. The sharp dry twigs caught and held her and scratched her like angry talons; the pitch made her thin little fingers clumsy and stiff as she went round and round the tree's great stem, higher and higher upward. The sparrows and robins in the woods below were beginning to wake and

20   twitter to the dawn, yet it seemed much lighter there aloft in the pine tree, and the child knew that she must hurry if her project were to be of any use.

    The tree seemed to lengthen itself out as she went up and to reach farther and farther upward. It was like a great mainmast to the voyaging earth; it must truly have been amazed that morning through all its ponderous frame

25   as it felt this determined spark of human spirit creeping and climbing from higher branch to branch. Who knows how steadily the least twigs held themselves to advantage this light, weak creature on her way! The old pine must have loved his new dependent. More than all the hawks and bats and moths and even the sweet-voiced thrushes was the brave, beating heart of the sol-

30   itary gray-eyed child. And the tree stood still and held away the winds that June morning while the dawn grew bright in the east.

—Sarah Orne Jewett

48. The girl's blood was tingling (line 3) because she was   (1) cold (2) frightened   (3) excited   (4) ill

49. Why did Sylvia climb the oak tree?   (1) to observe the birds   (2) to get closer to the pine tree   (3) to get to the ladder   (4) to chase a squirrel

50. Why was the first part of Sylvia's climb easy for her?   (1) The branches were close together.   (2) It was almost daylight.   (3) There was a ladder nearby.   (4) She had climbed the tree before.

51. In line 23, the tree is compared to   (1) a giant's hand   (2) the earth's axis   (3) a part of a ship   (4) a space shuttle

52. In lines 26 through 31, the pine tree is portrayed as a   (1) kindly protector   (2) solitary sentinel   (3) stern parent   (4) brave soldier

53. Which word in this passage is used in a unique way?   (1) "utmost" (line 2)   (2) "chafed" (line 10)   (3) "project" (line 21) (4) "advantage" (line 27)

Passage C

The Writer

In her room at the prow of the house
Where light breaks, and the windows are tossed with linden,
My daughter is writing a story.

I pause in the stairwell, hearing
5   From her shut door a commotion of typewriter-keys
Like a chain hauled over a gunwale.

Young as she is, the stuff
Of her life is a great cargo, and some of it heavy:
I wish her a lucky passage.

10   But now it is she who pauses,
As if to reject my thought and its easy figure.
A stillness greatens, in which

The whole house seems to be thinking,
And then she is at it again with a bunched clamor
15   Of strokes, and again is silent.

I remember the dazed starling
Which was trapped in that very room, two years ago;
How we stole in, lifted a sash

And retreated, not to affright it;
20   And how for a helpless hour, through the crack of the door,
We watched the sleek, wild, dark

And iridescent creature
Batter against the brilliance, drop like a glove
To the hard floor, or the desk-top,

25   And wait then, humped and bloody,
For the wits to try it again; and how our spirits
Rose when, suddenly sure,

It lifted off from a chair-back,
Beating a smooth course for the right window
30   And clearing the sill of the world.

It is always a matter, my darling,
Of life or death, as I had forgotten. I wish
What I wished you before, but harder.

—Richard Wilbur

54. The imagery in lines 7 and 8 suggests that the narrator's daughter (1) exaggerates her experiences   (2) has borne burdens in her life (3) is too young to be a writer   (4) takes her responsibilities seriously

55. In the first three stanzas, the narrator speaks of his daughter's world in terms of a   (1) ship   (2) lighthouse   (3) plane   (4) castle

56. Which poetic device is used in line 13?   (1) hyperbole (2) personification   (3) irony   (4) symbolism

57. The narrator's memory of the "helpless hour" (line 20) spent watching the starling was aroused by his   (1) fear for his daughter's life (2) frustration at being rejected   (3) wish that his daughter stop writing   (4) sympathy with his daughter's struggle

58. The phrase "Batter against the brillance" (line 23) refers to the bird's attempts to   (1) retreat through the open door   (2) fly through a closed window   (3) see in the bright sunlight   (4) keep its footing on the hard floor

59. The narrator used the phrase "drop like a glove" (line 23) to reinforce the bird's   (1) softness   (2) slipperiness   (3) limpness   (4) dryness

60. What effect does the bird's "clearing the sill" (line 30) have on the narrator and his daughter?   (1) disappointment   (2) amusement (3) disbelief   (4) joy

PART II OF THE EXAMINATION

The Literature Essay Test
[25 credits]

This is a test both of your knowledge of literature and your ability to write. It requires you to answer *one* of two questions dealing with some aspect of human behavior or experience. You are expected to develop your answer by referring not to people you know personally, but to characters you have met in *two* literary works. The works may be of any type or length. You can get the same credit for discussing a short short story or poem as for discussing a full-length novel or play, **as long as your discussion answers the question.** You are expected, of course, to show skill in organizing and developing your essay and to observe the conventions of standard written English in usage, spelling, punctuation, and so on.

TYPICAL COMPREHENSIVE ENGLISH LITERATURE ESSAY TEST

Directions: Write a well-organized essay of about 250 words on either *A* or *B*.   [25]

A. In many works of literature, a female character has a significant influence, positive or negative, on another character. From the literature you have read, choose *two* works in which a female character has a significant influence on another character. For *each* work, identify the female character and the other character and state whether the influence was positive or negative. Using specific references from *each* work, explain how the female character influenced the other character. Give titles and authors.

B. In many works of literature, an important theme is an individual's achievement of self-knowledge as a result of undergoing an ordeal. This self-knowledge may be a recognition of the individual's own strengths, weaknesses, values, prejudices, aspirations, or fears. From the literature you have read, choose *two* works in which an individual achieves self-knowledge as a result of undergoing an ordeal. For *each* work, identify the individual and the self-knowledge he or she achieves. Using specific references from *each* work, explain how the ordeal led the individual to the self-knowledge. Give titles and authors.

Let us begin by considering a model answer to Question *A*.

MODEL ANSWER TO QUESTION *A*

Two literary works in which a female character has a significant influence, positive or negative, on another character are *Macbeth* by William Shakespeare, and *Black Boy* by Richard Wright.

In *Macbeth*, Lady Macbeth has a significant negative influence on
5   her husband, Macbeth, a brave military leader, who has been told by three witches that he will be king of Scotland. She interprets this to mean that, to become king, her husband must kill King Duncan, and she urges him to do this while Duncan is a guest in their castle. At first, Macbeth agrees, but the idea troubles him because Duncan has
10 just made him thane of Cawdor and been like a father to him. When he balks at going ahead with the scheme, Lady Macbeth reproaches him for going back on his word and calls him a coward. To bolster his courage, she volunteers to get Duncan's bodyguards drunk and to help to plant incriminating evidence on them, so that they will appear
15 to be the murderers. Her powerful personality completely overwhelms Macbeth's humane instincts, and he commits the deed.

By contrast, Mrs. Wright, in the novel *Black Boy*, has a significant positive influence on her older son, Richard. When her husband abandons the family, she goes to work. Richard is given the responsibility
20 of doing the shopping. On two attempts to get to the grocery, he is beaten and robbed of his money by a gang of boys. After the second beating, Mrs. Wright refuses to let him into the house, despite his tearful pleading. Instead, she gives him some more money and a long, heavy stick, telling him to fight if the boys should bother him again.

25   This time, when they attack, he swings the stick with such blind fury that they run for their lives. Picking up the money he has dropped in the fight, Richard is able to complete the shopping. Thanks to his mother's positive influence, Richard can say, in recalling this incident, "That night I won the right to the streets of Memphis."

HOW THE MODEL ANSWER MEETS THE REQUIREMENTS OF QUESTION *A*

1. The model answer is well organized.

The first paragraph (lines 1–3) mentions the titles and authors of two works in which a female character has a significant influence, positive or negative, on another character.

> NOTE: Titles of full-length works are in **italics (underlined** in handwriting); titles of short works are enclosed in **quotation marks.**

The second paragraph (lines 4–16) explains, with specific references, how a female character has a negative influence on another character.

The third paragraph (lines 17–29) explains, with specific references, how a female character has a positive influence on another character.

2. The model answer has transitions between paragraphs.

A **transition** is a bridge by which a writer leads readers from one sentence or paragraph to the next, showing how they are logically connected.

Examples: "In *Macbeth*," (line 4) links paragraph 2 with paragraph 1.
           "By contrast" (line 17) connects paragraph 3 with paragraph 2.

Transitions help to unify an essay. Skill in transition is a characteristic of good writing.

3. The model answer is rich in specific references.

A **specific reference** can be a name ("Lady Macbeth"), a place ("Scotland"), a relationship ("guest"), a deed ("kill King Duncan"), an incident ("when he balks at going ahead"), a responsibility ("doing the shopping"), an object ("long, heavy stick")—in short, any relevant detail from the literary work that will give the reader a clearer idea of what the writer is trying to communicate.

EXERCISE 1. Rewrite the following paragraph, improving it by adding at least three specific references. See the model answer to Question *A* on page 125 for ideas.

Mrs. Wright has a strong influence on her son. When she gives him an errand to do, he is afraid to leave the house because he has been beaten up on the street. However, she teaches him how to deal with this problem.

QUESTION *B* OF THE TYPICAL LITERATURE ESSAY TEST

So far we have dealt only with Question *A*. Let us now give our attention to Question *B*, which, as you may recall, reads as follows:

In many works of literature, an important theme is an individual's achievement of self-knowledge as a result of undergoing an ordeal. This self-knowledge may be a recognition of the individual's own strengths, weaknesses, values, prejudices, aspirations, or fears. From the literature you have read, choose *two* works in which an individual achieves self-knowledge as a result of undergoing an ordeal. For *each* work, identify the individual and the self-knowledge he or she achieves. Using specific references from *each* work, explain how the ordeal led the individual to the self-knowledge. Give titles and authors.

MODEL ANSWER TO QUESTION *B*

Two literary works in which an individual achieves self-knowledge as a result of undergoing an ordeal are *The Pearl* by John Steinbeck and *The Red Badge of Courage* by Stephen Crane.

In *The Pearl*, Kino, a poor Mexican diver who has found an ex-
5   ceptionally beautiful pearl, learns that sudden wealth can distort a
person's sense of values. As news of his unusual find spreads in the
town, his ordeal begins. The unscrupulous pearl merchants refuse to
buy the pearl, except for a ridiculously low price; they claim it is ugly
because it is too large. Thieves try to rob Kino of the pearl; they attack
10 him day and night. He kills one, but others sabotage his canoe to
hamper his flight, and they burn his house to the ground. In the dead
of the night, with his wife Juana and infant son Coyotito, Kino heads
north into the mountains but is pursued by three assassins. A cry from

15 the infant gives away the family's hiding place. In the ensuing struggle, Kino kills the assassins, but not before Coyotito is fatally wounded by one of them. It is at this point that the grieving father achieves the self-knowledge that his sense of values has been wrong. The lives of his dear ones are far more important than any wealth the pearl can bring. Realizing that the pearl is evil, he flings it back into
20 the sea.

Similarly, Henry Fleming, in *The Red Badge of Courage*, achieves self-knowledge as the result of undergoing an ordeal. Henry, a young recruit in the Union Army, is worried about how he will behave under fire, and so are the other new enlistees. Asked if he will run when the
25 enemy attacks, he laughs and says "Of course not," but, truthfully, he is not sure that he is not a coward. When an attack does come, Henry suddenly sees some of his fellow recruits run. Thinking the whole regiment is in flight, he panics and takes to his heels, passing several dead and wounded soldiers on the way. But the rest of the
30 troops, as Henry later learns, hold their lines and repel the attackers. Too ashamed of his cowardice to rejoin his regiment, he plods deeper into the woods. Seeing a squirrel, he throws a pine cone at it, and the animal does what Henry had done—it runs away. This is Henry's moment of self-knowledge; he knows now that his fleeing—like the
35 squirrel's—was not cowardice but a perfectly natural response under the circumstances, and he feels much better about himself.

EXERCISE 2. Indicate what each of the following **specific references** does for the reader. The first answer has been entered as a sample.

1. **a poor Mexican diver** (line 4)
   (explains who Kino is)

2. **unscrupulous pearl merchants** (line 7)

3. **others sabotage his canoe** (line 10)

4. **a young recruit in the Union Army** (lines 22–23)

5. **how he will behave under fire** (lines 23–24)

6. **passing several dead and wounded soldiers** (lines 28–29)

IMPORTANT: (*a*) Turn now in this book to the pages indicated and read, or reread, these two short stories:

"Sixteen," by Maureen Daly (pages 163–166)
"Early Autumn," by Langston Hughes (pages 161–162)

(*b*) In your notebook, write a literature essay in response to Question *B* (page 127), using the above two short stories.

(*c*) Consult the following Checklist to make sure you have not omitted any of the requirements of Question *B*.

(*d*) Finally, check your literature essay with the Second Model Answer to Question *B* (page 130). It follows the Checklist.

CHECKLIST FOR YOUR LITERATURE ESSAY

In your **first paragraph,** did you

* state the titles and authors of two works in which—be sure to say—an individual achieves self-knowledge as the result of undergoing an ordeal?
* enclose the titles in quotation marks, as required for short story titles?
* use only one sentence for the entire paragraph?

In your **second paragraph,** did you

* provide a transition?
* mention the name of the first individual, and the title of the work in which he or she is a character, and—do not omit this—state that he or she achieves self-knowledge as the result of undergoing an ordeal?
* use specific references to explain not only the first individual's ordeal, but also the self-knowledge that he or she achieved as a result?

In your **third paragraph,** did you

* provide a transition?
* mention the name of the second individual, and the title of the work in which he or she is a character, and—do not omit this— state that he or she achieves self-knowledge as the result of undergoing an ordeal?
* use specific references to explain not only the second individual's ordeal, but also the self-knowledge he or she achieves as a result?

If you have overlooked any of the above recommendations, make the necessary change or changes in your literature essay now.

A SECOND MODEL ANSWER TO QUESTION *B*

Two literary works in which an individual achieves self-knowledge as a result of undergoing an ordeal are "Sixteen" by Maureen Daly and "Early Autumn" by Langston Hughes.

At the beginning of "Sixteen," a girl of that age insists she is "not
5 so dumb" because she has two older sisters, knows how to dress, and "gets around." Besides, she reads, listens to the radio, and keeps up with the gossip about the private lives of celebrities. But there is something about herself she does not know, and that is the point of the story. On a moonlit night she meets a boy at a skating rink who
10 asks, "Mind if I skate with you?" Holding hands, they circle the ice the rest of the evening, talking, laughing, and having a wonderful time. He walks her home, commenting on how nice she looks with snow in her hair. At parting, he says, "I'll call you." For several days, confidently, at first, she sits at the telephone, waiting for his
15 call; it never comes. The self-knowledge she gains from this ordeal is that she is too naive; she should not have put so much faith in the vague promise of someone she hardly knew. In the future, in a similar situation, perhaps she will be less trusting.

In the same hard way, Mary, in "Early Autumn," gains important
20 knowledge about herself. She and Bill are in love, but as the result of a petty argument, she impulsively leaves him to marry someone she "thinks" she loves. When she and Bill meet accidentally a few years later, he is shocked to see that she looks so old. She has to work to support her three small children. Apparently, life with a husband she

25   does not love has been hard for her. From her ordeal, she gains the self-knowledge that not only was she too impulsive, but she was a poor judge of character. If she had been aware of these weaknesses earlier, perhaps she would not have rushed into a bad marriage.

AN IMPORTANT TOOL: THE CORRECT USAGE APPENDIX

One area that we must not overlook is *correct usage*. In your literature essay (twenty-five points) and your composition (thirty points), you will be required to follow the "conventions (rules) of standard written English." This includes not only spelling, which we reviewed in the chapter beginning on page 48, but also such matters as punctuating correctly, making verbs agree with their subjects, using pronouns correctly, and avoiding run-on sentences, sentence fragments, double negatives, and superfluous words. For help with these matters, see the section **Review of Correct Usage** beginning on page 185.

EXERCISE 3. *Violations of the Conventions of Standard Written English*

Below are some common errors made by students in their literature essays. Correct these errors in your notebook. The first three corrections have been made as samples. If you need help in correcting a particular error, consult the page indicated.

1. When Duncan arrives. He is full of praise for Macbeth. (229, rule 2)
   When Duncan arrives, he is full of praise for Macbeth.

2. Beret should not of allowed her husband to leave in the blizzard. (206, #4)
   Beret should not have allowed her husband to leave in the blizzard.

3. Kino wanted a better life for his family, that was his dream. (228, rule 1)
   Kino wanted a better life for his family. That was his dream.

4. Mattie is young, beautiful, and sweet. While Zeena is old, ugly, and mean. (229, rule 2)

5. George is the one that takes care of Lenny. He looked after him. (200, rule 1)

6. Ahab wanted revenge on a white whale that tore his leg off. (201, rule 2)

7. In the play *Julius Caesar*, written by William Shakespeare, Brutus sacrificed something of great value to save his country. (227)
8. Willy Loman's lies drive him to the point where he took his own life. (200, rule 1)
9. Gatsby bought a big house and through parties for the wealthy. (195)
10. Romeo and Juliet come from familys that despise one another. (63, rule 21a)
11. Lady Macbeth threatens to kill the king herself if Macbeth didn't do so. (200, rule 1)
12. Willy is a failure at his job, he lies to his family. (228, rule 1)
13. Lady Macbeth was so upset by her guilt that she couldn't bear it no more. (220)
14. Romeo was in love with a girl, Juliet. (227)
15. Mama made many sacrifices. So that her family could build better lives for themselves. (229, rule 2)
16. Malcolm, one of Duncan's sons becomes king. (235, rule 4b)
17. She pressured her husband into doing evil so that he could acheive his goal (52, rule 3)
18. Macbeth looses all touch with reality. (207, #7)
19. We see a man who's character undergoes a remarkable change. (209, #16)
20. Macbeth used to be admired by everyone, he was a hero. (228, rule 1)

FORMER COMPREHENSIVE ENGLISH LITERATURE ESSAY TESTS

As part of your preparation, you should write answers to two or three questions from the following former tests, especially those suggested by your teacher.

Directions: Write a well-organized essay of about 250 words on either *A* or *B*.   [25]

Test 1

A. A character's search for happiness is the focus of many works of literature. However, the search may or may not be successful. From the literature you have read, select *two* works in which a character searches for happiness. For *each* work, identify the character and explain what happiness means to that character. Using specific references from *each* work, discuss whether or not the character's search for happiness was successful. Give titles and authors.

B. In some works of literature, setting contributes to the reader's understanding of the central conflict. From the literature you have read, choose *two* works in which setting contributes to the reader's understanding of the central conflict of the work. For *each* work, identify the setting and the central conflict. Using specific references for *each* work, explain how the setting contributes to the reader's understanding of the central conflict. Give titles and authors.

— Choose 2 works
— identify the mood.

— discuss incidents that
— explain the importance

Test 2

A. Authors often create a predominant mood in a work of literature. The mood may be happy, tense, fearful, mysterious, or any other mood. From the literature you have read, choose *two* works in which the author has created a predominant mood. For *each* work, identify the mood. Using specific references from *each* work, discuss incidents that illustrate that mood and explain the importance of the mood to the work. Give titles and authors.

B. The phrase "rite of passage" is used to describe a situation in which a young person is faced with an experience that results in the young person becoming mature. From the literature you have read, choose *two* works in which a young person goes through a "rite of passage." For *each* work, identify the young person. Using specific references from *each* work, explain the experience the young person faces and discuss how the young person matures as a result of the way in which he or she deals with the experience. Give titles and authors.

Choose 2 works
identify the young person
explain the experience

discuss - how
Give titles + authors

Test 3

A. Characters in works of literature frequently learn about life or themselves by taking risks. From the literature you have read, choose *two* works in which a character learns about life or self through risk taking. For *each* work, identify the character and the risk that character takes, state why it was a risk, and explain what the character learns about life or self as a result of taking that risk. Use specific references to the works. Give titles and authors.

B. In some works of literature, an object is sometimes used on a literal level in the development of the plot and on a symbolic level in the development of a theme of the work. From the literature you have read, choose *two* works in which an object is used in the development of both the plot and a theme of the work. For *each* work, identify the object. Using specific references from *each* work, show how the object, on a literal level, is used in the development of the plot and how the object, on a symbolic level, is used in the development of a theme of the work. Give titles and authors.

Test 4

A. Pride can be a virtue that strengthens an individual's character or a vice that weakens it, depending on the effect of that pride on the individual and on others. From the literature you have read, choose *two* works in which an individual's pride is either a virtue or a vice. For *each* work, identify the individual and state whether his or her pride is a virtue or a vice. Using specific references from *each* work, discuss the effect of that pride on the individual and on others. Give titles and authors.

B. In many works of literature, a character reaches a major turning point in his or her life. From that point onward, the character undergoes a significant change. From the literature you have read, choose *two* works in which a character reaches a major turning point. For *each* work, identify the character and the event that marks the turning point. Using specific references from *each* work, discuss how the character changes as a result of this turning point. Give titles and authors.

Test 5

A. Sometimes characters in literature experience conflict between their consciences and the standards of behavior expected by others. From the poems, plays, novels, short stories, biographies, and books of true experience you have read, choose *two* works in which a character faces a conflict between his or her conscience and the standards of behavior expected by others. For *each* work, identify the character, explain the specific nature of the conflict, and discuss how the character was affected by this conflict. Use specific references to the works. Give titles and authors.

B. Authors sometimes use foreshadowing to help develop the plot of a work of literature. Foreshadowing usually takes the form of incidents that seem to be unimportant at first, but take on added significance later in the work. From the novels, plays, and short stories you have read, choose *two* works in which foreshadowing is used to help develop the plot. For *each* work, explain how an incident that seems to be unimportant at first takes on added significance later in the work and explain how this incident helps develop the plot. Use specific references to the works. Give titles and authors.

PART III OF THE EXAMINATION

The Composition Test
[30 credits]

Since it has a weight of thirty points, this is the most important part of the Comprehensive Examination in English. With the help in this chapter, you should be able to earn a high score in the composition test.

Typical Comprehensive English Composition Test

Part III

Directions: Answer *A* <u>or</u> *B* <u>or</u> *C*.   [30]

A. A representative of a junior high school in your district has invited you to speak at the junior high graduation ceremonies on the topic "Getting Off to a Good Start in High School." Write a speech of about 250 words that you would give to the students, stating your recommendations for a successful start in high school. Use specific reasons, examples, or details to support your recommendations.

B. If you could choose a time and place in which to live, other than here and now, what would be your choice? In a composition of about 250 words, identify the time and place you would choose and explain why you would choose that time and place. Use specific reasons, examples, or details.

135

C. Write a well-organized composition of about 250 words on *one* of the following topics:

Music: a family affair	Information highway
A second chance	Today's explorers
Athletes as free agents: who benefits?	"It's a small world after all"

CHOICES OFFERED IN THE COMPOSITION TEST

As you can see, the test gives you the choice of writing your 250-word composition on either Question *A*, or Question *B*, or on one of the six topics in Question *C*. In all, you will have eight different topics to choose from. This chapter will provide a model composition for each of these eight topics.

Survey the eight topics to see which would be the best for you. Then, before beginning to write, devise a plan on scrap paper for what you are going to put into your composition.

SUGGESTED PLAN FOR A COMPOSITION ON QUESTION *A*

PARAGRAPH 1 (introductory paragraph): In a single sentence, state the purpose of your speech (to help the junior high graduates get off to a successful start in high school).

PARAGRAPH 2 (first of two main paragraphs): Make your most important recommendation and support it, as Question A requires, with specific reasons, examples, or details.

PARAGRAPH 3 (second main paragraph): Make another important recommendation and support it, too, with specific reasons, examples, or details.

PARAGRAPH 4 (concluding paragraph): In a single sentence, sum up your speech, and wish the graduates luck.

MODEL ANSWER TO QUESTION *A*

I am happy and honored to have been invited here today to help you get off to a successful start in high school.

My first recommendation is that you should make learning your top priority. Learning is the main reason for your being in high school. There is no
5   future in today's world for people without knowledge and skills. Therefore, pay attention in class, take notes, ask questions if something is unclear, and do your homework. Do not go to a party the night before an important test unless you have already done your studying. When you are unavoidably absent, call up a classmate to learn what happened in class and do the as-
10   signment if there is one. I can tell you that students who cut classes and treat schoolwork as a joke are shocked when they see their first report cards. Unless they quickly change their ways, they are not going to be able to get into a good college or qualify for a decent job.

My second recommendation to you is to get involved in an extracurricular
15   activity. Extracurricular activities not only enrich your social life by acquainting you with people of similar interests, they also teach you a great deal that you cannot learn in a classroom, and they help you to improve yourself. One of my best friends, for example, has been much less shy ever since she joined the Drama Club and began acting in school plays. As for
20   me, I joined the Journalism Club in my first semester and became a cub reporter on the school newspaper; now I am the sports editor. By the way, if you like sports, why not take part in the intramural program in basketball, volleyball, or handball, or try out for a varsity team?

I sincerely hope my speech has given you some ideas for a good start in
25   high school, and I wish you the best of luck.

EXERCISE 1. Specific Reasons, Examples, or Details

In your notebook, briefly note:

(*a*) three reasons mentioned above in paragraph 2 (lines 3–13) for making learning the top priority.

(*b*) three reasons mentioned above in paragraph 3 (lines 14–23) for getting involved in an extracurricular activity.

(*c*) an example from paragraph 2 of a bad start in high school.

(*d*) an example from paragraph 3 of an extracurricular activity that helped someone.

(*e*) two details from paragraph 2 of what to do when unavoidably absent.

AUDIENCE, PURPOSE, TONE, AND DICTION

In rating your composition, teachers are instructed to consider, among other things, your awareness of *audience*, *purpose*, *tone*, and *diction*.

Audience, as applied to a composition, means the person or persons that the writer is addressing.
Purpose refers to what the writer hopes to achieve.
Tone in a composition means the writer's attitude.
Diction means the writer's choice of words.

QUESTION: What is wrong with the following opening sentence of an answer to Question *A*?

I have been asked to give you kids some recommendations about getting off to a good start in high school.

ANSWER: The sentence shows the writer's unawareness of the importance of audience, purpose, tone, and diction. The audience here is the junior high school graduating class in their caps and gowns at one of the proudest moments of their lives. To address them as "kids" is an insult; besides, it clashes with the writer's purpose of helping them to a good start in high school. "Kids" (inappropriate diction) should be replaced by "graduates." Once that change is made, the writer's attitude (tone) will be perceived as helpful, instead of insulting.

PRECISE LANGUAGE

QUESTION: What is wrong with the following?

If you like sports, there is a basketball team and lots of other teams you can try out for.

ANSWER: "Lots of other teams" is vague. The student should be more precise about the choices available. For example:

If you like sports, there is a basketball team, a baseball team, a volleyball team, a bowling team, a soccer team, and several others you can try out for.

EXERCISE 2.   In your notebook, rewrite the following, making the necessary improvements:

(*a*) I am 19 and still in high school because in my first year I didn't do lots of the things I was supposed to do. I regret that now.

(*b*) First of all, I hope no one here is such a dope as to believe that when you get to high school, the seniors will steer you wrong if you ask them for directions.

EXERCISE 3. Common Errors in Standard Written English

In your notebook, correct the following common errors that students made in their Question *A* compositions. For help in correcting a particular error, see the page enclosed in parentheses. The first error has been corrected as a sample.

1. Even if you think you know your work, study, it's the only way to get a good grade. (228, rule 1)
   <u>Even if you think you know your work, study. It's the only way to get a good grade.</u>

2. Our team traveled to many other schools to play. That was quiet an experience. (73)

3. One of my friends who studied hard is getting into a real good college. (231, rule 20)

4. Hanging out with you're friends and not studying will not help you earn credits to graduate. (73)

5. Cutting classes leads to dropping out of school all together. (71)

6. While it is important to make friends with people. You must make sure they will not become a negative influence on you. (229, rule 2)

7. Everyone should do their homework every night. (214, rule 6, paragraph 11)

8. I wish I would of done things differently. (73)

9. Cutting class is like a drug, if you do it two or three times, it is hard to stop. (228, rule 1)

10. As a high school senior, I would like to advice you how to get off to a good start. (73)

ANSWERING QUESTION *B*

As we saw on page 135, Question *B* reads as follows:

B. If you could choose a time and place in which to live, other than here and now, what would be your choice? In a composition of about 250 words, identify the time and place you would choose and explain why you would choose that time and place. Use specific reasons, examples, or details.

SUGGESTED PLAN FOR A COMPOSITION ON QUESTION *B*

PARAGRAPH 1 (opening paragraph): In a single sentence, identify the time and place in which you would choose to live.

PARAGRAPH 2 (first of two main paragraphs): Discuss why you would want to live in your chosen time and place, using specific reasons, examples, or details.

PARAGRAPH 3 (second main paragraph): Discuss why you are less than satisfied with the time and place in which you are now living. Include specific reasons, examples, or details.

PARAGRAPH 4 (concluding paragraph): In a single sentence, end your composition in an interesting way.

MODEL ANSWER TO QUESTION *B*

If I could choose a place and time to live other than here and now, I would choose to be a member of a Native American tribe in the unspoiled Great Plains of North America of about 150 years ago.

Living in that place and time, I would have a deep appreciation of nature.
5 Almost every day, I would see the sun rise and set, and I would have plenty of opportunities to observe the habits of the animals—the hawks, antelope, badgers, snakes, coyotes, buffalo, and many others. I would grow up with a deep respect for my elders because they would teach me not only how to hunt and fish, but also how to make bows and arrows, fishhooks, moccasins,
10 and even a canoe, with my own hands. I would be taught how to interpret tracks and follow a trail, and how to recognize wild berries that are safe to eat. In short, I would know how to survive in my environment, and I would feel safe.

Right now in New York City and across the nation, efforts to stop the
15 illegal drug traffic have failed miserably. Each day there are reports of increasingly shocking drug-related crimes. Minor arguments often end in kill-
ings because there are so many guns in our society. Many people hesitate to
go out on the streets, especially at night, for fear of becoming the victim of
a stray bullet, or drunken driver, or mugger. Car owners worry all the time
20 that their vehicles may be stolen or vandalized. We also have an AIDS epi-
demic, a worsening pollution problem, and a homeless population of many
thousands; but the number one problem in America today is crime.

For these reasons, I can't help thinking how much more fortunate I would
be if I had been born at some other place and time, like the Great Plains of
25 about 1840 or 1850.

EXERCISE 4. Specific Reasons, Examples, or Details

In your notebook, answer briefly:

What reasons does the writer of the above composition give:
(*a*) in paragraph 2 (lines 4–13) for wanting to live in the Great Plains
of 150 years ago?
(*b*) in paragraph 3 (lines 14–22) for being dissatisfied with the time and
place of his or her life?

What examples does the writer give:
(*c*) in paragraph 2 of wildlife in the Great Plains?
(*d*) in paragraph 3 of people's fears and worries in their daily lives?

What details does the writer give:
(*e*) in paragraph 1 (lines 1–3) about the time and place he or she would
like to live?

EXERCISE 5: Common Errors in Standard Written English

In your notebook, correct the following common errors that students
made in their Question B compositions. If you need help, consult the page
enclosed in parentheses. The first error has been corrected as a sample.

1. Who would choose to live in a world like this? A world filled with
poverty and suffering? (229, rule 2)
Who would choose to live in a world like this, a world filled with
poverty and suffering?

2. Wouldn't it be nice if you could go to a place where you dont have to
face the problems of today? (62, rule 19)

3. The lifestyle was simpler, people didn't have cars. (228, rule 1)

4. The best time to live in would of been fifty years ago. (73)

5. She didn't stay in the house all day, she was out there working with her husband. (228, rule 1)

6. All of us have fantasys about living in the distant future. (63, rule 21)

7. It is just to upsetting to see and experience our own destruction. (73)

8. I was mugged and beaten on my way to my friend's house, I was hospitalized for a couple of days. (228, rule 1)

9. All of these things we live with today makes life stressful and frustrating. (211, rule 1)

10. Every time I leave my house, my mom says, "Olga, please don't wear your jewelery." (68, B, 4)

Question C Topics

MODEL COMPOSITION

Music: a Family Affair

From as early as I can remember, music has been an important part of our family life.

My parents tell me that when I was in my high chair, they sang nursery rhymes with me, and soon I was able to sing them by myself. Then, my sister was born. She enjoyed singing even more than I because at that time she had a very fine voice. As we were growing up, my father would often get down his guitar and lead the family in "Home on the Range," "What Shall We Do With the Drunken Sailor," "Greensleeves," and many other ballads. It was a lot of fun.

When my sister showed interest in the guitar, my parents arranged for her to take guitar lessons and for me to study the piano. I managed to learn the keyboard and to play a few tunes from *Fiddler on the Roof* and *West Side Story*, but my sister was the star of the family. She enchanted us with her singing and playing. Relatives always insisted that she give a performance when they came to visit. Her friends would ask her to play rock and pop tunes, like "I Want to Hold Your Hand" and "Blowin' in the Wind." She became very popular. Unfortunately, she developed a pain in the left wrist which doctors said was the beginning of carpal tunnel syndrome, and they advised her to rest. For more than a year, she has not seriously practiced the guitar.

The family's love for music, however, is still evident. At meals and in the car, we enjoy listening to tapes of classical, pop, and rock music. In the morning, my mother usually does aerobic exercises to tunes like "Electric Slide" and "Manhattan Shuffle," and if my sister and I are home, we join her in this activity. My sister, as you can well imagine, just can't wait for the doctor's permission to go back to her favorite instrument, the guitar.

MODEL COMPOSITION

A Second Chance

It happened very unexpectedly. Up until that moment, it had been one of the most enjoyable days of my life. We had been to a birthday party at his cousin's house, where we had a wonderful time. The weather was ideal. As we walked back to my house, talking and laughing, he said something that hurt my feelings. I started to cry, and before I knew it, the words were out of my mouth. "How could you say a thing like that? You're mean! Get out of my sight! I never want to see you again! Never! I hate you!"

He was shocked. The blood went out of his face, and tears gathered in his eyes. He was unable to say a word. After a minute, he just turned and walked away without looking back, and I said nothing to stop him. Only then did I realize how deeply my words must have hurt him. I had lost my boyfriend, my first true love, and the best friend I ever had. Entering the house, I went straight to my room, locked the door, threw myself on the bed, and cried for the rest of the afternoon.

The phone rang several times that afternoon, but none of the calls were for me. I kept thinking of all the good times we had enjoyed together, and this made me only more miserable. Just when I had about given up all hope, the phone rang again. Tremblingly, I picked it up. "Stella," he said, "I want you to know that no matter what has happened, I still love you and will always love you. If I have said or done anything wrong, I am very sorry, and I hope you will forgive me." "I love you, too, Joe," I said. He wanted to come over for a while to talk to me, and I said, "There is nothing I would like better, Joe."

Fate was kind to me that day for giving me a second chance.

MODEL COMPOSITION

Athletes as Free Agents: Who Benefits?

In 1974, pitcher Jim (Catfish) Hunter had a contract dispute with the San Diego Padres. The arbitrator ruled in his favor, declaring him a free agent. This meant he could sign with any team he wanted. Since he had won 25 games that season, and the Cy Young Award, almost every team in the majors competed for his services. As a result, Hunter signed a 3.1 million-dollar contract with the New York Yankees. That is how free agency began in baseball.

The other players were astonished that club owners were willing to pay so much, and many of them became free agents as soon as possible. The result has been a bonanza for the players. Even the least talented now get fat salaries, and the stars who are free agents earn as much as seven million a year. Equally important is the greater freedom that players enjoy. An athlete who feels overshadowed by a teammate, or is not getting a chance to play regularly, now has a much better chance of changing teams, and so does the one who is homesick and wants to play closer to home.

The fans have not benefited too much. It is now very expensive to go to a ball game. Not only have ticket prices soared, but the cost of refreshments in ballparks has become exorbitant.

Many of the team owners have continued to prosper because they have been able to generate vast amounts of new revenue, especially from television, but they can be hurt. The loss of a star through free agency, for example, can change a pennant contender to a second division team. On the other hand, some teams have been able to climb out of the cellar in just a year or two, thanks to free agency and the draft, and the owners are well aware of this.

For the players' agents, however, free agency has been a windfall; they just sit back and continue to collect a percentage of the fabulous salaries that they helped the players to negotiate.

MODEL COMPOSITION

Information Highway

My assignment was to write a research paper on a recent discovery in the field of health or medicine. I chose cholesterol as my topic because it is on so many people's minds. Then I headed for the local library for information about recent research in cholesterol. As usual, I found the reference librarian an excellent guide to the information highway.

I explained my assignment and told her I had to read some recent magazine articles on cholesterol. She introduced me to a new research tool that saved me a great deal of time and effort, the computerized form of the Readers' Guide to Periodical Literature. It consists of a computer, a monitor, and a printer. I typed in CHOLESTEROL, and immediately the author, title, and source of the most recent of 472 articles on cholesterol appeared on the screen. When I found a promising article, I directed the computer to print its author, title, and source. With this helpful information, I secured and read articles on cholesterol research in *Newsweek*, the *New York Times, Business Week, Science News*, and several other periodicals. The paper I finally wrote dealt with a recent Harvard study reported in the *American Journal of Public Health*. The gist of it is that consuming partially hydrogenated fats in margarine and shortening increases the risk of heart disease.

By writing this paper, I learned not only about nutrition and a new research tool, but also about the library's plans to provide greater access to the information highway. In the not too distant future, it hopes to be able to give library users access to the information stored in the INTERNET, a network of thousands of computers owned by the government and many universities, colleges, and other institutions. This will not happen tomorrow, but when it does it will be something to celebrate.

MODEL COMPOSITION

Today's Explorers

Almost all of the earth's terrain has already been mapped, but that does not mean that the age of exploration is over. In fact, there are more explorers today than ever before. They are working night and day in thousands of laboratories all over the world to try to discover solutions for the causes of human suffering.

One of the finest examples of today's explorers is Barry Marshall, the young Australian physician who recently discovered a permanent, inexpensive cure for ulcers. Until just a couple of years ago, the medical profession firmly believed that most ulcers were caused by stomach acid and nervous tension. Dr. Marshall's curiosity was aroused, however, when he found H-pylori bacteria in the stomach of every one of his ulcer patients. This led him to investigate the possibility that the bacteria might be causing the ulcers. At one point he even swallowed a culture of these bacteria to give himself ulcers, so that he might prove that he could rid himself of the ulcers by taking antibiotics, as indeed he did.

At first, the medical profession and the drug companies scoffed at Dr. Marshall's discovery, even though he had already cured a large number of Australians of their ulcers. But he was finally able to convince them that most ulcers are caused by H-pylori bacteria, and that they can be cured with antibiotics. Think of all the misery and all the billions of dollars of expense for ulcer pills that will no longer be necessary. Think, also, of the many millions who will now be able to lead more healthful, more productive lives, thanks to Barry Marshall.

Dr. Marshall's brilliant discovery is not only an inspiration to medical researchers seeking cures for cancer, heart disease, diabetes, AIDS, multiple sclerosis, arthritis, and other serious maladies; it also gives hope to every sufferer from an incurable disease that a cure will be found.

MODEL COMPOSITION

"It's a Small World After All."

When I was in the first grade, I was a very shy girl. The only real friend I had was Patricia; the others in the class were just acquaintances. Patricia's family and mine had known each other for years, and she and I grew up like sisters. We traveled to school together, and after school we usually played in my house or in hers. Unfortunately, we were separated when I was only seven because my family decided to move upstate. I was too young then to know what this would entail, but it slowly dawned on me that I would no longer be in the same class as Patricia.

In the new town to which we moved, it took me a couple of years to get settled. Gradually, I overcame my shyness and made some new friends. Just as I was beginning to feel at home in my surroundings, my family moved again. In fact, by the time I was twelve, we had moved three times. Each time I went through the same ordeal of losing friends and learning to get along with new classmates and teachers.

Eventually we moved back to the city, to a neighborhood not far from where we had once lived. There, in my first term in high school, I saw a girl in my gym class who called herself Trisha. Something about her seemed familiar, but I could not understand what it was, until one day, in discussing our childhood, we realized that we had been in the same first-grade class. This is how Patricia and I redis-covered each other. Now, we are like sisters again.

Who would have thought that friends who hadn't heard about or seen each other since the first grade would end up in the same high school gym class? It's a small world after all.

EXERCISE 6: COMMON ERRORS IN STANDARD WRITTEN ENGLISH

In your notebook, correct the following common errors made by students in Question *C* compositions. If you need help with a particular error, refer to the page enclosed in parentheses. The first error has been corrected as a sample.

1. If the organization is making a great deal of money off of you, you are entitled to a raise. (231, rule 19)
   If the organization is making a great deal of money off you, you are entitled to a raise.

2. My parents like to listen to soft, gentle music because its relaxing. (206, rule 5)

3. It happened in 1992, for me that was an unforgettable year. (228, rule 1)

4. Today however, exploration has a different meaning. (237, rule *r*)

5. Sometimes, if your lucky, you may get a second chance. (210, rule 17)

6. Soon, I came to a turning point in my life. A turning point that would change my life for the better. (229, rule 2)

7. Most of the people who were their were drinking and seemed to be having a good time. (209, rule 14)

8. Some teams spend to much to get a good player. (209, rule 15)

9. Today's explorers are trying to solve the mysteries of life. Through research and experimentation. (229, rule 2)

10. The reason I was so hurt was because the person I considered my best friend had lied to me. (231, rule 15)

11. Last summer, me and my family made a trip to California. (231, rule 17)

12. Right now, even country music is making a comeback, I can't stand it. (228, rule 1)

13. Often, many teams compete for a players services. (66, rule 26)

14. The fact is that without a second chance, you are going to be left behind. While everyone else in the world goes ahead. (229, rule 2)

15. On my first try, I didn't do too good, but I was lucky to get a second chance. (231, rule 8)

FORMER COMPREHENSIVE ENGLISH COMPOSITION TESTS

Directions: **Answer *A* or *B* or *C*.** [30]

A. The editor of your local newspaper has proposed that businesses that hire high school graduates pay them salaries in proportion to their grades from the last two years of high school; that is, the higher a graduate's grades for the last two years of high school, the higher the salary. Write a letter of about 250 words to the editor in which you state your opinion of the proposal that graduates be paid salaries in proportion to their grades for the last two years of high school. Use specific reasons, examples, or details. *Write only the body of the letter.*

B. A community center in your area recently advertised that a rock concert will be held there this summer. The concert is expected to attract over 5,000 teenagers to this quiet suburban community. In recent letters to the editor of the local paper, residents of the community have protested the use of the community center for a rock concert, and the writers have demanded that the concert be canceled. Write a letter of about 250 words to the editor of the paper in which you give your view on holding the rock concert at the community center. Support your position with specific reasons, examples, or details. *Write only the body of the letter.*

C. Write a well-organized composition of about 250 words on *one* of the following topics:

All the world's a stage	Forever mine
Sports have been good to me	End of the cold war
Morality today	Curfews

Directions: **Answer *A* or *B* or *C*.** [30]

A. You have been asked to write an article for the next issue of the school literary magazine. The theme of the next issue is "Those who ignore the past are condemned to repeat it." Write an article of about 250 words for the magazine in which you discuss the implications of this statement either for you personally or for society in general. Use specific reasons, examples, or details.

B. Some educators have suggested that all public high school students wear school uniforms just as students in many private schools do. They cite some advantages of this suggestion—most notably a deemphasis on personal appearance and an emphasis on academic achievement. In a composition of about 250 words, state your opinion of the suggestion that all public high school students wear school uniforms. Support your opinion with specific reasons, examples, or details.

C. Write a well-organized composition of about 250 words on *one* of the following topics:

Space probes: Are they worth the cost?	Should art be censored? You don't have to be a
The new immigrants	star to play
Out of order	Preserving the wilderness

Directions: **Answer *A* or *B* or *C*.** [30]

A. Some people are opposed to using animals as subjects for scientific experiments and medical research. Others support this practice. In a composition of about 250 words, state your opinion about the use of animals as subjects for scientific experiments and medical research. Use specific reasons, examples, or details to support your opinion.

B. The approach of the 21st century may arouse feelings of hope or despair. Optimists will see the new century as a time of potential achievement in areas such as the quality of life for all individuals, social progress, international peace, economic development, environmental issues, or other areas. Pessimists, however, will see the new century as a time of continuing stress and turmoil. In a composition of about 250 words, state whether you agree with the optimists or the pessimists in your expectations for the 21st century. Support your opinion with specific reasons, examples, or details.

C. Write a well-organized composition of about 250 words on *one* of the following topics:

The price of liberty	Raising the speed limit to
Mars: the next frontier?	65 miles per hour
An important milestone	The me I want to be
	Athletics as big business

Directions: **Answer *A* or *B* or *C*.** [30]

A. As a sportswriter for your school newspaper, you have decided your next article will focus on the question, What makes an athlete exceptional? In an article of about 250 words, explain what qualities, in your opinion, make an athlete exceptional, both on and off the playing field. Support your opinion with specific reasons, examples, or details.

B. Your student government has begun a campaign to get students more actively involved in helping homeless people. They have asked the student body to suggest ways that students can take an active role in helping the homeless. In a letter of about 250 words to the members of the student government, suggest ways in which students can become more actively involved in helping the homeless. Support your suggestions with specific examples and details. *Write only the body of the letter.*

C. Write a well-organized composition of about 250 words on *one* of the following topics:

The other side of the fence	The greenhouse effect
Racism: everybody loses	Do my grades reflect me?
City lights	Getting started

Directions: **Answer A or B or C.** [30]

A. The editor of your school newspaper is planning to publish a special issue that deals with important problems facing young people today. In an article of about 250 words for the school newspaper, identify the problem that you believe is the most important one facing young people today. Discuss why you think the problem is the most important one facing young people today, and suggest a possible solution. Use specific reasons, examples, or details.

B. A friend of yours who is adopted is thinking about trying to locate his or her biological parents. Your friend has asked for your advice on this matter. In a letter of about 250 words to your friend, state your opinion about whether or not your friend should try to locate his or her biological parents. Support your opinion with specific reasons, examples, or details. *Write only the body of the letter.*

C. Write a well-organized composition of about 250 words on *one* of the following topics:

A minority report	Rituals
An experience I'd rather forget	New York State's most
The right to dissent	scenic area
	On being left-handed

A Little Anthology of Short Stories, Poems, and Essays

A short literary work, such as a short story, poem, or essay deals with essentially the same material as a longer work, such as a novel, a play, a biography, or a book of true experience. It may make important observations about life, death, human nature, or the world around us. It may present a universal theme, provide insight into human behavior, or use language in an exceptional way. For these reasons, past examinations have almost always given students the option of writing their literature essay about short works, like short stories, poems, and essays.

The main purpose of this little anthology is to give you the opportunity to read, or reread, the following excellent short literary works:

Short Stories

Poems

Essays

The Gift of the Magi
by O. Henry

One dollar and eighty-seven cents. That was all. And sixty cents of it was in pennies. Pennies saved one and two at a time by bulldozing the grocer and the vegetable man and the butcher until one's cheeks burned with the silent imputation of parsimony that such close dealing implied. Three times Della counted it. One dollar and eighty-seven cents. And the next day would be Christmas.

There was clearly nothing to do but flop down on the shabby little couch and howl. So Della did it. Which instigates the moral reflection that life is made up of sobs, sniffles, and smiles, with sniffles predominating.

While the mistress of the home is gradually subsiding from the first stage to the second, take a look at the home. A furnished flat at $8 per week. It did not exactly beggar description, but it certainly had that word on the lookout for the mendicancy squad.

In the vestibule below was a letterbox into which no letter would go, and an electric button from which no mortal finger could coax a ring. Also appertaining thereunto was a card bearing the name "Mr. James Dillingham Young."

The "Dillingham" had been flung to the breeze during a former period of prosperity when its possessor was being paid $30 per week. Now, when the income was shrunk to $20, the letters of "Dillingham" looked blurred, as though they were thinking seriously of contracting to a modest and unassuming D. But whenever Mr. James Dillingham Young came home and reached his flat above, he was called "Jim" and greatly hugged by Mrs. James Dillingham Young, already introduced to you as Della. Which is all very good.

Della finished her cry and attended to her cheeks with the powder rag. She stood by the window and looked out dully at a gray cat walking a gray fence in a gray backyard. Tomorrow would be Christmas Day and she had only $1.87 with which to buy Jim a present. She had been saving every penny she could for months, with this result. Twenty dollars a week doesn't go far. Expenses had been greater than she had calculated. They always are. Only $1.87 to buy a present for Jim. Her Jim. Many a happy hour she had spent planning for something nice for him. Something fine and rare

Reprinted by permission of DOUBLEDAY a division of Bantam, Doubleday, Dell Publishing Group, Inc.

and sterling—something just a little bit near to being worthy of the honor of being owned by Jim.

There was a pier glass between the windows of the room. Perhaps you have seen a pier glass in an $8 flat. A very thin and very agile person may, by observing his reflection in a rapid sequence of longitudinal strips, obtain a fairly accurate conception of his looks. Della, being slender, had mastered the art.

Suddenly she whirled from the window and stood before the glass. Her eyes were shining brilliantly, but her face had lost its color within twenty seconds. Rapidly she pulled down her hair and let it fall to its full length.

Now, there were two possessions of the James Dillingham Youngs in which they both took a mighty pride. One was Jim's gold watch that had been his father's and his grandfather's. The other was Della's hair. Had the Queen of Sheba lived in the flat across the airshaft, Della would have let her hair hang out the window some day to dry just to depreciate Her Majesty's jewels and gifts. Had King Solomon been the janitor, with all his treasures piled up in the basement, Jim would have pulled out his watch every time he passed, just to see him pluck at his beard from envy.

So now Della's beautiful hair fell about her rippling and shining like a cascade of brown waters. It reached below her knee and made itself almost a garment for her. And then she did it up again nervously and quickly. Once she faltered for a minute and stood still while a tear or two splashed on the worn red carpet.

On went her old brown jacket; on went her old brown hat. With a whirl of skirts and with the brilliant sparkle still in her eyes, she fluttered out the door and down the stairs to the street.

Where she stopped the sign read: "Mme. Sofronie. Hair Goods of All Kinds." One flight up Della ran, and collected herself, panting. Madame, large, too white, chilly, hardly looked the "Sofronie."

"Will you buy my hair?" asked Della.

"I buy hair," said Madame. "Take yer hat off and let's have a sight at the looks of it."

Down rippled the brown cascade.

"Twenty dollars," said Madame, lifting the mass with a practiced hand.

"Give it to me quick," said Della.

Oh, and the next two hours tripped by on rosy wings. Forget the hashed metaphor. She was ransacking the stores for Jim's present.

She found it at last. It surely had been made for Jim and no one else. There was no other like it in any of the stores, and she had turned all of them inside out. It was a platinum fob chain simple and chaste in design, properly proclaiming its value by substance alone and not by meretricious ornamentation—as all good things should do. It was even worthy of The Watch. As soon as she saw it she knew that it must be Jim's. It was like him. Quietness and value—the description applied to both. Twenty-one dollars they took from her for it, and she hurried home with the 87 cents. With that chain on his watch Jim might be properly anxious about the time in any company. Grand as the watch was, he sometimes looked at it on the sly on account of the old leather strap that he used in place of a chain.

When Della reached home her intoxication gave way a little to prudence and reason. She got out her curling irons and lighted the gas and went to work repairing the ravages made by generosity added to love. Which is always a tremendous task, dear friends—a mammoth task.

Within forty minutes her head was covered with tiny, close-lying curls that made her look wonderfully like a truant schoolboy. She looked at her reflection in the mirror long, carefully, and critically.

"If Jim doesn't kill me," she said to herself, "before he takes a second look at me, he'll say I look like a Coney Island chorus girl. But what could I do—oh! what could I do with a dollar and eighty-seven cents?"

At 7 o'clock the coffee was made and the frying pan was on the back of the stove hot and ready to cook the chops.

Jim was never late. Della doubled the fob chain in her hand and sat on the corner of the table near the door that he always entered. Then she heard his step on the stair away down on the first flight, and she turned white for just a moment. She had a habit of saying little silent prayers about the simplest everyday things, and now she whispered: "Please God, make him think I am still pretty."

The door opened and Jim stepped in and closed it. He looked thin and very serious. Poor fellow, he was only twenty-two—and to be burdened with a family! He needed a new overcoat and he was without gloves.

Jim stepped inside the door, as immovable as a setter at the scent of quail. His eyes were fixed upon Della, and there was an expression in them that she could not read, and it terrified her. It was not anger, nor surprise, nor disapproval, nor horror, nor any of the sentiments that she had been prepared for. He simply stared at her fixedly with that peculiar expression on his face.

Della wriggled off the table and went for him.

"Jim, darling," she cried, "don't look at me that way. I had my hair cut off and sold it because I couldn't have lived through Christmas without giving you a present. It'll grow out again—you won't mind, will you? I just had to do it. My hair grows awfully fast. Say 'Merry Christmas!', Jim, and let's be happy. You don't know what a nice—what a beautiful, nice gift I've got for you."

"You've cut off your hair?" asked Jim, laboriously, as if he had not arrived at that patent fact yet even after the hardest mental labor.

"Cut it off and sold it," said Della. "Don't you like me just as well, anyhow? I'm me without my hair, ain't I?"

Jim looked about the room curiously.

"You say your hair is gone?" he said, with an air almost of idiocy.

"You needn't look for it," said Della. "It's sold, I tell you—sold and gone, too. It's Christmas Eve, boy. Be good to me, for it went for you. Maybe the hairs of my head were numbered," she went on with a sudden, serious sweetness, "but nobody could ever count my love for you. Shall I put the chops on, Jim?"

Out of his trance Jim seemed quickly to wake. He enfolded his Della. For ten seconds let us regard with discreet scrutiny some inconsequential object in the other direction. Eight dollars a week or a million a year—what is the difference? A mathematician or a wit would give you the wrong answer. The magi brought valuable gifts, but that was not among them. This dark assertion will be illuminated later on.

Jim drew a package from his overcoat pocket and threw it upon the table.

"Don't make any mistake, Dell," he said, "about me. I don't think there's anything in the way of a haircut or a shave or a shampoo that could make me like my girl any less. But if you'll unwrap that package you may see why you had me going a while at first."

White fingers and nimble tore at the string and paper. And then an ecstatic scream of joy; and then, alas! a quick feminine change to hysterical tears and wails, necessitating the immediate employment of all the comforting powers of the lord of the flat.

For there lay The Combs—the set of combs, side and back, that Della had worshiped for long in a Broadway window. Beautiful combs, pure tortoise shell, with jeweled rims—just the shade to wear in the beautiful vanished hair. They were expensive combs, she knew, and her heart had simply craved and yearned over them without the least hope of possession. And now, they were hers, but the tresses that should have adorned the coveted adornments were gone.

But she hugged them to her bosom, and at length she was able to look up with dim eyes and a smile and say: "My hair grows so fast, Jim!"

And then Della leaped up like a little singed cat and cried, "Oh, oh!"

Jim had not yet seen his beautiful present. She held it out to him eagerly upon her open palm. The dull precious metal seemed to flash with a reflection of her bright and ardent spirit.

"Isn't it a dandy, Jim? I hunted all over town to find it. You'll have to look at the time a hundred times a day now. Give me your watch. I want to see how it looks on it."

Instead of obeying, Jim tumbled down on the couch and put his hands under the back of his head and smiled.

"Dell," said he, "let's put our Christmas presents away and keep 'em a while. They're too nice to use just at present. I sold the watch to get the money to buy your combs. And now suppose you put the chops on."

The magi, as you know, were wise men—wonderfully wise men—who brought gifts to the Babe in the manger. They invented the art of giving Christmas presents. Being wise, their gifts were no doubt wise ones, possibly bearing the privilege of exchange in case of duplication. And here I have lamely related to you the uneventful chronicle of two foolish children in a flat who most unwisely sacrificed for each other the greatest treasures of their house. But in a last word to the wise of these days let it be said that of all who give gifts these two were the wisest. Of all who give and receive gifts, such as they are wisest. Everywhere they are wisest. They are the magi.

Bill

by Zona Gale

Bill was thirty when his wife died, and little Minna was four. Bill's carpenter shop was in the yard of his house, so he thought that he could keep up his home for Minna and himself. All day while he worked at his bench, she played in the yard, and when he was obliged to be absent for a few hours, the woman next door looked after her. Bill could cook a little, coffee and bacon and fried potatoes and flapjacks, and he found bananas and sardines and crackers useful. When the woman next door said this was not the diet for four-year-olds, he asked her to teach him to cook oatmeal and vegetables, and though he always burned the dishes in which he cooked these things, he cooked them every day. He swept, all but the corners, and he dusted, dabbing at every object; and he complained that after he had cleaned the windows he could not see out as well as he could before. He washed and patched Minna's little garments and mended her doll. He found a kitten for her so that she wouldn't be lonely. At night he heard her say her prayer, kneeling in the middle of the floor with her hands folded, and speaking like lightning. If he forgot the prayer, he either woke her up, or else he made her say it the first thing next morning. He himself used to try to pray: "Lord, make me do right by her if you see me doing wrong." On Sundays he took her to church and sat listening with his head on one side, trying to understand, and giving Minna peppermints when she rustled. He stopped work for a day and took her to the Sunday school picnic. "Her mother would of," he explained. When Minna was old enough to go to kindergarten, Bill used to take her morning or afternoon, and he would call for her. Once he dressed himself in his best clothes and went to visit the school. "I think her mother would of," he told the teacher, diffidently. But he could make little of the colored paper and the designs and games, and he did not go again. "There's some things I can't be any help to her with," he thought.

Minna was six when Bill fell ill. On a May afternoon he went to a doctor. When he came home he sat in his shop for a long time and did nothing. The sun was beaming through the window in bright squares. He was not

---

going to get well. It might be that he had six months. . . . He could hear
Minna singing to her doll.

When she came to kiss him that night, he made an excuse, for he must
never kiss her now. He held her at arm's length, looked in her eyes, said:
"Minna's a big girl now. She doesn't want papa to kiss her." But her lip
curled and she turned away sorrowful, so the next day Bill went to another
doctor to make sure. The other doctor made him sure.

He tried to think what to do. He had a sister in Nebraska, but she was a
tired woman. His wife had a brother in the city, but he was a man of many
words. And little Minna . . . there were things known to her which he
himself did not know—matters of fairies and the words of songs. He wished
that he could hear of somebody who would understand her. And he had
only six months. . . .

Then the woman next door told him bluntly that he ought not to have the
child there, and him coughing as he was; and he knew that his decision
was already upon him.

One whole night he thought. Then he advertised in a city paper:

> A man with a few months more to live would like nice people
> to adopt his little girl, six, blue eyes, curls. References required.

They came in a limousine, as he had hoped that they would come. Their
clothes were as he had hoped. They had with them a little girl who cried:
"Is this my little sister?" On which the woman in the smart frock said
sharply:

"Now then, you do as mama tells you and keep out of this or we'll leave
you here and take this darling little girl away with us."

So Bill looked at this woman and said steadily that he had now other
plans for his little girl. He watched the great blue car roll away. "For the
land sake!" said the woman next door when she heard. "You done her out
of a fortune. You hadn't the right—a man in your health." And when other
cars came, and he let them go, this woman told her husband that Bill ought
to be reported to the authorities.

The man and woman who walked into Bill's shop one morning were still
mourning their own little girl. The woman was not sad—only sorrowful,
and the man, who was tender of her, was a carpenter. In a blooming of his
hope and his dread, Bill said to them: "You're the ones." When they
asked: "How long before we can have her?" Bill said: "One day more."

That day he spent in the shop. It was summer and Minna was playing in
the yard. He could hear the words of her songs. He cooked their supper
and while she ate, he watched. When he had tucked her in her bed, he

stood in the dark hearing her breathing. "I'm a little girl tonight—kiss me," she had said, but he shook his head. "A big girl, a big girl," he told her.

When they came for her the next morning, he had her ready and her little garments were ready, washed and mended, and he had mended her doll. "Minna's never been for a visit!" he told her buoyantly. And when she ran toward him, "A big girl, a big girl," he reminded her.

He stood and watched the man and woman walking down the street with Minna between them. They had brought her a little blue parasol in case the parting should be hard. This parasol Minna held bobbing above her head, and she was so absorbed in looking up at the blue silk that she did not remember to turn and wave her hand.

Early Autumn
by Langston Hughes

When Bill was very young, they had been in love. Many nights they had spent walking, talking together. Then something not very important had come between them, and they didn't speak. Impulsively, she had married a man she thought she loved. Bill went away, bitter about women.

Yesterday, walking across Washington Square, she saw him for the first time in years.

"Bill Walker," she said.

He stopped. At first he did not recognize her, to him she looked so old. "Mary! Where did you come from?"

Unconsciously, she lifted her face as though wanting a kiss, but he held out his hand. She took it.

"I live in New York now," she said.

"Oh"—smiling politely. Then a little frown came quickly between his eyes.

"Always wondered what happened to you, Bill."

"I'm a lawyer. Nice firm, way downtown."

"Married yet?"

"Sure. Two kids."

"Oh," she said.

A great many people went past them through the park. People they didn't know. It was late afternoon. Nearly sunset. Cold.

"And your husband?" he asked her.

"We have three children. I work in the bursar's office at Columbia."

"You're looking very . . ." (he wanted to say *old*) ". . . well," he said.

She understood. Under the trees in Washington Square, she found herself desperately reaching back into the past. She had been older than he then in Ohio. Now she was not young at all. Bill was still young.

"We live on Central Park West," she said. "Come and see us sometime."

"Sure," he replied. "You and your husband must have dinner with my family some night. Any night. Lucille and I'd love to have you."

The leaves fell slowly from the trees in the Square. Fell without wind. Autumn dusk. She felt a little sick.

"We'd love it," she answered.

"You ought to see my kids." He grinned.

Suddenly the lights came on up the whole length of Fifth Avenue, chains of misty brilliance in the blue air.

"There's my bus," she said.

He held out his hand. "Good-by."

"When . . ." she wanted to say, but the bus was ready to pull off. The lights on the avenue blurred, twinkled, blurred. And she was afraid to open her mouth as she entered the bus. Afraid it would be impossible to utter a word.

Suddenly she shrieked very loudly, "Good-by!" But the bus door had closed.

The bus started. People came between them outside, people crossing the street, people they didn't know. Space and people. She lost sight of Bill. Then she remembered she had forgotten to give him her address—or to ask him for his—or tell him that her youngest boy was named Bill, too.

"Sixteen"
by Maureen Daly

NOW DON'T get me wrong. I mean, I want you to understand from the beginning that I'm not really so dumb. I know what a girl should do and what she shouldn't. I get around. I read. I listen to the radio. And I have two older sisters. So you see, I know what the score is. I know it's smart to wear tweedish skirts and shaggy sweaters with the sleeves pushed up and pearls and ankle-socks and saddle shoes that look as if they've seen the world. And I know that your hair should be long, almost to your shoulders, and sleek as a wet seal, just a little fluffed on the ends, and you should wear a campus hat or a dink or else a peasant hankie if you've that sort of face. Properly, a peasant hankie should make you think of edelweiss, mist and sunny mountains, yodeling and Swiss cheese. You know, that kind of peasant. Now, me, I never wear a hankie. It makes my face seem wide and Slavic and I look like a picture always in one of those magazine articles that run—"And Stalin says the future of Russia lies in its women. In its women who have tilled its soil, raised its children—" Well, anyway. I'm not exactly too small-town either. I read Winchell's column. You get to know what New York boy is that way about some pineapple princess on the West Coast and what Paradise pretty is currently the prettiest, and why someone, eventually, will play Scarlett O'Hara. It gives you that cosmopolitan feeling. And I know that anyone who orders a strawberry sundae in a drugstore instead of a lemon coke would probably be dumb enough to wear colored ankle-socks with high-heeled pumps or use Evening in Paris with a tweed suit. But I'm sort of drifting. This isn't what I wanted to tell you. I just wanted to give you the general idea of how I'm not so dumb. It's important that you understand that.

You see, it was funny how I met him. It was a winter night like any other winter night. And I didn't have my Latin done either. But the way the moon tinseled the twigs and silverplated the snow drifts, I just couldn't stay inside. The skating rink isn't far from our house—you can make it in five minutes if the sidewalks aren't slippery, so I went skating. I remember it took me a long time to get ready that night because I had to darn my skating socks first. I don't know why they always wear out so fast—just in the toes, too. Maybe it's because I have metal protectors on the toes of my skates. That probably *is* why. And then I brushed my hair—hard, so hard it clung to my hand and stood up around my head in a hazy halo.

My skates were hanging by the back door all nice and shiny, for I'd just gotten them for Christmas and they smelled so queer—just like fresh-smoked ham. My dog walked with me as far as the corner. She's a red chow, very polite and well-mannered, and she kept pretending it was me she liked when all the time I knew it was the ham smell. She panted along beside me and her hot breath made a frosty little balloon balancing on the end of her nose. My skates thumped me good-naturedly on the back as I walked and the night was breathlessly quiet and the stars winked down like a million flirting eyes. It was all so lovely.

It was all so lovely I ran most of the way and it was lucky the sidewalks had ashes on them or I'd have slipped surely. The ashes crunched like crackerjack and I could feel their cindery shape through the thinness of my shoes. I always wear old shoes when I go skating.

I had to cut across someone's back garden to get to the rink and last summer's grass stuck through the thin ice, brown and discouraged. Not many people came through this way and the crusted snow broke through the little hollows between corn stubbles frozen hard in the ground. I was out of breath when I got to the shanty—out of breath with running and with the loveliness of the night. Shanties are always such friendly places. The floor all hacked to wet splinters from skate runners and the wooden wall frescoed with symbols of dead romance. There was a smell of singed wool as someone got too near the glowing isinglass grid of the iron stove. Girls burst through the door laughing with snow on their hair and tripped over shoes scattered on the floor. A pimply-faced boy grabbed the hat from the frizzled head of an eighth-grade blonde and stuffed it into an empty galosh to prove his love and then hastily bent to examine his skate strap with innocent unconcern.

It didn't take me long to get my own skates on and I stuck my shoes under the bench—far back where they wouldn't get knocked around and would be easy to find when I wanted to go home. I walked out on my toes and the shiny runners of my new skates dug deep into the sodden floor.

It was snowing a little outside—quick, eager little Lux-like flakes that melted as soon as they touched your hand. I don't know where the snow came from for there were stars out. Or maybe the stars were in my eyes and I just kept seeing them every time I looked up into the darkness. I waited a moment. You know, to start to skate at a crowded rink is like jumping on a moving merry-go-round. The skaters go skimming round in a colored blur like gaudy painted horses and the shrill musical jabber reechoes in the night from a hundred human calliopes. Once in, I went all right. At least, after I found out exactly where that ɹough ice was. It was "round, round, jump the rut, round, round, round, jump the rut, round, round—"

And then he came. All of a sudden his arm was around my waist so warm and tight and he said very casually, "Mind if I skate with you?" and then he took my other hand. That's all there was to it. Just that and then we were skating. It wasn't that I'd never skated with a boy before. Don't be silly. I told you before I get around. But this was different. He was a smoothie! He was a big shot up at school and he went to all the big dances and he was the best dancer in town except Harold Wright who didn't count because he'd been to college in New York for two years! Don't you see? This was different.

At first I can't remember what we talked about, I can't even remember if we talked at all. We just skated and skated and laughed every time we came to that rough spot and pretty soon we were laughing all the time at nothing at all. It was all so lovely.

Then we sat on the big snow bank at the edge of the rink and just watched. It was cold at first even with my skating pants on, sitting on that hard heap of snow, but pretty soon I got warm all over. He threw a handful of snow at me and it fell in a little white shower on my hair and he leaned over to brush it off. I held my breath. The night stood still.

The moon hung just over the warming shanty like a big quarter-slice of muskmelon and the smoke from the pipe chimney floated up in a sooty fog. One by one the houses around the rink twinked out their lights and somebody's hound wailed a mournful apology to a star as he curled up for the night. It was all so lovely.

Then he sat up straight and said, "We'd better start home." Not "Shall I take you home?" or "Do you live far?" but "We'd better start home." See, that's how I know he wanted to take me home. Not because he *had* to but because he *wanted* to. He went to the shanty to get my shoes. "Black ones," I told him. "Same size as Garbo's." And laughed again. He was still smiling when he came back and took off my skates and tied the wet skate strings in a soggy knot and put them over his shoulder. Then he held out his hand and I slid off the snow bank and brushed off the seat of my pants and we were ready.

It was snowing harder now. Big, quiet flakes that clung to twiggy bushes and snuggled in little drifts against the tree trunks. The night was an etching in black and white. It was all so lovely I was sorry I lived only a few blocks away. He talked softly as we walked as if every little word were a secret

"Did I like Wayne King, and did I plan to go to college next year and had I a cousin who lived in Appleton and knew his brother?" A very respectable Emily Post sort of conversation, and then finally—"how nice I looked with snow in my hair and had I ever seen the moon so—close?" For the moon was following us as we walked and ducking playfully behind a chimney every time I turned to look at it. And then we were home.

The porch light was on. My mother always puts the porch light on when I go away at night. And we stood there a moment by the front steps and the snow turned pinkish in the glow of the colored light and a few feathery flakes settled on his hair. Then he took my skates and put them over my shoulder and said, "Good night now. I'll call you," he said.

I went inside then and in a moment he was gone. I watched him from my window as he went down the street. He was whistling softly and I waited until the sound faded away so I couldn't tell if it was he or my heart whistling out there in the night. And then he was gone, completely gone.

I shivered. Somehow the darkness seemed changed. The stars were little hard chips of light far up in the sky and the moon stared down with a sullen yellow glare. The air was tense with sudden cold and a gust of wind swirled his footprints into white oblivion. Everything was quiet.

But he'd said, "I'll call you." That's what he said, "I'll call you." I couldn't sleep all night.

And that was last Thursday. Tonight is Tuesday. Tonight is Tuesday and my homework's done, and I darned some stockings that didn't really need it, and I worked a cross-word puzzle, and I listened to the radio and now I'm just sitting. I'm just sitting because I can't think of anything else to do. I can't think of anything, anything but snowflakes and ice skates and yellow moons and Thursday night. The telephone is sitting on the corner table with its old black face turned to the wall so I can't see its leer. I don't even jump when it rings anymore. My heart still prays but my mind just laughs. Outside the night is still, so still I think I'll go crazy and the white snow's all dirtied and smoked into grayness and the wind is blowing the arc light so it throws weird, waving shadows from the trees onto the lawn— like thin, starved arms begging for I don't know what. And so I'm just sitting here and I'm not feeling anything. I'm not even sad because all of a sudden I know. I can sit here now forever and laugh and laugh while the tears run salty in the corners of my mouth. For all of a sudden I know, I know what the stars knew all the time—he'll never, never call—never.

The Little Cask
by Guy de Maupassant

M. CHICOT, the innkeeper of Epreville, stopped his cart in front of the farmhouse of Mother Magloire. He was a jovial fellow, about forty years old, ruddy and corpulent, and he gave the impression of being crafty. He hitched his horse to the gatepost and entered the court.

M. Chicot owned property adjoining the old woman's land, and, for a long time, he had coveted hers. Many times he had tried to buy it, but Mother Magloire obstinately refused to sell.

"I was born here, and here I shall die," she always said.

He found her outside her door paring potatoes. She was seventy-two years old, dried up, lined and bent, but untiring as a young girl. Chicot gave her a friendly clap on the back and then sat down on a stool beside her.

"Well! Mother, and how's your health, still fine?"

"Not so bad, and yours, Master Prosper?"

"Oh, a few aches; outside of that, pretty fair."

"Well, that's good!"

And she said nothing more. Chicot watched her doing her task. Her fingers, bent, knotted, hard as crabs' claws, seized the grayish tubercles in one hand like pincers, and quickly turned them around, paring off long strips of peel with the blade of an old knife which she held in the other hand. When the potato had become entirely yellow, she would throw it in a pail of water. Three daring chickens crept one after the other as far as the hem of her skirts to pick up the parings, and then scuttled off, carrying their booty in their beaks.

Chicot seemed troubled, hesitating, anxious, as if he had something on his mind that he did not wish to say. Finally he remarked,

"Tell me, now, Mother Magloire, this farm of yours—don't you ever want to sell it to me?"

"Certainly not. You can make up your mind in that score. What I have said, I mean, so let's not refer to the matter again."

"All right, only I think I have devised a scheme which we shall both like."

"What is it?"

"Just this: you can sell me the farm and retain it just the same. You don't understand? Just listen to this."

The old woman stopped paring her vegetables and looked at the innkeeper attentively from under her shaggy eyebrows. He continued:

"Let me explain. I shall give you a hundred and fifty francs every month. Do you understand? Every month! I shall bring here in my wagon thirty crowns. And it won't make the least bit of difference to you, not the least! You will stay in your home; you won't trouble yourself with me; you won't do anything for me: you will only take my money. How does that appeal to you?"

He looked at her with a happy, good-natured expression but the old woman glanced back at him with distrust, as if she were searching for some trap.

"It is all right as far as I can see, but," she asked, "you don't think it is going to get the farm for you, do you?"

"Don't you worry about that. You will stay here just as long as God Almighty is willing that you should live. You will stay in your own home, only you will sign a paper before a notary, that, after you are finished with the farm, it will come to me. You have no children—only a few nephews who have scarcely any hold on you. Is that all right for you? You keep your property during your life, and I give you thirty crowns a month. It is all gain for you."

The old woman was still surprised and puzzled, but inclined to accept. She replied:

"I don't say 'no,' but I want to think it over. Come back sometime next week and we will talk it over. I will give you my answer then."

Master Chicot went away as happy as a king who had just conquered an empire.

Mother Magloire kept thinking about it. She did not sleep that night, and for four days she was in a fever of hesitation. She detected something in the offer which was not to her advantage, but the thought of thirty crowns a month, of all that beautiful jingling money that would come to roll around in her apron pocket, which would fall as if from Heaven, without any effort on her part, filled her with covetousness. Then she went to hunt for a notary and tell him her case. He advised her to accept Chicot's proposition, but to ask for fifty crowns instead of thirty because her farm was worth sixty thousand francs at the lowest estimate.

"If you live fifteen years," the notary said, "in that way he will pay even then only forty-five thousand."

The old woman trembled at the thought of fifty crowns a month, but she was still suspicious, fearing a thousand unforseen tricks and she stayed till evening asking questions, unable to make up her mind to leave. Finally she gave the notary instructions to draw up the deed, and went home with her head in a whirl, just as if she had drunk four jugs of new cider.

When Chicot came to get her answer, she took a lot of persuading and declared she could not make up her mind what to do, but all the time she was distracted by the idea that he might not consent to give the fifty crowns a month. Finally, when he became insistent, she told him what she wanted for her farm.

He looked surprised and disappointed, and refused. Then, in order to win him over, the old woman began to argue on the probable duration of her life.

"I can't have but five or six years more to live. Here I am nearly seventy-three and none too hearty at that. The other evening I thought I was going to die. It seemed to me that my soul was being dragged out of my body and I could scarcely crawl to my bed." But Chicot didn't let himself be taken in.

"Come, now," he said, "old woman, you are as solid as a church bell. You will live to be a hundred at least. You will see me buried, I'm sure."

They spent the whole day in discussion, but as the old woman would not give in, the innkeeper finally consented to give her the fifty crowns a month. They signed the deed the next day, and Mother Magloire drew out ten crowns from her wine jug.

Three years rolled by. The old woman lived as if protected by a charm. She seemed not to have aged a day, and Chicot was in despair. It seemed to him that he had been paying this rent for fifty years, and that he had been tricked, cheated, ruined. From time to time he paid a visit to the old farmer woman, as in July we go into the fields to see if the wheat is ripe enough to harvest. She received him with a malicious gleam in her eye. One would say that she was congratulating herself on the good trick she had played on him, and he would quickly get back into his wagon murmuring, "You won't die then, you old brute!"

He didn't know what to do. When he saw her, he wanted to strangle her. He hated her with a ferocious, crafty hatred, with the hatred of a peasant who has been robbed, and he began to think of ways to get rid of her.

Finally, one day, he came to see her, rubbing his hands as he did the first time when he had proposed the bargain. After he had talked for some time, he said,

"Tell me, now, Mother, why haven't you stopped for dinner at my inn when you have been at Epreville? People have been talking about it; they say that we are not good friends, and that grieves me. You know at my place you don't pay anything. Just stop in whenever you feel like it. It will give me a great deal of pleasure."

Mother Magloire didn't make him repeat his offer, but the next day, as she was going to market in her carriage driven by her servant Celestin, without any hesitancy she had her horse put in Chicot's stable, and went into the inn to claim the promised dinner.

The delighted innkeeper treated her like a great lady. He served her with chicken, black pudding, chitterlings, leg of mutton, and bacon and cabbage. But, as she had always been a very moderate eater since childhood, she ate almost nothing. Her usual fare had always been a little soup and a crust of bread and butter. Chicot was disappointed, but he kept insisting that she eat. Neither could he prevail upon her to drink anything; she refused even coffee.

Finally he said, "Surely you always accept a small glass of wine."

"Oh, yes! I won't say 'no'!"

And he shouted as loudly as he could across the room, "Rosalie, bring the extra-fine brandy—you know, the special."

The servant appeared, bringing a long bottle decorated with a paper wine leaf. He filled two liqueur glasses.

"Taste that, Mother; it is some of the famous brand."

The good woman began to drink very slowly, in little swallows to make the pleasure last. When she had emptied her glass, she held it up again to get the last drop; then she exclaimed,

"Yes, that is very excellent."

She had not finished speaking before Chicot had poured out a second glass for her. She wanted to refuse, but it was too late, and she drank it slowly, as she had the first. Then he wanted her to accept a third glass, but she declined. He insisted, adding,

"Why, that is just as weak as milk. See *I* drink ten or twelve glasses without any embarrassment. It goes down like sugar and leaves no unpleasant effects in the stomach or the head. One would say that it evaporates on the tongue. There is nothing better for one's health!"

As she was very anxious to have it, she gave in, but she took only half of the glassful.

Then acting from an impulse of generosity, Chicot exclaimed,

"Look here, since you like it so well, I am going to give you a little cask of it, a little token to show that we are good friends."

The good woman did not say "no," and she went away a little unsteadily.

The next day the innkeeper drove into the courtyard of Mother Magloire and took from the bottom of his wagon a small barrel with iron hoops. Then he wanted her to taste the contents to be sure that it was some of the same fine brandy. When they had both had three glasses, he reminded her as he was going away,

"Now, you know, when that is gone, there is still more where that came from. Don't be bashful. The sooner it is finished, the better pleased I shall be."

And he got up into his wagon.

He came back four days later. The old woman was near her door cutting bread for supper. He went up to where she was and greeted her, getting close enough to be able to smell her breath. When he caught a whiff of alcohol, he was pleased.

"Aren't you going to offer me a glass of brandy?" he asked. Then they clinked glasses two or three times.

Soon there was a report going about that occasionally Mother Magloire was getting drunk all by herself. She was picked up first in her kitchen, later in the courtyard, then in the country roads, and she had to be carried home lifeless as a log.

Chicot never went to her house now, and when anyone spoke to him about the peasant woman, with a sad expression in his face he murmured,

"It is too bad, at her age, to have become addicted to a habit like that! You know, when one is old, there isn't any remedy. It will end up by playing a bad trick on her!"

And it did play a bad trick on her. She died the following winter, about Christmas time. She fell intoxicated in the snow.

When Master Chicot took possession of the farm, he remarked, "You know, it wasn't at all necessary. She could easily have lived ten years more."

The Daffodils
by William Wordsworth

I wandered lonely as a cloud
That floats on high o'er vales and hills,
When all at once I saw a crowd,
A host of golden daffodils,
Beside the lake, beneath the trees,
Fluttering and dancing in the breeze.

Continuous as the stars that shine
And twinkle on the Milky Way,
They stretched in never-ending line
Along the margin of a bay:
Ten thousand saw I at a glance
Tossing their heads in sprightly dance.

The waves beside them danced, but they
Outdid the sparkling waves in glee:—
A Poet could not but be gay
In such a jocund company!
I gazed—and gazed—but little thought
What wealth the show to me had brought;

For oft, when on my couch I lie
In vacant or in pensive mood,
They flash upon that inward eye
Which is the bliss of solitude;
And then my heart with pleasure fills,
And dances with the daffodils.

The Blind Men and the Elephant
(A Hindoo Fable)
by John Godfrey Saxe

It was six men of Indostan
   To learning much inclined,
Who went to see the Elephant
   (Though all of them were blind),
That each by observation
   Might satisfy his mind.

The *First* approached the Elephant,
   And happening to fall
Against his broad and sturdy side,
   At once began to bawl:
"God bless me! but the Elephant
   Is very like a wall!"

The *Second*, feeling of the tusk,
   Cried, "Ho! what have we here
So very round and smooth and sharp?
   To me 'tis mighty clear
This wonder of an Elephant
   Is very like a spear!"

The *Third* approached the animal,
   And happening to take
The squirming trunk within his hands,
   Thus boldly up and spake:
"I see," quoth he, "the Elephant
   Is very like a snake!"

The *Fourth* reached out an eager hand,
   And felt about the knee.
"What most this wondrous beast is like
   Is mighty plain," quoth he;
"'Tis clear enough the Elephant
   Is very like a tree!"

The *Fifth,* who chanced to touch the ear,
    Said: "E'en the blindest man
Can tell what this resembles most;
    Deny the fact who can,
This marvel of an Elephant
    Is very like a fan!"

The *Sixth* no sooner had begun
    About the beast to grope,
Than, seizing on the swinging tail
    That fell within his scope,
"I see," quoth he, "the Elephant
    Is very like a rope!"

And so these men of Indostan
    Disputed loud and long,
Each in his own opinion
    Exceeding stiff and strong,
Though each was partly in the right,
    And all were in the wrong!

After Blenheim
by Robert Southey

It was a summer evening,
  Old Kaspar's work was done,
And he before his cottage door
  Was sitting in the sun,
And by him sported on the green
His little grandchild Wilhelmine.

She saw her brother Peterkin
  Roll something large and round,
Which he beside the rivulet
  In playing there had found;
He came to ask what he had found
That was so large, and smooth, and round.

Old Kaspar took it from the boy,
  Who stood expectant by;
And then the old man shook his head,
  And with a natural sigh,
"'Tis some poor fellow's skull," said he,
"Who fell in the great victory.

"I find them in the garden,
  For there's many here about;
And often when I go to plow,
  The plowshare turns them out!
For many thousand men," said he,
"Were slain in that great victory."

"Now tell us what 'twas all about,"
  Young Peterkin, he cries;
And little Wilhelmine looks up
  With wonder-waiting eyes;
"Now tell us all about the war,
  And what they fought each other for."

"It was the English," Kaspar said,
  "Who put the French to rout;
But what they fought each other for
  I could not well make out;
But everybody said," quoth he,
"That 'twas a famous victory.

"My father lived at Blenheim then,
  Yon little stream hard by;
They burnt his dwelling to the ground,
  And he was forced to fly;
So with his wife and child he fled,
Nor had he where to rest his head.

"With fire and sword the country round
  Was wasted far and wide,
And many a childing mother then,
  And new-born baby died;
But things like that, you know, must be
At every famous victory.

"They say it was a shocking sight
  After the field was won;
For many thousand bodies here
  Lay rotting in the sun;
But things like that, you know, must be
After a famous victory.

"Great praise the Duke of Marlbro' won,
  And our good Prince Eugene."
"Why, 'twas a very wicked thing!"
  Said little Wilhelmine.
"Nay . . . nay . . . my little girl," quoth he,
"It was a famous victory.

"And everybody praised the Duke
  Who this great fight did win."
"But what good came of it at last?"
  Quoth little Peterkin.
"Why, that I cannot tell," said he,
"But 'twas a famous victory."

Richard Cory
by Edwin Arlington Robinson

Whenever Richard Cory went down town,
We people on the pavement looked at him:
He was a gentleman from sole to crown,
Clean favored, and imperially slim.

And he was always quietly arrayed,
And he was always human when he talked;
But still he fluttered pulses when he said,
"Good-morning," and he glittered when he walked.

And he was rich—yes, richer than a king—
And admirably schooled in every grace:
In fine, we thought that he was everything
To make us wish that we were in his place.

So on we worked, and waited for the light,
And went without the meat, and cursed the bread;
And Richard Cory, one calm summer night,
Went home and put a bullet through his head.

"Richard Cory," from THE CHILDREN OF THE NIGHT by Edwin Arlington Robinson (New York: Charles Scribner's Sons, 1897)

Any Human to Another
by Countee Cullen

The ills I sorrow at
Not me alone
Like an arrow,
Pierce to the marrow,
Through the fat
And past the bone.

Your grief and mine
Must intertwine
Like sea and river,
Be fused and mingle,
Diverse yet single,
Forever and forever.

Let no man be so proud
And confident,
To think he is allowed
A little tent
Pitched in a meadow
Of sun and shadow
All his little own.

Joy may be shy, unique,
Friendly to a few,
Sorrow never scorned to speak
To any who
Were false or true.

Your every grief
Like a blade
Shining and unsheathed
Must strike me down.
Of bitter aloes wreathed,
My sorrow must be laid
On your head like a crown.

When in Disgrace with Fortune and Men's Eyes

by William Shakespeare

When in disgrace with fortune and men's eyes
I all alone beweep my outcast state,
And trouble deaf heaven with my bootless cries,
And look upon myself, and curse my fate;

Wishing me like to one more rich in hope,
Featured like him, like him with friends possessed,
Desiring this man's art, and that man's scope,
With what I most enjoy contented least;

Yet in these thoughts myself almost despising,
Haply I think on thee—and then my state,
Like to the lark at break of day arising
From sullen earth, sings hymns at heaven's gate;

For thy sweet love remembered such wealth brings
That then I scorn to change my state with kings.

When I Heard the Learn'd Astronomer
by Walt Whitman

When I heard the learn'd astronomer,
When the proofs, the figures, were ranged in columns
    before me,
When I was shown the charts and diagrams, to add,
    divide, and measure them,
When I, sitting, heard the astronomer where he lectured
    with much applause in the lecture room,
How soon unaccountable I became tired and sick,
Till rising and gliding out I wandered off by myself,
In the mystical moist night air, and from time to time,
Look up in perfect silence at the stars.

Opportunity
by Edward Rowland Sill

This I beheld, or dreamed it in a dream:—
There spread a cloud of dust along a plain;
And underneath the cloud, or in it, raged
A furious battle, and men yelled, and swords
Shocked upon swords and shields. A prince's banner
Wavered, then staggered backward, hemmed by foes.
A craven hung along the battle's edge,
And thought, "Had I a sword of keener steel—
That blue blade that the king's son bears—but this
Blunt thing!" he snapped and flung it from his hand,
And lowering crept away and left the field.
Then came the king's son, wounded, sore bestead,
And weaponless, and saw the broken sword,
Hilt-buried in the dry and trodden sand,
And ran and snatched it, and with battle-shout
Lifted afresh he hewed his enemy down,
And saved a great cause that heroic day.

The Gettysburg Address
by Abraham Lincoln

Four score and seven years ago our fathers brought forth on this continent a new nation, conceived in liberty, and dedicated to the proposition that all men are created equal.

Now we are engaged in a great civil war, testing whether that nation, or any nation so conceived and so dedicated, can long endure. We are met on a great battlefield of that war. We have come to dedicate a portion of that field as a final resting place for those who here gave their lives that that nation might live. It is altogether fitting and proper that we should do this.

But, in a larger sense, we cannot dedicate—we cannot consecrate—we cannot hallow—this ground. The brave men, living and dead, who struggled here, have consecrated it far above our poor power to add or detract. The world will little note nor long remember what we say here, but it can never forget what they did here. It is for us, the living, rather, to be dedicated here to the unfinished work which they who fought here have thus far so nobly advanced. It is rather for us to be here dedicated to the great task remaining before us—that from these honored dead we take increased devotion to that cause for which they gave the last full measure of devotion—that we here highly resolve that these dead shall not have died in vain—that this nation, under God, shall have a new birth of freedom—and that government of the people, by the people, for the people, shall not perish from the earth.

The Hibernation of the Woodchuck
by Alan Devoe

The woodchuck's hibernation usually starts about the middle of September. For weeks he has been foraging with increased appetite among the clover blossoms and has grown heavy and slow-moving. Now, with the coming of mid-September, apples and corn and yarrow tops have become less plentiful, and the nights are cool. The woodchuck moves with slower gait, and emerges less and less frequently for feeding trips. Layers of fat have accumulated around his chest and shoulders, and there is thick fat in the axils of his legs. He has extended his summer burrow to a length of nearly thirty feet, and has fashioned a deep nest-chamber at the end of it, far below the level of the frost. He has carried in, usually, a little hay. He is ready for the Long Sleep.

When the temperature of the September days falls below 50 degrees or so, the woodchuck becomes too drowsy to come forth from his burrow in the chilly dusk to forage. He remains in the deep nest-chamber, lethargic, hardly moving. Gradually, with the passing of hours or days, his coarse-furred body curls into a semicircle, like a foetus, nose-tip touching tail. The small legs are tucked in, the handlike clawed forefeet folded. The woodchuck has become a compact ball. Presently the temperature of his body begins to fall.

In normal life the woodchuck's temperature, though fluctuant, averaged about 97 degrees. Now, as he lies tight-curled in a ball with the winter sleep stealing over him, this body heat drops ten degrees, twenty degrees, thirty. Finally, by the time the snow is on the ground and the woodchuck's winter dormancy has become complete, his temperature is only 38 or 40. With the falling of the body heat there is a slowing of his heartbeat and his respiration. In normal life he breathes thirty or forty times each minute; when he is excited, as many as a hundred times. Now he breathes slower and slower—ten times a minute, five times a minute, once a minute, and at last only ten or twelve times in an hour. His heartbeat is a twentieth of normal. He has entered fully into the oblivion of hibernation.

The Long Sleep lasts, on an average, about six months. For half a year the woodchuck remains unmoving, hardly breathing. His pituitary gland is inactive; his blood is so sluggishly circulated that there is an unequal distribution in the chilled body; his sensory awareness has wholly ceased. It is almost true to say that he has altered from a warm-blooded to a cold-blooded animal.

Then, in the middle of March, he wakes. The waking is not a slow and gradual thing, as was the drifting into sleep, but takes place quickly, often in an hour. The body temperature ascends to normal, or rather higher for a while; glandular functions instantly resume; the respiration quickens and steadies at a normal rate. The woodchuck has become himself again, save only that he is a little thinner, and is ready at once to fare forth into the pale spring sunlight and look for grass and berries.

Such is the performance each fall and winter, with varying detail, of bats and worms and bears, and a hundred other kinds of creature. It is a marvel less spectacular than the migration flight of hummingbirds or the flash of shooting stars, but it is not much less remarkable.

A Review of Correct Usage

WHAT IS CORRECT USAGE?

To answer this question, we must realize that there are several levels of usage. Examples:

NONSTANDARD: "Dey ain't done nothin'."
INFORMAL: "They've done nothing."
FORMAL: "They have done nothing."

The correct level of usage is the one that is appropriate for the occasion. Suppose you are writing dialogue in a play or story in which some of the characters have not been influenced by schooling. To represent their speech, you will use *nonstandard* English.

For ordinary conversation and friendly letters, you will use *informal* English. But for reports, term papers, minutes, letters of application, business letters, speeches, lectures—in short, for formal writing and speaking—you will use *formal* English.

Both *informal* and *formal* English are considered *standard usage*.

Our review will deal with the following topics:

1. Pronouns

WHAT IS A PRONOUN?

A pronoun is a word that stands for a noun. The word *it* in the following sentence is a pronoun:

> Food is essential because *it* provides energy.

You can tell *it* is a pronoun because it stands for the noun *food*.

WHY ARE PRONOUNS TROUBLESOME?

Pronouns have different forms for different uses. Notice that the following pronouns have one form as a subject, another as an object, and a third as a possessive:

AS SUBJECT (*Nominative Case*)	AS OBJECT (*Objective Case*)	AS POSSESSIVE (*Possessive Case*)
I	me	my, mine
you	you	your, yours
he	him	his
she	her	her, hers
it	it	its
we	us	our, ours
they	them	their, theirs
who	whom	whose
whoever	whomever	whosever

In reviewing the rules for using pronouns, we shall use examples that offer two choices. Note that the correct choice is italicized.

Rule 1: A pronoun used as a subject takes the nominative case.

1. I know of no other person in the club who is as kindhearted as (*she*, her).

> ANSWER EXPLAINED: *She* is subject of the understood verb *is*. ("I know of no other person in the club who is as kindhearted as she *is*.")

2. (*Who*, Whom) do you believe is the most capable?

> ANSWER EXPLAINED: *Who* is subject of the verb *is*. ("*Who*...is the most capable?") Ignore interrupting expressions like *do you believe* (*do you suppose, think, say*, etc.). They do not affect the case of *who* and *whom*.

3. He voted against (*whoever*, whomever) favored that proposal.

> ANSWER EXPLAINED: *Whoever* is subject of the verb *favored*. Don't choose *whomever* in the belief that it is the object of the preposition *against*. It isn't. The object of *against* is the entire clause *whoever favored that proposal*.

Exception to Rule 1: A pronoun used as the subject of an infinitive takes the objective case.

> (The infinitive is the form of the verb preceded by *to: to be, to tell, to read*, etc.)

4. Father expects Fred and (I, *me*) to pass.

> ANSWER EXPLAINED: *Me* (together with *Fred*) is the subject of the infinitive *to pass*—not the object of *expects*. The entire phrase *Fred and me to pass* is the object of *expects*.

> In an instance like the above, construct two sentences. Then combine them for the correct answer.
> Sentence 1: Father expects Fred to pass.
> Sentence 2: Father expects *me* (not *I*) to pass.
> Answer: Father expects Fred and *me* to pass.

Rule 2: A pronoun used as a predicate nominative takes the nominative case.

> [A noun or pronoun after some form of *to be* (*is, was, might have been*, etc.) is called a predicate nominative.]

5. It was (*we*, us) girls who decorated the gym for the dance.

> ANSWER EXPLAINED: *We* is a predicate nominative after the verb *was*.

Remember that the verb *to be*, in all its forms, is the same as an equals sign (=). Whatever case comes before it (practically always nominative case) must also follow it:

| | It | was | we. |
| | (nominative) | = | (nominative) |

Rule 3: A pronoun used as direct object of a verb, object of an infinitive, object of a preposition, or indirect object takes the objective case.

6. "(Who, *Whom*) can you send to help us?" inquired Aunt May.

> ANSWER EXPLAINED: In formal English, *whom* is direct object of the verb *can send*.

> With a *who-whom* question, mentally change the word order: You can send *whom* to help us? Obviously, *you* is subject and *whom* is object of *can send*.

7. The lawyer promised to notify my mother and (I, *me*) of his plans for a new trial.

> ANSWER EXPLAINED: *Me* (together with *mother*) is object of the infinitive *to notify*.

> In a case like the above, construct two sentences. Then combine them for the correct answer.
> Sentence 1: The lawyer promised to notify my mother.
> Sentence 2: The lawyer promised to notify *me* (not *I*).
> Answer: The lawyer promised to notify my mother and *me* of his plans for a new trial.

8. It is always a pleasure for (we, *us*) boys to visit a firehouse.

> ANSWER EXPLAINED: *Us* is object of the preposition *for*.

> When a pronoun is combined with a noun (*we boys, we girls,* etc.), temporarily omit the noun.
> Noun omitted: It is always a pleasure for *us* (not *we*) to visit a firehouse.
> Noun added: It is always a pleasure for *us boys* to visit a firehouse.

9. All the pupils except George and (she, *her*) plan to order the book.

> ANSWER EXPLAINED: *Her* (together with *George*) is object of the preposition *except*. (*Except* is a preposition, as are *to*, *by*, *of*, *for*, *with*, *between*, etc. Prepositions are followed by the objective case.)

In a situation like the above, construct two sentences. Then combine them for the correct answer.

> Sentence 1: All the pupils except George plan to order the book.
> Sentence 2: All the pupils except *her* (not *she*) plan to order the book.
> Answer: All the pupils except George and *her* plan to order the book.

10. Grandfather gave my sister and (I, *me*) a year's subscription to a magazine.

> ANSWER EXPLAINED: *Me* (together with *my sister*) is the indirect object of the verb *gave*. (An indirect object tells *to* or *for* whom something is done.)

In a case like the above, construct two sentences. Then combine them for the correct answer.

> Sentence 1: Grandfather gave my sister a year's subscription to a magazine.
> Sentence 2: Grandfather gave *me* (not *I*) a year's subscription to a magazine.
> Answer: Grandfather gave my sister and *me* a year's subscription to a magazine.

You can tell that a word is an indirect object if you can temporarily insert *to* or *for* before it without changing the meaning:

> Grandfather gave (*to*) *my sister* (indirect object) and (*to*) *me* (indirect object) a year's *subscription* (direct object).
> Grandmother baked (*for*) *us* (indirect object) a *cake* (direct object).

Rule 4: A pronoun used in apposition with a noun is in the same case as that noun.

11. Two contestants, Martha and (*she*, her), were disqualified by the judges.

> ANSWER EXPLAINED: The pronoun must be in the nominative case (*she*) because it is in apposition with the noun *contestants*, which is in the nominative case.
>
> The noun *contestants* is in the nominative case because it is the subject of *were disqualified*.

12. The judges disqualified two contestants, Martha and (she, *her*).

> ANSWER EXPLAINED: The pronoun must be in the objective case (*her*) because it is in apposition with the noun *contestants*, which is in the objective case.
>
> The noun *contestants* is now in the objective case because it is the object of *disqualified*.

Rule 5: A pronoun that expresses ownership is in the possessive case.

13. The girl refused to admit that the note was (her's, *hers*).

> ANSWER EXPLAINED: *Hers* (*belonging to her*) is the correct spelling of the possessive case, which is needed here to express ownership.
>
> Personal pronouns that express ownership (*yours, his, hers, its, ours, theirs*) never require an apostrophe.

14. He became an authority on the theater and (*its*, it's) great personalities.

> ANSWER EXPLAINED: *Its* (*belonging to it*) is the correct spelling of the possessive case, which is needed here to express ownership. Do not confuse possessive pronouns with contractions.

POSSESSIVE PRONOUNS		CONTRACTIONS	
its	(belonging to it)	*it's*	(it is)
yours, your	(belonging to you)	*you're*	(you are)
theirs, their	(belonging to them)	*they're*	(they are)
whose	(belonging to whom)	*who's*	(who is)

15. Father disapproves of (me, *my*) staying up late before examinations.

> ANSWER EXPLAINED: *My* (possessive case) is required by the meaning.
>
> Of what does Father disapprove? *Me?* Certainly not. He disapproves of *my* (*belonging to me*) *staying up late.*

Rule 6: *Who* is used for persons, *that* for persons or things, and *which* for things only.

16. The character (which, *who*) suffered the most was Laura.

> ANSWER EXPLAINED: Since *character* is a person, it can not be referred to by *which*.

EXERCISE 1: *Pronouns*. Write the correct choice, and state the reason for your choice.

1. I wonder whether that scheme of (yours, your's) will work.
2. (It's, Its) a pleasure to see you looking so well.
3. In the first row of the orchestra sat Emily and (he, him).
4. Did you know that Frank can sew better than (she, her)?
5. Are you willing to allow (we, us) boys to form a cooking class?
6. There was a serious difference of opinion between her and (me, I).
7. (Us, We) two boys have been very close friends for a long time.
8. The committee consisted of Nora, Henry, Juan, and (I, me).
9. The audience gave our opponents and (we, us) a rousing ovation.
10. It was (they, them) who objected to the decision.
11. There was no chance of (them, their) planning an attack.
12. Divide the responsibilities between Jane and (her, she).
13. This is John (who, whom), I am sure, will be glad to serve you.
14. Few student officers have served as conscientiously as (she, her).
15. (Whom, Who) shall we invite to the Arista installation?
16. Time did not permit José and (I, me) to go swimming today.
17. Please let her and (I, me) do it.
18. The money found on the stairs proved to be neither Gary's nor (our's, ours).
19. (Who, Whom) do you think will be designated "most likely to succeed"?
20. I don't know what I would do if I were (him, he).
21. "(It's, Its) victory for them or (I, me)," he shouted.
22. Hattie criticized (me, my) playing the radio when I do my homework.
23. (We, Us) seniors always have a greater share of responsibility.
24. When the dance was held, all came except (she, her).
25. Is this term paper (your's, yours) or Helen's?
26. We have room in the car for only two people, you and (he, him).

27. Gerald and (he, him) are always dependable in emergencies.
28. Mary and Paul wish to go because (their, they're, there) eager to visit the museum.
29. Alex was the only one of the boys (who, whom), as you know, was not eligible.
30. I shall ask my parents to let Lola and (he, him) come with us to the game.
31. See (who's, whose) at the door.
32. Between you and (I, me) there have never been any serious misunderstandings.
33. Such a comment about anyone (who, whom) we know to be thoughtful is unfair.
34. The co-captains, Nick and (he, him), will sit on the platform.
35. It was (they, them) who first suggested that we need a computer.
36. She is the artist (who's, whose) poster was chosen.
37. I have always been able to read a map better than (she, her).
38. It must have been (they, them) who purchased the class gift.
39. Call on (whoever, whomever) raises his or her hand.
40. The house looked (its, it's) age.
41. Why were Jane and (him, he) permitted to go?
42. It would not be safe for you or (me, I) to travel through the jungle.
43. Father does not approve of (you, your) studying so late.
44. That is the man (who, whom), I believe, was the driver of the car.
45. The girls stated that the dresses were (theirs, their's).
46. This is the story of a girl (who's, whose) mother was a scientist.
47. I am not so good in trigonometry as (she, her).
48. I find that an essential item for (we, us) beginners is missing.
49. I am certain that these books are not (our's, ours).
50. If you will describe (it's, its) color, perhaps we can find it.

2. Irregular Verbs

HOW TO RECOGNIZE A VERB

You can in most cases tell that a word is a verb if you can add *s*, *ing*, and *ed* to its basic form.

The word *play* in "We *play* games" is a verb. Proof: *plays*, *playing*, *played*.

Similarly, *smile* in "Please *smile*" is a verb. Proof: *smiles*, *smiling*, *smiled*.

IRREGULAR VERBS

Some verbs cannot add *ed*, but they are verbs nevertheless. The word *bring* in "*Bring* your lunch" is a verb. Proof: *brings, bringing, brought* (not "bringed").

Verbs that cannot add *ed* are irregular verbs. You must know the principal parts of common irregular verbs if you are to speak and write good English.

PRINCIPAL PARTS

The principal parts of a verb are:

1. The present tense: *break*
2. The past tense: *broke*
3. The past participle: *broken* (This principal part comes after a helping verb, such as *is, are, was, were, has been, would have been, might have been*, etc.)

One of the most common verb errors is the use of the past tense instead of the past participle:

When I first saw the car, its steering wheel was *broke*.

To correct this sentence, you must change *broke* (past tense) to *broken* (past participle). Obviously, you should know your principal parts. The following list is well worth reviewing:

PRINCIPAL PARTS OF IRREGULAR AND TROUBLESOME VERBS

PRESENT TENSE	PAST TENSE	PAST PARTICIPLE
arise	arose	arisen
bear	bore	borne, or born
beat	beat	beaten
become	became	become
begin	began	begun
bend	bent	bent
bite	bit	bitten
blow	blew	blown
break	broke	broken
bring	brought	brought

burst	burst	burst
catch	caught	caught
choose	chose	chosen
come	came	come
creep	crept	crept
dig	dug	dug
dive	dived, or dove	dived
do	did	done
draw	drew	drawn
drink	drank	drunk
drive	drove	driven
eat	ate	eaten
fall	fell	fallen
fight	fought	fought
flee	fled	fled
fly	flew	flown
forget	forgot	forgotten
forgive	forgave	forgiven
freeze	froze	frozen
get	got	got, or gotten
give	gave	given
go	went	gone
grow	grew	grown
hang (suspend a thing)	hung	hung
hang (execute a person)	hanged	hanged
hide	hid	hidden
hold	held	held
hurt	hurt	hurt
kneel	knelt	knelt
know	knew	known
lay (put down)	laid	laid
lead	led	led
lend	lent	lent
lie (be in a horizontal position)	lay	lain
lie (tell a lie)	lied	lied
lose	lost	lost
mistake	mistook	mistaken
pay	paid	paid
prove	proved	proved, or proven
rid	rid	rid

ride	rode	ridden
ring	rang	rung
rise	rose	risen
run	ran	run
say	said	said
see	saw	seen
set	set	set
sew	sewed	sewed, or sewn
shake	shook	shaken
show	showed	showed, or shown
shrink	shrank	shrunk
sing	sang	sung
sink	sank	sunk
sit	sat	sat
slay	slew	slain
slide	slid	slid
speak	spoke	spoken
spend	spent	spent
spring	sprang	sprung
steal	stole	stolen
strike	struck	struck
swear	swore	sworn
sweep	swept	swept
swim	swam	swum
take	took	taken
teach	taught	taught
tear	tore	torn
throw	threw	thrown
wake	waked, or woke	waked, or woken
wear	wore	worn
weep	wept	wept
wind	wound	wound
wring	wrung	wrung
write	wrote	written

SOLVING PROBLEMS OF IRREGULAR VERBS

Study these two samples:

1. If you had been more patient, you might not have (tore, *torn*) it.

   ANSWER EXPLAINED: The helping verb *might have* requires the third principal part (tear, tore, *torn*).

2. There were fewer candidates than we had been (*led*, lead) to expect.

   ANSWER EXPLAINED: The helping verb *had been* requires the third principal part (lead, led, *led*).

   Do not confuse *led* with an altogether different word that happens to sound the same—*lead* (a metal).

EXERCISE 2: *Irregular and troublesome verbs.* Write the correct choice, and state the reason for your choice.

1. I could not do the assignment because the pages were (tore, torn) from my book.
2. Last night the stranger (lead, led) us down the mountain.
3. After Roscoe had (ran, run) the mile, he was breathless.
4. In all the confusion, nobody took the trouble to find out who had (rung, rang) the bell.
5. I can assure you that he has always (spoke, spoken) well of you.
6. When was the last time your picture was (took, taken)?
7. This problem would never have (arose, arisen) if you had done the work on time.
8. I had (rode, ridden) over the same course many times before.
9. Your sweater has (laid, lain) on the floor for a week.
10. Mary, aren't you (suppose, supposed) to take part in the play?
11. Jack no sooner (laid, lay) down than he fell asleep.
12. My dog has never (bit, bitten) anyone, except when provoked.
13. How can you be so sure that he (did, done) it?
14. We were not allowed to skate on the pond until the ice had (froze, frozen) to a depth of ten inches.
15. Richard concluded that his pen must have (fell, fallen) from his pocket as he was running for the bus.
16. How much have food costs (raised, risen) during the past year?
17. When he (began, begun) to give us advice, we stopped listening.
18. Evita was so thirsty that she (drank, drunk) two glasses of water.

19. My cousin framed the photographs and (hung, hanged) them on the wall of his den.
20. They are (use, used) to living very quiet lives.

3. Verbs Often Confused

Does air pollution *affect* (or *effect*) our health? Did the dog *lie* (or *lay*) asleep at your feet?

Because pairs of verbs like *affect—effect* and *lie—lay* are so commonly confused, they have been the subject of frequent errors.

Review the following verb pairs, giving special attention to those that you may not yet have mastered.

1. to *accept:* to receive, agree to
   He *accepted* my apology.

   to *except:* to leave out
   Food purchases were *excepted* from the sales tax.

2. to *affect:* to influence
   His dog's death *affected* him deeply.

   to *effect:* to bring about
   The enemy *effected* a quick retreat.

3. to *borrow:* to take with the intention of returning
   May I *borrow* your pen?

   to *lend:* to give with the intention of getting back
   I shall gladly *lend* you my pen.

4. to *bring:* to carry toward the speaker
   Bring the newspaper when you return from shopping.

   to *take:* to carry from the speaker
   Take these shirts to the laundry.

5. *can:* a helping verb expressing ability
   Can you (Are you able to) swim across the pool?

   may: a helping verb expressing permission or possibility
   You *may* (not *can*) have another chance.
   It *may* rain tomorrow.

6. to *learn:* to receive knowledge
   I *learned* safe driving from Dad.

   to *teach:* to impart knowledge
   Dad *taught* me safe driving.

7. to *leave:* to depart, let remain
   When you *leave*, please shut the door.
   Leave the key under the mat.

   to *let:* to permit, allow
   Let (not *Leave*) them do their work without interruption.

8. to *lie:* to be in a horizontal position
   Present: The dog *lies* (*is lying*) on the ground.
   Future: The dog *will lie* on the ground.
   Past: The dog *lay* on the ground.
   Perfect Tenses: The dog *has lain* (*had lain, will have lain*) on the ground.

   to *lay:* to put down
   Present: The player *lays* (*is laying*) his cards on the table.
   Future: The player *will lay* his cards on the table.
   Past: The player *laid* his cards on the table.
   Perfect Tenses: The player *has laid* (*had laid, will have laid*) his cards on the table.

9. to *precede:* to go before in rank or time
   Evening *precedes* night.

   to *proceed:* to move forward, advance
   Proceed to the main entrance.

10. to *raise:* to lift, elevate
   How can I *raise* my grades?

   to *rise:* to go up, get up
   Will the cost of living *rise?*
   To ask a question, please *rise* and face the class.

REMOVING THE CONFUSION

Note the reasoning involved in solving the following two typical problems:

1. Overnight the river had (raised, *risen*) another foot.

   ANSWER EXPLAINED: The meaning of the sentence requires *risen*, which is the third principal part of *to rise*, meaning "to go up"; *raised* is the third principal part of another verb, *to raise*, meaning "to lift."

2. Where have you (lain, *laid*) the book I was reading?

   ANSWER EXPLAINED: The meaning of the sentence requires *laid*, the third principal part of *to lay*, meaning "to put down"; *lain* is the third principal part of another verb, *to lie*, meaning "to be in a horizontal position."

EXERCISE 3: *Verbs often confused.* Write the correct choice, and state the reason for your choice:

1. Have you ever tried to (learn, teach) anyone to tie knots?
2. Although he had (accepted, excepted) a deposit on the new automobile, he refused to deliver it for the agreed price.
3. May I (borrow, lend) your French dictionary over the weekend?
4. I had (lain, laid) awake all night, worrying about the final test.
5. The cost of living is (raising, rising) again.
6. (Bring, Take) these books to the library, as they will soon be overdue.
7. Where did you (lay, lie) the magazine I was reading?
8. When operas are performed on radio or television, they (effect, affect) listeners, so that after hearing them they want to buy recordings of the music.
9. My parents didn't (leave, let) me go to the last dance because I had failed two subjects.
10. Weekly dances have become a popularly (accepted, excepted) feature of the summer schedule.

11. (Can, May) I have another helping of ice cream?
12. A blanket of fresh snow (lays, lies) on the ground.
13. The news of his narrow escape (affected, effected) her visibly.
14. In these ways we are (preceding, proceeding) toward the goal of an educated and informed public.
15. At first, passengers were forbidden to enter the lifeboats, women and children (accepted, excepted).
16. Please (bring, take) these visitors to the main desk.
17. If you won't (let, leave) her solve the problem by herself, she will never learn.
18. With the new advances in medicine, physicians have been able to (affect, effect) some remarkable recoveries.
19. I could not recall where I had (lain, laid) my glasses.
20. When the fire alarm sounds, (precede, proceed) calmly to the nearest exist.

4. Tenses of Verbs

A *tense* is the *time* of a verb action. Verbs have six tenses, each expressing a different time.

PRESENT TENSE:	he *answers*
PAST TENSE:	he *answered*
FUTURE TENSE:	he *will answer*
PERFECT TENSE:	he *has answered*
PAST PERFECT TENSE:	he *had answered*
FUTURE PERFECT TENSE:	he *will have answered*

SOME RULES GOVERNING THE TENSES OF VERBS

Rule 1: Do not shift unnecessarily from one tense to another.

1. Whenever I asked him to explain, he (says, *said*), "Later, not now."

   ANSWER EXPLAINED: *Said* (past tense) is required because the sentence begins in the past tense (*asked*).

   The present tense, *says*, would be correct only if the sentence were to begin in the present tense: Whenever I *ask* him to explain, he *says*, "Later, not now."

Exception to Rule 1: Use the present tense to express a universal truth (something that is true regardless of time).

2. She said that health (was, *is*) better than riches.

>ANSWER EXPLAINED: *Is* (present tense) is required to express a universal truth. It has been, is, and always will be true that "health *is* better than riches."

Rule 2: In describing two past actions in the same sentence, use the past perfect tense for the earlier action.

3. In the bus I realized that I (took, *had taken*) my brother's notebook by mistake.

>ANSWER EXPLAINED: *had taken* (past perfect tense) is needed to describe an action earlier than that of *realized* (past tense).

Rule 3: After *if*, do not use the helping verb *would have;* use *had*.

4. If he (would have, *had*) studied harder, he would have received a passing grade.

>ANSWER EXPLAINED: *Had* (not *would have*) is required after *if*.

>Note that *would have* may be used in a main clause (He *would have* received a passing grade) but never in an *if* clause.

Rule 4: Use the present infinitive to express action not completed at the time of the preceding verb.

Verbs have a present infinitive (*to do, to tell*, etc.) and a past infinitive (*to have done, to have told*, etc.).

5. We intended (*to go*, to have gone) before Tuesday.

>ANSWER EXPLAINED: *To go* (the present infinitive) is required because the action of "going" had not yet happened at the time of the preceding verb *intended*.

>Note the correct use of the past infinitive: I am sorry *to have scolded* you yesterday. The past infinitive *to have scolded* is required because the action of "scolding" had already happened at the time of the preceding verb *am*.

EXERCISE 4: *Tenses.* Write the correct choice, and state the reason for your choice.

1. Magellan's voyage proved that the world (was, is) round.
2. If you (would have, had) called me earlier, I would unquestionably have gone with you.
3. Suddenly he yelled "George!" and (dashes, dashed) up the stairs.
4. The doctor suspected that I (sprained, had sprained) my ankle.
5. From that experience I learned that a friend in need (is, was) a friend indeed.
6. If he (had, would have) stopped smoking, his health would have been better.
7. At the box office I realized that I (forgot, had forgotten) to bring my credit card.
8. Our teacher explained that the Grand Canyon (was, is) in Arizona.
9. I am sorry to (cause, have caused) so much trouble yesterday.
10. She could not recall the title of any one-act play that she (read, had read) in previous terms.
11. Karen would gladly have set an extra place for dinner if she (had, would have) known you were coming.
12. Aren't you sorry to (be, have been) so discourteous when she phoned?
13. If it (had not, would not have) rained, the mishap would never have occurred.
14. Does Phil plan to (finish, have finished) the essay before he rides down to the beach?
15. If more nations (had, would have) fought against tyranny, the course of history would have been different.
16. As soon as Mother learned of my plan, she (begins, began) to worry.
17. If the game had gone into extra innings, the lights would (be, have been) turned on.
18. Mr. Lopez was reputed to (be, have been) an outstanding athlete in his youth.
19. You are expected to (graduate, have graduated) next June.
20. Jim is ashamed to (be, have been) so rude to your guests last Saturday.

5. Active and Passive Verbs

ACTIVE VERBS

A verb is *active* when its subject is the doer of the action.

Marie *answered* the question.

The verb *answered* is active because its subject, *Marie*, is the doer: she did the answering.

PASSIVE VERBS

A verb is *passive* when the action is done to its subject.

The question *was answered* by Marie.

The verb *was answered* is passive because it describes an action done to its subject, *question*. The doer of the action, *Marie*, is now the object of the preposition *by*.

FURTHER EXAMPLES OF ACTIVE AND PASSIVE VERBS

ACTIVE: Storms *damage* crops.
PASSIVE: Crops *are damaged* by storms.
ACTIVE: Frank *will make* the sandwiches.
PASSIVE: The sandwiches *will be made* by Frank.
ACTIVE: The audience *applauded* the speaker.
PASSIVE: The speaker *was applauded* by the audience.

FORMING PASSIVE VERBS

To form the passive, add some form of *to be* (*is, was, will be, has been,* etc.) to the past participle (third principal part) of a verb. Examples:

is broken   *was collected*   *are being kept*
has been told *had been sent*   *were introduced*

USING ACTIVE VERBS

In general, *use active verbs*. They will allow you to express yourself clearly, naturally, and briefly. Compare these sentences:

PASSIVE: Our business was minded by us.   (6 words)
ACTIVE: We minded our business.   (4 words)

Note that the sentence with the active verb is clearer, more natural, and briefer.

Active verbs, like *minded*, are much more common in English than passive verbs, like *was minded*. Except for a few special situations, like those noted below, *use active verbs*.

USING PASSIVE VERBS

Among the situations when the passive may be used effectively are the following:

1. When you wish not to mention the doer.

   A word *has been misspelled.*

2. When necessary to avoid vagueness.

   Furniture *is manufactured* in Grand Rapids.
   (Instead of "They *manufacture* furniture in Grand Rapids," where the subject *They* is vague.)

3. When the doer is not known.

   The store *was robbed.*

4. When the result of the action is more important than the doer.

   The driver *was arrested* for speeding.

TYPICAL PROBLEM INVOLVING ACTIVE AND PASSIVE VERBS

Below, the same idea is expressed in four different ways. Which way is the best?

1. It was decided by the team that the post-season game would be played by them.
2. Having been decided, the team will play the post-season game.
3. The team decided that they would play the post-season game.
4. The team having decided, the post-season game would be played by them.

ANSWER: (3)

ANSWER EXPLAINED: Sentence 3 is clearer and more direct than any of the other choices because it uses active verbs—"The team *decided*...they *would play.*"

WRONG CHOICES:

> Sentence 1 is less effective because it uses passive verbs—"It *was decided*...the post-season game *would be played* by them."

> Sentence 4 is poor because it, too, uses a passive verb—"the post-season game *would be played* by them."

> Sentence 2 is spoiled by the dangling construction "Having been decided," which is vague because it cannot be attached to anything in the rest of the sentence. (See pages 245, 246 for a fuller discussion of dangling constructions.)

EXERCISE 5: *Active and passive verbs.* Rewrite the sentence with an active or passive verb, if necessary. If the sentence is correct, write "Correct."

1. An agreement with Aunt Martha was entered into by my brothers and me.
2. Eight kittens were had by our cat.
3. They grow oranges in Florida and California.
4. The players wore their old uniforms.
5. Another look at my examination paper was taken by Mrs. Benson.
6. A terrible mistake has been made.
7. In high school, knowledge is gained and plans for the future are formulated by the students.
8. The implications of what he had heard were considered by the judge.
9. They sell hot dogs and soda at the ball game.
10. I hope that a good time will be had by you.

6. Troublesome Words

A word may be troublesome because it sounds like, or almost like, another word or two. Learn to distinguish between the following:

advise, advice

1. In schools, teachers (*advise*, advice) their students to listen to, or to view, certain programs.

   ANSWER EXPLAINED: *Advise*, a verb, is required by the sentence.

   OTHER WORD: *Advice* is a noun. (The teacher gave us good *advice*.)

altogether, all together

2. I am not (*altogether*, all together) in agreement with the author's point of view.

ANSWER EXPLAINED: *Altogether*, meaning "completely," is required by the sentence.

OTHER WORD: *All together*, written as two words, means "all at one time." (We decided we would leave *all together*.)

effect, affect

3. We expect the (affects, *effects*) of the trip to be beneficial.

ANSWER EXPLAINED: *Effects*, a noun meaning "results," is required by the sentence.

OTHER WORD: *Affect* is used mostly as a verb meaning "to influence." (Alcohol *affects* the brain.)

have, of

4. If people had helped Burns, instead of talking about him, he might (of, *have*) become a greater poet.

ANSWER EXPLAINED: *Have*, a verb, is required as a helping verb.

OTHER WORD: *Of* is a preposition. (The rest *of* us protested.)

its, it's

5. When that program is over, the children know (its, *it's*) time for bed.

ANSWER EXPLAINED: *It's* (contraction for "it is") is required by the sentence.

OTHER WORD: *Its* means "belonging to it." (The dog injured *its* leg.)

lead, led

6. The general (lead, *led*) his troops into battle.

ANSWER EXPLAINED: *Led*, the past tense of *to lead*, is required as a verb for the subject *general*.

OTHER WORD: *Lead*, as a noun, is a metal. (These boots are as heavy as *lead*.)

loose, lose

7. How did you (loose, *lose*) your wallet?

ANSWER EXPLAINED: *Lose*, a verb meaning "part with accidentally," is required by the subject *you*.

OTHER WORD: *Loose* is an adjective meaning, "free, not fastened." (Who turned the dog *loose?*)

passed, past

8. We (*passed*, past) the bus stop.

ANSWER EXPLAINED: *Passed*, the past tense of *to pass*, a verb meaning "to go by," is required by the subject *We*.

OTHER WORD: *Past* may be
a. an adjective. (He presided at *past* meetings.)
b. a noun. (Forget the *past*.)
c. a preposition. (We went *past* the bus stop.)

personal, personnel

9. All the (personal, *personnel*) involved, even the lowest paid "extra," are glad when the picture is finished.

ANSWER EXPLAINED: *Personnel*, a noun meaning "employees," is required as a subject.

OTHER WORD: *Personal* is an adjective meaning "private." (Every student will be assigned a *personal* locker.)

principal, principle

10. The teacher explained the (principal, *principle*) of refrigeration.

   ANSWER EXPLAINED: *Principle*, a noun meaning "underlying rule" or "general truth," is required by the context. Notice that the last two letters of principle and rule are the same.

   OTHER WORD: *Principal*, as a noun, means "main teacher." (The *principal* has been helping the new teachers.)

   Principal, as an adjective, means "main." (Broadway is our city's *principal* street.)

quiet, quite

11. When the teacher spoke, the room became (quite, *quiet*).

   ANSWER EXPLAINED: *Quiet*, meaning "silent," is required by the context.

   OTHER WORD: *Quite* means "completely." (By bedtime the children were *quite* exhausted.)

respectfully, respectively

12. The blue, red, and yellow sweaters belong to Jean, Marie, and Alice (respectfully, *respectively*).

   ANSWER EXPLAINED: *Respectively*, an adverb meaning "in the order stated," is required by the context.

   OTHER WORD: *Respectfully*, also an adverb, means "with proper respect." (As the principal rose to speak, the audience applauded *respectfully*.)

than, then

13. Try to find one that is shorter (*than*, then) this one.

> ANSWER EXPLAINED: *Than*, a conjunction used in comparisons, is required by the sentence.

> OTHER WORD: *Then*, an adverb, means "at that time." (He was *then* a lad of twelve.)

their, they're, there

14. The enemy fled in many directions, leaving (*their*, they're, there) weapons on the battlefield.

> ANSWER EXPLAINED: *Their* (*belonging to them*) is required to show ownership.

> OTHER WORDS: *They're* is a contraction for "they are." (*They're* altogether right.)

> *There* means "in that place." (Have you ever been *there?*)

to, too, two

15. He felt that he had paid (to, *too*, two) high a price for one mistake.

> ANSWER EXPLAINED: *Too*, meaning "excessively," is required by the context. (Sometimes *too* means "also": Donald is ill and his brother, *too*.)

> OTHER WORDS:
> *To* is a preposition. (Give it *to* me.)
> *Two* is a number. (One and one are *two*.)

who's, whose

16. (Who's, *Whose*) money is on this desk?

> ANSWER EXPLAINED: *Whose* (*belonging to whom*) is required to show ownership.

> OTHER WORD: *Who's* is a contraction for "Who is." (*Who's* there?)

your, you're

17. Do not hand in the report until (your, *you're*) certain that it is complete.

   ANSWER EXPLAINED: *You're*, a contraction for "you are," is required by the context.

   OTHER WORD: *Your* means "belonging to you." (What is *your* principal worry?)

EXERCISE 6: *Troublesome word pairs.* Write the correct choice, and state the reason for your choice.

1. Jules and Hector wish to go because (their, there, they're) eager to visit the museum.
2. Is that (your, you're) jacket on the floor?
3. Have you successfully (passed, past) all your final examinations?
4. The article describes the (principal, principle) (affects, effects) of the new law.
5. (Who's, Whose) at the door?
6. In the violent storm, the boat broke (loose, lose) from its moorings.
7. We did not realize that the children had not fed (there, their, they're) puppy.
8. We want to go to the movies, (to, too, two).
9. In the (passed, past) we have always held our commencement exercises in the evening.
10. He is taller (then, than) his brother.
11. She is the artist (who's, whose) poster was chosen for the contest.
12. I was advised to review the (principals, principles) of correct usage.
13. Dora, Richard, and Sandy scored ninety, eighty, and seventy-five (respectfully, respectively).
14. She was (quite, quiet) breathless from running upstairs.
15. Her puppy's death (effected, affected) her deeply.
16. There were fewer candidates (then, than) we had been (led, lead) to expect.
17. Your interpretation of the results of the test is (all together, altogether) inaccurate.
18. Did you see that truck speed (passed, past) the red light?
19. How will the new tax (affect, effect) your business?
20. The (principle, principal) cause of failure is excessive absence.
21. The reward must (of, have) pleased them very much.
22. The pages in my old dictionary are (loose, lose) and dog-eared.
23. The horse lifted (its, it's) head and snorted.
24. My English teacher gave me ample opportunity to make up for (passed, past) mistakes.
25. You have been (led, lead) astray by your own carelessness.
26. (You're, Your) coming to visit me in the hospital cheered me up.

27. (Who's, Whose) car is that?
28. Doing a task promptly is better (than, then) worrying about it.
29. It's (your, you're) turn to drive now, if you're ready.
30. The alumni have announced that (their, there, they're) sending a representative to our graduation.
31. You should (of, have) been at the game yesterday.
32. (Who's, Whose) going to make the arrangements for the dance?
33. What is the (affect, effect) of sunlight on plants?
34. (It's, Its) advisable to apply to at least three colleges early in your senior year.
35. (They're, There, Their) altogether overjoyed with the results.
36. Let them try to do it (there, their, they're) own way.
37. Tell me (who's, whose) on third base; I don't recognize him.
38. On his physician's (advice, advise), he resumed a full program of physical activities.
39. The dog wagged (its, it's) tail and barked happily.
40. The merchant promised to refund my money if I were not (all together, altogether) satisfied.

7. Agreement

Should you say that a pint of strawberries *costs*, or *cost*, a dollar?

Should you ask everyone to open *his or her*, or *their*, book?

To help you answer such questions, let us review some of the rules of agreement.

Rule 1: A singular subject requires a singular verb. A plural subject requires a plural verb.

1. Too many commas in a passage often (*cause*, causes) confusion in the reader's mind.

    ANSWER EXPLAINED: The plural subject *commas* requires the plural verb *cause*.

    Note that *causes* is singular—don't be misled by the final *s*.

    Notice how we conjugate a verb in the present tense:

SINGULAR	PLURAL
I cause	we cause
you cause	you cause
he (she, it) causes	they cause

2. There ('s, *are*) several ways to solve that problem.

ANSWER EXPLAINED: The plural subject *ways* requires the plural verb *are*.

When an expression such as *There is* (*There are*), *Here is* (*Here are*), or *It is* begins a sentence, look for the real subject to appear further along in the sentence. In the sentence above, for example, the real subject is not *There* but *ways*.

3. A box of materials (*is*, are) in the cabinet.

ANSWER EXPLAINED: The singular subject *box* requires the singular verb *is*.

Disregard *of-* phrases that come between subject and verb (example: *of materials* in the sentence above). They do not affect agreement.

4. The leader of the flock, as well as most of his followers, (*has*, have) jumped the fence.

ANSWER EXPLAINED: The singular subject *leader* requires the singular helping verb *has*.

Interrupting expressions beginning with *as well as*, *together with*, *in addition to*, *rather than*, etc., do not affect agreement between subject and verb.

Rule 2: Subjects that are singular in meaning but plural in form (*news, economics, measles,* etc.) require a singular verb.

5. Mathematics (*is*, are) extremely important in today's world.

ANSWER EXPLAINED: The singular subject *Mathematics* requires the singular verb *is*.

ADDITIONAL EXAMPLE: The United States *has* (not *have*) many beautiful national parks.

Rule 3: Singular subjects connected by *or, nor, either...or,* or *neither...nor* require a singular verb.

6. Either the witness or the defendant (*is*, are) lying.

>   ANSWER EXPLAINED: The singular subjects *witness* and *defendant* are connected by *either...or* and require the singular verb *is*.

>   ADDITIONAL EXAMPLE: Neither the sergeant nor the corporal *was* (not *were*) off duty.

Rule 4: A compound subject connected by *and* requires a plural verb.

7. The arrival and departure (was, *were*) on schedule.

>   ANSWER EXPLAINED: The compound subject *arrival and departure* requires the plural verb *were*.

>   ADDITIONAL EXAMPLE: Her study and preparation for the test *were* (not *was*) thorough.

Exception to Rule 4: A compound subject regarded as a single entity requires a singular verb.

8. Spaghetti and meatballs (*is*, are) a popular dish.

>   ANSWER EXPLAINED: *Spaghetti and meatballs*, regarded as a single entity, requires the singular verb *is*.

>   ADDITIONAL EXAMPLE: The long and short of the matter *is* (not *are*) that we won the game.

Rule 5: If a subject consists of two or more nouns or pronouns connected by *or* or *nor*, the verb agrees with the nearer noun or pronoun.

9. Neither my cousins nor Marie (*is*, are) leaving for the summer.

>   ANSWER EXPLAINED: The verb *is* agrees in number with the nearer noun *Marie*.

ALSO CORRECT: "Neither Marie nor my cousins *are* (not *is*) leaving for the summer." In this case the verb *are* agrees in number with the nearer noun *cousins*.

10. Either she or you (is, *are*) to blame.

ANSWER EXPLAINED: The verb *are* agrees in person with the nearer pronoun *you*.

ALSO CORRECT: "Either you or she *is* to blame." In this case the verb *is* agrees in person with the nearer pronoun *she*.

Rule 6: Make a pronoun agree with its antecedent.

Definition: An antecedent is the previous word to which a pronoun refers.

11. If anyone has any doubt about the value of this tour, refer (*him or her*, them) to me.

ANSWER EXPLAINED: The singular antecedent *anyone* requires a singular pronoun.

Remember that the following words are singular: *anyone, everyone, someone, no one, one, each, each one, either, neither, anybody, everybody, nobody, somebody, every* (person, etc.), *many a* (person, etc.).

12. *Hamlet* is the greatest of all the plays that (has, *have*) ever been written.

ANSWER EXPLAINED: The plural subject *that* requires the plural helping verb *have*. We know *that* is plural because its antecedent is *plays*.

To determine whether *that*, *which*, or *who* is singular or plural, look at the antecedent.

13. He is one of those persons who (*deserve*, deserves) great credit for perseverance.

ANSWER EXPLAINED: The plural pronoun *who* requires the plural verb *deserve*. We know *who* is plural because its antecedent is *persons*.

EXERCISE 7: *Agreement*. Write the correct choice, and state the reason for your choice.

1. The lieutenant, with all his soldiers, (was, were) captured.
2. Both the body and the mind (need, needs) exercise.
3. Each of the papers (has, have) been photocopied.
4. There ('s, are) several reasons for that girl's popularity.
5. The new movie has a number of actors (which, who) have been famous.
6. A sight to inspire fear (are, is) wild animals on the loose.
7. How much (has, have) food costs risen?
8. Jackson is one of the few sophomores who (has, have) ever made the varsity team.
9. Gladys' presence in her aunts' household resulted in many changes that (was, were) not to their liking.
10. I found that one of the brackets (was, were) broken.
11. There, crouching in the grass, (was, were) four enemies.
12. There (was, were) a dog and a cat in the chair.
13. Calisthenics (is, are) a part of Bob's morning routine.
14. The books they read (show, shows) their taste in literature.
15. He (don't, doesn't) speak very well on formal occasions.
16. Children's health (is, are) a serious concern of all parents.
17. Each applicant was asked for (their, his or her) name and address.
18. Neither he nor we (was, were) aware of the nature of your illness.
19. The number of foursomes on the course today (was, were) very small.
20. Macbeth himself, rather than the witches, (was, were) responsible for his downfall.
21. Everybody (was, were) asked to remain seated.
22. There, Alice, (is, are) some of my classmates.
23. Emily Dickinson is one of the poets (which, that) we studied last term.
24. Corned beef and cabbage (is, are) on tonight's menu.
25. The present series of discussions on current events (was, were) started in January.
26. One of the girls lost (their, her) books as a result of the confusion.
27. (Are, Is) each of the pies the same size?
28. An important ingredient of high school life (is, are) intramural athletics.
29. Either your mother or your father (is, are) supposed to sign the report card.
30. (Doesn't, Don't) either of you girls want this?
31. The dog together with its puppies (has, have) come into the den again.
32. She is one of the juniors who (was, were) nominated for the G.O. presidency.
33. Each of the men did (his, their) duty with exemplary courage.
34. Interesting news (is, are) what sells our paper.
35. Juan was the only one of the boys who, as you know, (was, were) not eligible.
36. If anyone wants the book, tell (him or her, them) that it is in my desk.
37. A bushel of peaches (cost, costs) five dollars.

38. Many a person had to earn (his or her, their) way through college.
39. The combination of the three colors (give, gives) a pleasing effect.
40. Your approach and delivery (is, are) faulty and need improvement.
41. Being both observant and curious about things (promote, promotes) learning.
42. A box of cookies (was, were) found on the porch, unopened.
43. Radio and television programs, along with other media of communication, (helps, help) us to appreciate the arts and to keep informed.
44. A magazine and a book (was, were) lying in disorder on the floor.
45. Neither of you (seem, seems) to be paying the slightest attention.
46. Each of the girls (has, have) an individual locker.
47. Will everyone please open (their, his or her) book to the preface.
48. The captain as well as six of his men (was, were) wounded in the skirmish.
49. The students' ingenuity (was, were) particularly challenged by the third question on the physics test.
50. Such a rapid succession of unfortunate events (is, are) enough to discourage anybody.

8. Adjectives and Adverbs

WHAT IS AN ADJECTIVE?

An *adjective* is a word that modifies a noun or a pronoun.

Buy a *new* hat.   (adjective *new* modifies noun *hat*)
I am *tired*.   (adjective *tired* modifies pronoun *I*)

WHAT IS AN ADVERB?

An *adverb* is a word that modifies a verb, an adjective, or another adverb.

Did she speak *clearly?*   (adverb *clearly* modifies verb *did speak*)
I am *extremely* tired.   (adverb *extremely* modifies adjective *tired*)
She spoke *very* clearly.   (adverb *very* modifies adverb *clearly*)

Review the following rules. They will help you to make proper use of adjectives and adverbs.

Rule 1: Use an adverb to modify a verb.

1. Mathematics problems must be done (accurate, *accurately*).

   ANSWER EXPLAINED: We need the adverb *accurately* to modify the verb *must be done*.

   An adverb answers such questions about a verb as *How? To what extent? Where?* or *When?* To tell *how* the "problems must be done," we need the adverb *accurately* (not the adjective *accurate*).

   An adjective describes a noun or pronoun. In "accurate clock," the adjective *accurate* describes the noun *clock*. In "*It* is *accurate*," the adjective *accurate* describes the pronoun *It*.

Rule 2: Use an adverb to modify an adjective.

2. The campers had an (unbelievable, *unbelievably*) large capacity for food.

   ANSWER EXPLAINED: We need the adverb *unbelievably* to modify the adjective *large*.

   Note that *unbelievably* tells "how" large the campers' capacity for food was.

Rule 3: Use an adjective after a linking verb.

   [A linking verb is a verb that "links" or connects the subject with a modifier. The following are linking verbs: *be* (*is, am, was, were,* etc.), *seem, appear, look, feel, smell, sound, taste, become, grow, remain, stay, turn.*]

3. Food prepared in this manner tastes more (*delicious*, deliciously).

   ANSWER EXPLAINED: The adjective *delicious* is required after the linking verb *tastes*.

   Study these further examples of the same rule:

The flowers smell *sweet*.	(not *sweetly*)
This sounds *strange*.	(not *strangely*)
The food looks *good*.	(not *well*)

Rule 4: Use the comparative degree (the *-er* or *more* form) for comparing two persons or things; use the superlative degree (the *-est* or *most* form) for comparing more than two.

Adjectives and adverbs have three degrees, as follows:

POSITIVE	COMPARATIVE	SUPERLATIVE
(adj.) wide	wider	widest
(adv.) widely	more widely	most widely
(adj.) faithful	more faithful	most faithful
(adv.) faithfully	more faithfully	most faithfully

Good and *bad* have irregular forms:

(adj.) good	better	best
(adv.) well	better	best
(adj.) bad	worse	worst
(adv.) badly	worse	worst

4. It was the (worse, *worst*) storm that the inhabitants of the island could remember.

ANSWER EXPLAINED: The superlative *worst* is needed because the sentence compares more than two storms.

The comparative *worse* can be used when only two persons or things are compared, as in the following: This storm was *worse* than the last one.

Rule 5: Use the adjective *other* when you compare a person or thing with the rest of his, her, or its group.

5. Peter is younger than any of (the, *the other*) boys.

ANSWER EXPLAINED: *Other* must be included because the sentence compares Peter with the rest of his group (*boys*). Peter is a boy, too.

Note that *other* is not required in the following: Pauline is younger than any of the boys. Pauline is not a member of the group *boys*.

EXERCISE 8: *Adjectives and adverbs.* Write the correct choice, and state the reason for your choice.

1. I wish he would take his work more (serious, seriously).
2. At the picnic, the young children behaved very (good, well).
3. The food looks (delicious, deliciously) and is quite reasonable.
4. Our old television set does not work so (good, well) as our new one.
5. Did you notice how (beautiful, beautifully) the sky looked?
6. The birds' morning song sounded (sweet, sweetly) to our ears.
7. A person who works as (efficient, efficiently) as Celina deserves high praise.
8. The butter tastes (rancidly, rancid).
9. Da Vinci was more brilliant than (any, any other) person in his century.
10. Yes, my brother can do this work as (good, well) as I.
11. How (strange, strangely) the noise sounded in the quiet, abandoned house!
12. I am (real, really) sorry to have disturbed you, Mrs. Jones.
13. Clara's piano playing seems no (worse, worst) than yours.
14. You are not likely to encounter another pupil who studies as (diligent, diligently) as Anne.
15. He has always done his work (well, good) and cheerfully.
16. This material feels so (soft, softly) that it reminds me of fur.
17. He was voted the most (handsome, handsomely) dressed boy in the class.
18. Pam (sure, surely) appeared glad to see me receive the award.
19. Notice how (rapid, rapidly) that boiling water dissolves sugar.
20. Sam should have received a trophy too, for he played just as (good, well).
21. I felt (bad, badly) when my car was damaged.
22. José could throw a fast ball and field a bunt as (good, well) as Luis.
23. If you try a slice, you'll see how (delicious, deliciously) the melon tastes.
24. When Paul first joined the team, he was no better than any of (the, the other) players.
25. That oriental music sounded (strange, strangely) to my ears.
26. Our car has always run (good, well) on ordinary unleaded gasoline.
27. Willa Cather is one of the (real, really) distinguished authors in American literature.
28. Your conduct during this period has been the (worse, worst) in the class.
29. Our teacher (sure, surely) knows how to recite a poem.
30. Florence listened (attentively, attentive) to the music.
31. The sun made us feel (warm, warmly) and glad to be alive.
32. You must admit, Dorothy, that you behaved very (rude, rudely).
33. Nothing smells as (tempting, temptingly) as Mother's homemade pie.
34. Ben was brighter than (any, any other) pupil in his class.
35. No other character behaved more (faithful, faithfully) than Diggory Venn.
36. Be sure that the list is copied (accurately, accurate).

37. To the terrified wedding guest, the ancient mariner looked very (strange, strangely).
38. Jack does not swim so (good, well) as Betty.
39. Please turn down the radio; it is altogether too (loud, loudly).
40. He works more (diligently, diligent) now that he has become vice president of the company.

9. Double Negatives

"I *didn't* do *nothing*" is nonstandard English because it uses two negatives: (1) the *n't* in *didn't*, and (2) *nothing*.

To make the sentence acceptable as standard English, we must remove one of the negatives. Either of the following is correct:

> I did *nothing*.   (*n't* removed)
> I *didn't* do anything.   (*nothing* removed)

RECOGNIZABLE NEGATIVES

We can easily recognize these negatives:

no	*nobody*	*nowhere*
not	*no one*	*never*
n't	*nothing*	*neither*

HARD-TO-RECOGNIZE NEGATIVES

The following five words, too, are negatives, and unless we realize this we are likely to make the double-negative error:

> *barely, hardly, scarcely, only,* and *but* (when it means "only," as in "I had *but* one dollar").

Rule: Use only one negative word to express a negative idea.

1. He (*has*, hasn't) hardly a friend.

> ANSWER EXPLAINED: *Has* is correct because the sentence already has one negative (*hardly*).

2. You haven't (no one, *anyone*) to blame but yourself for your financial difficulties.

> ANSWER EXPLAINED: Since *haven't* is a negative word, do not use *no one*, which is also a negative expression. Use *anyone*.

3. Although he searched all over for the glue, he couldn't find (*any*, none).

> ANSWER EXPLAINED: Since *couldn't* is a negative word, do not use *none*, which is also a negative expression. Use *any*.

4. The child is short; he (*is*, isn't) barely able to reach the first shelf.

> ANSWER EXPLAINED: *Is* is correct because the sentence has another negative (*barely*).

5. I saw Jane and Frances at the party, but I didn't get a chance to speak to (*either*, neither) one all evening.

> ANSWER EXPLAINED: Since *didn't* is a negative word, do not use *neither*, which is also negative. Use *either*.

EXERCISE 9: *Double negatives.* Write the correct choice, and state the reason for your choice.

1. I (could, couldn't) hardly believe that she would desert the cause.
2. With their best player disqualified, Lincoln High (can, can't) barely hope to tie us in Saturday's game.
3. Ginette has scarcely (an, no) equal on the tennis courts.
4. Jody (had, hadn't) no reason to doubt his father's judgment.
5. I don't have (anything, nothing) left in my savings account.
6. They stayed home and didn't go (nowhere, anywhere) all summer.
7. Jack looked everywhere for earthworms, but he didn't see (none, any).
8. Her older brother scarcely (ever, never) works harder than necessary.
9. Where are Debbie and Alice? I haven't seen (either, neither) one all week.
10. The term (had, hadn't) hardly begun when we got our first full-period test.
11. At the dance, there wasn't (anybody, nobody) from our club.
12. If you haven't (anything, nothing) better to do, why not join us at the beach?
13. There (is, isn't) barely an hour left before the plane leaves.
14. Margaret's illness hadn't (nothing, anything) to do with this problem.
15. Our high-jump star had hardly (a, no) rival during the whole season.
16. How can you plan to go bowling if you (have, haven't) but two days to study?
17. I looked at all the passengers on the train, but I didn't recognize (no one, anyone).

18. Eva gets the highest grades, yet she scarcely (ever, never) studies.
19. When my grandfather arrived in this country, he (had, hadn't) only ten dollars in his pocket.
20. I don't know why the dean questioned me because I didn't have (nothing, anything) to do with the incident.

10. Parallel Structure

To express yourself clearly and effectively, put ideas of the same rank into the same (parallel) grammatical structure.

DO NOT SAY: TV is good for *news* (noun), *movies* (noun), and *to watch sports* (infinitive phrase).

SAY: TV is good for *news* (noun), *movies* (noun), and *sports* (noun).

Because *news* and *movies* are nouns, the sentence requires a third noun, *sports* (rather than the infinitive phrase *to watch sports*), to achieve parallel structure.

Rule: Put ideas of the same rank into the same grammatical structure.

1. Mailing a letter a few days early is better than (to run, *running*) the risk of its arriving late.

    ANSWER EXPLAINED: The verbal noun *running* is required for parallel structure with the verbal noun *mailing*.

    If the sentence had begun with the infinitive *to mail*, the correct answer would have been the infinitive *to run*: "*To mail* a letter a few days early is better than *to run* the risk of its arriving late."

2. You should select foods that are nourishing and (*tasty*, taste good).

    ANSWER EXPLAINED: The adjective *tasty* is required for parallel structure with the adjective *nourishing*.

3. Brian doesn't know whether he should watch TV or (to go, *go*) to the movies.

    ANSWER EXPLAINED: The verb *go*, rather than the infinitive *to go*, is required for parallel structure with the verb *watch*.

4. Cotton is comfortable and (one can wash it, *washable*).

ANSWER EXPLAINED: The adjective *washable* is needed for parallel structure with the adjective *comfortable*.

5. To do the job at hand takes more character than (planning, *to plan*) heroic deeds.

ANSWER EXPLAINED: The infinitive *to plan* is required for parallel structure with the infinitive *to do*.

EXERCISE 10: *Parallel structure.* Write the correct choice, and state the reason for your choice.

1. A stenographer's job is better paying than a grocery (clerk, clerk's).
2. The modern automobile has the advantages of strength and (being speedy, speed, moving swiftly).
3. To do a task promptly is better than (worrying, to worry) about doing it.
4. She likes dancing, skating, and (to go swimming, swimming).
5. Nylon dresses wash easily, drip-dry readily, and (you can wear them a long time, wear durably).
6. He appeared tired and (disappointed, a disappointed man).
7. George was unruly, inattentive, and (had no patience, impatient).
8. They promised me a good job and (to pay me a fair salary, a fair salary).
9. Last-minute studying is not so effective as (keeping up, to keep up) with the daily assignments.
10. My ambition is to be a physician and (specializing, to specialize) in surgery.
11. Our neighbor is helpful, friendly, and (she talks a great deal, talkative).
12. To be outclassed is not so annoying as (losing, to lose) by one point.
13. We plan to go to college to study, to prepare for a career, and (for the purpose of making, to make) new friends.
14. The pioneers were industrious, ambitious, and (courageous, they had a great deal of courage).
15. A computer offers the benefits of speed and (you can get accurate results, accuracy).
16. In the summer we enjoy picnicking, outdoor camping, and (to go sightseeing, sightseeing).
17. Paperback books are handy, inexpensive, and (you can get them anywhere, easily available).
18. Her marks were higher than her (sister, sister's).
19. To climb the mountain is much more fun than (to go, going) up by the scenic railway.
20. Henderson, the president of the class and (who is also captain of the team, captain of the team), will lead the rally.

11. Dangling Constructions

WHAT IS A DANGLING CONSTRUCTION?

Coming up the stairs, the clock struck twelve.

The phrase *Coming up the stairs* has nothing to modify and is therefore *dangling*. It would appear to modify *clock*, but it obviously doesn't, for clocks can't climb stairs.

Coming up the stairs is a dangling construction because it cannot be attached to any word in the sentence.

CORRECTING A DANGLING CONSTRUCTION

The way to correct the error is to provide a noun or pronoun to which the dangling construction can be attached. Examples:

1. Coming up the stairs, *he* heard the clock strike twelve.
2. As *he* was coming up the stairs, the clock struck twelve.

Note that in both of the above examples we stopped the construction from dangling by providing the pronoun *he*.

Rule: Be sure to include the noun or pronoun to which a phrase or a clause refers. Otherwise, you will have a *dangling construction*.

1. (After preparing, After having prepared, *After I had prepared*) all day for Jane's visit, my desire to see her increased.

   ANSWER EXPLAINED: Because *After I had prepared* has the pronoun *I*, it tells who did the preparing. The other choices do not; they are dangling constructions.

2. While driving along the highway, (a fatal head-on collision was seen, *we saw a fatal head-on collision*).

   ANSWER EXPLAINED: The italicized clause is correct because it includes the pronoun *we*, telling who saw the collision.

3. Although (tired, *they were tired*) of climbing, it was cheering to see their goal just ahead.

> ANSWER EXPLAINED: The pronoun *they*, in the clause *they were tired*, tells who was tired.

4. While (at, *he was at*) lunch, the soup bowl slid onto his lap.

> ANSWER EXPLAINED: The pronoun *he*, in the phrase *he was at*, identifies the person at lunch. The other phrase would suggest that the soup bowl was at lunch.

5. To succeed in life, (hard work can't be escaped, *you can't escape hard work*).

> ANSWER EXPLAINED: The pronoun *you*, in the clause *you can't escape hard work*, tells who is *to succeed in life*.

EXERCISE 11: *Dangling constructions.* Some of the following sentences are correct, but most are incorrect. Rewrite the incorrect sentences.

1. All the next week, while driving back and forth to work, the scene remained vivid in my mind.
2. Diving into the water, my goggles came off.
3. The tomb of an Egyptian pharaoh commanded attention coming into the museum.
4. As she hurried down the stairs, her shoe fell off.
5. While passing a large boulder, a sudden noise made me jump.
6. While shopping in the supermarket, their parking lights remained on.
7. Humbled by the loss of prestige, her plans changed.
8. After failing the examination, the teacher advised them to study regularly.
9. Sailing up the harbor, the Statue of Liberty was seen.
10. The five-o'clock whistle blew as we came down the avenue.

12. Misplaced Modifiers

Through carelessness we sometimes place a phrase, clause, or word too far from the word, or words, it modifies. As a result, the sentence fails to convey our exact meaning and may produce a kind of amusement that we did not intend.

CASES OF MISPLACED MODIFIERS

MISPLACED PHRASE: Francis caught sight of the train passing *through the kitchen door.*

Obviously, the train did not pass through the kitchen door. The phrase *through the kitchen door* modifies *caught sight of* and should be placed nearer to it, rather than next to *passing.*

ERROR CORRECTED: *Through the kitchen door,* Francis caught sight of the train passing.

MISPLACED CLAUSE: They brought a puppy for my sister *that they call Rex.*

The clause *that they call Rex* modifies *puppy*, not *sister.*

ERROR CORRECTED: They brought a puppy *that they call Rex* for my sister.

MISPLACED WORD: To get to the beach, we *nearly* traveled six miles.

The word *nearly* modifies *six.*

ERROR CORRECTED: To get to the beach, we traveled *nearly* six miles.

EXERCISE 12: *Misplaced modifiers.* If a modifier has been misplaced, rewrite the sentence to correct the error.

 1. Crossing the street, a car almost struck us.
 2. The plant was given to us by a friend that was supposed to flower in the spring.
 3. A qualified physician can only prescribe medicine.
 4. Occurring in April, we were surprised by the event.
 5. Through the corner of my eye, I saw a squirrel approaching.
 6. Reserve a room for the gentleman with a bath.
 7. I caught a glimpse of the old piano walking down the hall.
 8. Joe found a letter in his mailbox that doesn't belong to him.
 9. My brother nearly earned five hundred dollars by cutting our neighbors' lawns.
10. Coming up the hill, we saw the moon rising.
11. Her mother is the woman talking to the policeman in the red dress.
12. He discovered a bird's nest trimming the hedges.
13. Brenda put the books on the bed that she borrowed from the library.
14. We made a profit of almost ten dollars.
15. Karen bought a coat in the department store with a detachable lining.

13. Superfluous Words

Always revise your writing to remove superfluous (unnecessary) words, such as those in italics:

Doesn't she have a beautiful smile *on her face?*
On my next birthday I will be seventeen *years old.*
We rowed to a small island *surrounded by water* and pitched our tent.

Rule: Omit words that add unnecessary details or repeat ideas already expressed.

1. This is a club with which I wouldn't want to be (*associated*, associated with).

   ANSWER EXPLAINED: *Associated* ends the sentence correctly. The preposition *with* should not be repeated.

   Do not end a clause with the same preposition with which you began it.

2. He refused (to accept my invitation, *my invitation*) to our club party.

   ANSWER EXPLAINED: *To accept* adds nothing to the meaning of the sentence.

3. Your answer is correct; please (*repeat it*, repeat it again) for the class.

   ANSWER EXPLAINED: *Again* is unnecessary. If the student repeated his answer *again*, he would be giving it for the *third* time.

4. Are you telling me the (*truth*, real truth)?

   ANSWER EXPLAINED: *Real* adds nothing to the meaning of *truth* and should be eliminated.

EXERCISE 13: *Removing superfluous words.* Rewrite the following sentences, omitting the unnecessary words:

1. A girl of about nine years old opened the door.
2. Dennis, where will the game be held at?
3. A heavy dew lay on the surface of the grass.
4. On his head he wore a hunting cap.

5. She feels better, now that the operation is over with.
6. Susan found the old hairstyles of bygone days amusing.
7. My new car is heavier in weight than yours.
8. They didn't know to whom to give the supplies to.
9. We can't make a decision until we know the true facts.
10. The headline at the top of the main article says: "Fire Out of Control."
11. After each stanza, repeat the chorus again.
12. Take this prescription over to the nearest pharmacy.
13. Tell me for whom you are now working for.
14. Most department stores run special sales in the month of January.
15. Only one of their starting players was shorter in height than our athletes.
16. My brother Tim slept throughout the entire performance.
17. I cannot remember where I met him at.
18. We received a letter from Ruth written on her personal stationery.
19. In my opinion, I think you are wrong.
20. He thought that, if he apologized, that he would be excused.
21. The end result was that I was given a new test.
22. Fresh fruit and vegetables are more expensive in price now.
23. The secretary declined to accept my offer to type the report.
24. Maxine, why are you so upset for?
25. Parents prefer small children to play indoors when it rains outside.

14. Run-on Sentences and Sentence Fragments

Two of the more serious errors encountered in written English are *run-on sentences* and *sentence fragments*.

1. A *run-on sentence* is the running together of two or more sentences.

TYPICAL RUN-ON:

The people are what makes Ithaca <u>great, they</u> are different, special, and most of all, exciting.

RUN-ON CORRECTED:

The people are what makes Ithaca <u>great. They</u> are different, special, and most of all, exciting.

EXPLANATION:

Since <u>great</u> ends the first sentence, it must be followed by a period. Since the next word starts a new sentence, it should begin with a capital (<u>They</u>).

2. A *sentence fragment* **results from writing a piece (fragment) of a sentence as if it were a whole sentence.**

TYPICAL SENTENCE FRAGMENT (from the end of a sentence):

Nassau has beautiful beaches and parks. That provide year-round recreation for every member of the family.

SENTENCE FRAGMENT CORRECTED:

Nassau has beautiful beaches and parks that provide year-round recreation for every member of the family.

EXPLANATION:

"That provide year-round recreation for every member of the family" is merely a piece (*fragment*) of the previous sentence. Therefore (1) there must be no period before that, and (2) that must begin with a small "t."

TYPICAL SENTENCE FRAGMENT (from the beginning of a sentence):

When people from other countries come to live in New York City. They always bring a part of their culture with them.

SENTENCE FRAGMENT CORRECTED:

When people from other countries come to live in New York City, they always bring a part of their culture with them.

EXPLANATION:

"When people from other countries come to live in New York City" is merely a piece (*fragment*) of the next sentence. Therefore (1) the period after City must be replaced by a comma, and (2) the next word (they) must begin with a small "t."

EXERCISE 14: *Run-on sentences and sentence fragments.* Some of the excerpts below are run-ons. Others contain sentence fragments. Rewrite each of the following, removing the error.

1. I am very interested in studying music, for the past six years I have been in the chorus in my high school and junior high school.
2. I would very much like to attend your summer school course in the arts. Particularly your film program.

3. Also, I received a score of 1400 on the S.A.T. Which places me in the top fifth of the country.
4. There are also students who just wonder what happened. Like those who ask the teacher why they failed.
5. It is not good for you just to watch and not participate, you never get that feeling of pleasure that comes when you succeed at something.
6. Many people come to New York. Just to become famous or make a great deal of money.
7. Getting revenge on the white whale meant a great deal to Captain Ahab, it did not mean that much to the rest of the crew.
8. People today are in a constant rush, they have no time for the simple things in life.
9. There are many excellent openings. Especially for someone with a good education.
10. Traffic moved very slowly on the highway, there had been a serious accident.

15. Some Expressions to Avoid

Below are some common expressions—most of them nonstandard—that you should learn to avoid.

1. AVOID: He wants that tape deck _irregardless_ of cost.
   SAY: He wants that tape deck _regardless_ of cost.

2. AVOID: What kind (sort, type) of _a book_ are you reading?
   SAY: What kind (sort, type) of _book_ are you reading?

3. AVOID: She _graduated_ high school last year.
   SAY: She _graduated from_ high school last year.

4. AVOID: _Being that_ I'm older, I'll go first.
   SAY: _Since_ I'm older, I'll go first.

5. AVOID: He (She, It) _don't_ appear to be old.
   SAY: He (She, It) _doesn't_ appear to be old.

6. AVOID: Credit is _when you trust somebody._
   SAY: Credit is _trust._

7. AVOID: I was _sure_ happy to meet her.
   SAY: I was _surely_ happy to meet her.

8. AVOID: He dances *good.*
   SAY: He dances *well.*

9. AVOID: We *had ought* to go in now.
   SAY: We *ought* to go in now.

10. AVOID: My *father, he* says I'm lazy.
    SAY: My *father* says I'm lazy.

11. AVOID: *This here* book was just published.
    SAY: *This* book was just published.

12. AVOID: He will help *hisself* if they will help *theirselves.*
    SAY: He will help *himself* if they will help *themselves.*

13. AVOID: *In "Sea-Fever" it* tells about the lure of the sea.
    SAY: *"Sea-Fever"* tells about the lure of the sea.

14. AVOID: Try *and* do better.
    SAY: Try *to* do better.

15. AVOID: The reason is *because* I was sick.
    SAY: The reason is *that* I was sick.

16. AVOID: *Like* I told you, he moved to Seattle.
    SAY: *As* I told you, he moved to Seattle.

17. AVOID: *Me and my friend* went to the circus.
    SAY: *My friend and I* went to the circus.

18. AVOID: *Most* always April is cool there.
    SAY: *Almost* always April is cool there.

19. AVOID: Please get *off of* the platform.
    SAY: Please get *off* the platform.

20. AVOID: That was a *real* good movie.
    SAY: That was a *really* good movie.

21. AVOID: Would you hand me *them* tools?
    SAY: Would you hand me *those* tools?

22. AVOID: His project is different *than* mine.
    SAY: His project is different *from* mine.

23. AVOID: *That there* boy is my cousin.
    SAY: *That* boy is my cousin.

24. AVOID: Eleanor seems *kind (sort) of* tired.
    SAY: Eleanor seems *rather* tired.

25. AVOID: I read in the newspaper *where* the coach resigned.
    SAY: I read in the newspaper *that* the coach resigned.

EXERCISE 15: *Expressions to avoid.* Some of the following sentences are correct, but most are incorrect. Rewrite the incorrect sentences.

1. Being that he was the best qualified person, he received the appointment.
2. You had ought to return this book before it becomes overdue.
3. Musicals most always attract large audiences.
4. What kind of ending does *Moby Dick* have?
5. When will your sister graduate law school?
6. The reason for my refusal is that you're undependable.
7. He hurriedly took the luggage off of the bus rack.
8. Would you please lend me them notes for tonight?
9. What type of a jacket are you interested in?
10. My teacher, he said we should memorize that table.
11. Give me that there book lying on the desk.
12. All of us were kind of upset when we heard the news.
13. Most everyone there wore a campaign button.
14. Try and call me up before ten-thirty.
15. We always get a friendly welcome in that there place.
16. I'm going to the party irregardless of what you say.
17. Being that she broke the watch, she should pay for the repairs.
18. They went to bed early, as little children should.
19. It don't make the slightest difference to us.
20. Bliss is when you are perfectly happy.
21. They did it theirselves in less than an hour.
22. In *The Return of the Native*, it tells about a beautiful girl named Eustacia.
23. Me and my brother have always attended the same schools.
24. Can you recommend a really good short story?
25. The second problem was hardly different than the first.
26. Henry took all the old magazines off the shelf.
27. The reason I failed my driving test was because I passed a stop sign.
28. This here apparatus is certainly quite complicated.
29. Most always we have a dance before the final examinations.
30. Did you read in the sports column where the Rovers are getting a new manager?
31. The reason is because we were unavoidably delayed in leaving the house.
32. The club members prepared the stage setting all by theirselves.
33. I checked all my answers, like my teacher had suggested.
34. After the first marking period, Helen resolved that she would try to do better.
35. My uncle, he says that fishing is the most relaxing sport.

16. Punctuation

If you know the rules of correct punctuation, you will be both a better writer and a better reader. In your writing you will be unlikely to commit such blunders as "After eating grandmother washed the dishes." When you encounter a colon [:] in your reading, you will immediately sense the author's next move: he will either present a series or explain more fully an idea he has just stated. To improve your punctuation skill, review the rules and do the exercises on the following pages.

REVIEW OF PUNCTUATION RULES

1. USE THE PERIOD [.]

a. After a statement.

Our school has a new physics laboratory.

b. After a command.

Put your pens down.

c. After most abbreviations.

Mr.   etc.   p.m.   op. cit.

Use *only one period* after an abbreviation that ends a sentence.

The sports editor is William Harris, Jr.

The period following *Jr* performs *two* functions:

(1) it shows *Jr* is an abbreviation, and
(2) it ends the sentence.

WITH CLOSING QUOTATION MARKS: The period is inside.

Mother said, "Dinner is ready."

2. USE THE QUESTION MARK [?] after a question.

When will you hand in your report?
"Where are you going?" asked Dad.

EXCEPTION: After a request phrased as a question for the sake of politeness, you may use a period.

Will you please detach the stub and return it with your payment.

WITH CLOSING QUOTATION MARKS: The question mark is inside if it belongs to the quotation only.

Mr. Rossi asked, "Who would like to volunteer?"

The question mark is outside if it belongs to the sentence as a whole.

Do you know who wrote "The Death of the Hired Man"?

3. USE THE EXCLAMATION POINT [!] after an exclamation.

What a fine throw Sally made!
"Look out!" someone shouted.

WITH CLOSING QUOTATION MARKS: The exclamation point is inside if it belongs to the quotation only.

She exclaimed, "What a delightful surprise!"

The exclamation point is outside if it belongs to the sentence as a whole.

How thrilling it was to hear the band play "Stars and Stripes Forever"!

EXERCISE 16: *Punctuation.* Rewrite each sentence, inserting omitted periods, question marks, and exclamation points.

1. Suddenly someone screamed, "Help me"
2. Have you read "Annabel Lee"
3. Place hands on shoulders
4. Susan asked, "Is Tom coming"
5. *Punctual* means "on time"
6. What a beautiful day
7. Didn't George Gershwin write *Rhapsody in Blue*
8. The official replied, "No comment"
9. Fasten your seat belts
10. Asked to apologize, she screamed, "Never"

4. USE THE COMMA [,]

　　a. To set off words of direct address (words that tell to whom a remark is addressed).

　　　Mr. Jones, that is the reason for my absence. (one comma)
　　　That is the reason for my absence, *Mr. Jones.* (one comma)
　　　That, *Mr. Jones,* is the reason for my absence.

　　　　(Use two commas to set off a word or expression that neither begins nor ends a sentence.)

b. To set off words in apposition (words that give additional information about the preceding or following word or expression).

A light sleeper, Mom is the first to awake. (one comma)
The first to awake is Mom, *a light sleeper*. (one comma)
Mom, *a light sleeper*, is the first to awake. (two commas)

CAUTION: Use no commas when the appositive is so closely associated with the word it modifies that the two are pronounced as one expression, with no pause between them.

Do you know my friend *Louise?*
Alexander *the Great* died of a fever.
Some consider the number *thirteen* unlucky.

c. To set off a direct quotation.

The chairperson said, *"The meeting is adjourned."*
"The meeting is adjourned," said the chairperson.
"The meeting," said the chairperson, *"is adjourned."*

(Use two commas to set off a divided quotation.)

d. To set off an interrupting, or parenthetic, expression.

My sister, *Heaven help her*, has three finals on Friday.
These prices, *we are well aware*, are the lowest in town.

e. After such words as *yes, no, ah, oh, well*, etc., at the beginning of a sentence.

Oh, I'm sorry to hear it.

f. Before the conjunction (*and, but, or, for*) in a compound sentence.

Geraldine was the first to leave the examination room, *and* I followed about five minutes later.

NOTE: The comma is unnecessary in a short compound sentence:

Sarah washed the dishes and I dried them.

EXCEPTION: Use the comma before the conjunction *for* to prevent misreading.

Dad stopped the car, *for* Emma was ill.

g. After each item in a series, except after the last item.

The fruit bowl contained *peaches, pears, nectarines, plums, grapes,* and *bananas* in an attractive arrangement.

(The comma before *and* may be omitted.)

h. To set off a contrasting expression.

The girls did most of the work, *not the boys.*

The girls, *not the boys*, did most of the work.

i. After an introductory prepositional phrase.

Along the route from the airport to City Hall, the hero was wildly acclaimed.

NOTE: The comma may be omitted if the phrase is short:

Along the route the hero was wildly acclaimed.

j. After an introductory subordinate clause.

When I brought home a report card with three A's, Dad was surprised.

k. After an introductory participial phrase.

Frightened by our approach, the burglar fled.

l. To set off a nonessential clause (a clause that *can be omitted* without making the sentence illogical or changing its basic meaning).

Franklin D. Roosevelt, *who was elected President four times*, was an avid stamp collector.

CAUTION: Do not set off an essential clause (a clause that *cannot be omitted*).

Franklin D. Roosevelt is the only American *who was elected President four times.*

(Note that if we omit the clause "who . . . times," we are left with the illogical sentence "Franklin D. Roosevelt is the only American." This proves the clause "who . . . times" is *essential;* therefore, *no comma before "who."*)

m. To set off a nonessential participial phrase.

The patient, *weakened by loss of blood*, lapsed into unconsciousness.

CAUTION: Do not set off an essential participial phrase.

People *weakened by loss of blood* need transfusions. (no commas)

n. After the salutation in a friendly letter.

Dear Joe,   Dear Agnes,   Dear Dad,

   o. After the complimentary close in a friendly or business letter.
   Your friend,   Sincerely yours,   Yours truly,

   p. Between the day of the month and the year.
   November 11, 1918   October 12, 1492

   q. Before the state in an address.
   Fort Lauderdale, FL 33310   St. Louis, MO 63166

   r. To set off such expressions as *however, moreover, furthermore, nevertheless, on the other hand, incidentally, of course, for example,* etc.
   The results, *nevertheless*, were quite satisfactory.

   WITH CLOSING QUOTATION MARKS: The comma is inside.
   ''Remember to revise your paper,'' Mr. Brown concluded.

EXERCISE 17: *Punctuation.* Rewrite each sentence, adding the necessary punctuation.

   1. Mary a girl with little talent for cooking enjoys preparing pizza
   2. No I have never been there
   3. Have you ever considered Mr. Jones began how exciting it is to operate a computer
   4. Jackson High is the only school that beat us last year but we expect to beat them this year
   5. At the start of our hike up the mountain everybody was in a good mood
   6. For these reasons my fellow students I ask you to vote for me
   7. The first orbital flight was made on April 12 1961
   8. Anthony Gallo the captain of the track team is in my chemistry class
   9. The results I am happy to say took us completely by surprise
   10. Don't you agree that the parents not the children should be held responsible
   11. My favorite pastime unless I am in a hurry is walking
   12. Encouraged by her success in Spanish Marian is now planning to begin French
   13. My shopping list included aluminum foil cereal milk sugar and potatoes
   14. We left Chicago at midnight hoping for better weather by morning
   15. It is not possible however that the judge will suspend the sentence
   16. He was eager to work for Mrs. Bailey had praised his attitude
   17. As I entered my friend George exclaimed Look who's here
   18. Beverly Edwards our class representative will make a brief report
   19. When did Ivan the Terrible reign
   20. Every home destroyed in the storm is being rebuilt

5. USE THE SEMICOLON [;]

a. To separate items in a series when the items contain commas.

The following officers were elected: *Eleanor Bloch, president; Marvin Swenson, vice president;* and *Mildred White, secretary.*

b. Between main clauses that contain commas.

Sydney Carton, the hero, worships Lucie Manette; and he eventually sacrifices his life to save Charles Darnay, Lucie's husband.

c. Between main clauses when the conjunction (*and, but, for, or*) has been left out.

We have made many suggestions to your committee; not a single one has been accepted.

d. Between main clauses connected by *however, moreover, nevertheless, for example, consequently,* etc.

It was really a comfortable seat; *consequently,* she felt no inclination to move.

WITH CLOSING QUOTATION MARKS: The semicolon is outside.

Edna St. Vincent Millay was only nineteen when she wrote "Renascence"; nevertheless, it is an outstanding poem.

6. USE THE COLON [:]

a. After the word *following* and similar expressions that introduce a list or series.

The dinner menu offered a choice of the *following:* broiled chicken, roast beef, liver and bacon, or baked mackerel.

b. Before a long quotation, especially a formal one.

Article VIII of the Constitution states: "Excessive bail shall not be required, nor excessive fines imposed, nor cruel and unusual punishments inflicted."

c. Before a part of a sentence that merely restates, explains, or gives an example of what has just been stated.

Our firm has a fixed policy: we will not be undersold.

A Shakespearean sonnet consists of four parts: three quatrains and a couplet.

    d. After the salutation of a business letter.

      Dear Sir or Madam: Dear Ms. O'Brien:

      WITH CLOSING QUOTATION MARKS: The colon is outside.

      There are three characters in ''The Death of the Hired Man'': Mary, Warren, and Silas.

7 USE THE DASH [—]

    a. To show a sudden change in thought.

      We have a democratic student government—*of course, we don't make all the rules*—that gives us a voice in school affairs.

    b. Before a summary of what has just been stated in the sentence.

      Staying on the team, graduating, going to college—*everything depended on my getting better marks.*

8. USE PARENTHESES ( )

    a. To enclose information added to the sentence to guide the reader.

      The decline in exports in the past two years has been considerable (*see graph*).

    b. To enclose numbers or letters used to list items in a sentence.

      A book owned by a library is usually represented in the card catalog by (1) a title card, (2) an author card, and (3) a subject card.

9. USE BRACKETS [ ] to enclose a comment that interrupts a direct quotation.

      She said, ''I helped Tom occasionally with his Latin [*in fact, she saved him from failing*] when he had Mrs. Brown.''

10. USE QUOTATION MARKS ['' '']

    a. To set off titles of short works: poems, essays, short stories, one-act plays, songs, magazine articles, etc.

      ''The Rime of the Ancient Mariner'' (poem)
      ''On Doors'' (essay)
      ''The Gift of the Magi'' (short story)
      ''The Star-Spangled Banner'' (song)

NOTE: In handwritten or typewritten matters, underline titles of full-length works (novels, biographies, full-length plays, anthologies, nonfiction books, etc.) and titles of newspapers, magazines, operas, and motion pictures.

<u>Macbeth</u> (full-length play)
<u>Modern American and British Poetry</u> (anthology)
<u>Giants in the Earth</u> (novel)
<u>Newsweek</u> (magazine)

b. To set off a definition. (The word or expression being defined should be underlined.)

The expression <u>to aggravate</u> means "to make worse."

c. To set off a direct quotation (a speaker's exact words).

The principal said, *"We have been informed that our cafeteria will be renovated."* (Capitalize the first word of a direct quotation: use *We*, not *we*.)

"We have been informed that our cafeteria will be renovated," the principal said.

"We have been informed," the principal said, *"that our cafeteria will be renovated."* (Two sets of quotation marks are needed when a direct quotation is divided.)

CAUTION: Do not use quotation marks with an indirect quotation.

The principal said that we had been informed that our cafeteria would be renovated. (no quotation marks)

NOTE: To set off a quotation within a direct quotation, use single quotation marks.

"Please explain," the prosecutor asked, "what you mean by *'I don't remember exactly.'*"

EXERCISE 18: *Punctuation.* Rewrite each of the following sentences, correcting the errors in punctuation.

1. Four words may be unfamiliar to you in "The Man With the Hoe:" stolid, seraphim, Pleiades, and immedicable.
2. "If we don't hurry, said Marcia, we will miss our bus."
3. Give dollars, quarters, dimes, pennies anything you can spare.
4. One of Poe's finest short stories is *The Tell-Tale Heart.*
5. The expression *a baker's dozen* means "thirteen".

6. Your outline should provide for three parts; an introduction, a body, and a conclusion.
7. Ms. Burke stated "Wednesday is absolutely [she stressed this word] the last day for handing in reports".
8. The manager is very busy: nevertheless, he will try to help you.
9. To qualify you must be a senior have at least an 85% average, and present recommendations from three teachers.
10. The Gift of the Magi is a short story by O. Henry.

17. Capitalization

Review your capitalization rules. They are essential for good writing technique.

Should you write *the Reader's Digest* or *The Reader's Digest?* Which is correct—*my Uncle John* or *my uncle John?* Are the names of the seasons capitalized (*spring* or *Spring*)? Is it *Seventy-second Street* or *Seventy-Second Street?*

The answers to these and other capitalization problems appear in the next few pages. Study the examples. Then do the exercises.

REVIEW OF CAPITALIZATION RULES

1. CAPITALIZE the opening words:

   a. Of a sentence.

   It is a pleasure to go hiking in spring.

   b. Of a direct quotation.

   The officer explained, "**If** you go two blocks north, you will see the main entrance."

   DO NOT CAPITALIZE the opening word of the second half of a divided quotation, unless it begins a new sentence.

   "If you go two blocks north," the officer explained, "you (*no capital*) will see the main entrance."

   "Go two blocks north," the officer explained. "**There** (*a capital is used to begin the new sentence*) you will see the main entrance."

c. Capitalize the opening word of a line of poetry.

"Tomorrow, and tomorrow, and tomorrow
Creeps in this petty pace from day to day."
— *William Shakespeare*

DO NOT CAPITALIZE the opening word of a line if the poet himself did not do so.

"The fog comes
on (*no capital*) little cat feet."
— *Carl Sandburg*

d. Capitalize the opening word of the salutation in a letter. In addition, capitalize a *noun* or a *title* in the salutation.

Dear Pat,   **My dear Ms. Lopez:**
Dear Uncle Mike,   **Dear Sir or Madam:**

e. Capitalize the opening word of the complimentary close of a letter. (Capitalize the opening word only.)

Your friend,   **Sincerely yours,**
Your best pal,   **Very truly yours,**
Your former pupil,   **Yours very truly,**

f. Capitalize the opening word of each item in an outline. (Note these items from an outline on "How I Learned to Drive.")

I. Driver-training course
  A. In the classroom
  B. Behind the wheel
II. Practice in the family car

2. CAPITALIZE proper nouns (names of particular persons, places, things, etc.) and proper adjectives (adjectives formed from proper nouns).

A *common noun* refers to no particular person, place, or thing and is not capitalized. Examples: **man, country, building**.

A *proper noun* refers to a particular person, place, or thing and is always capitalized. Examples: **Shakespeare** (a particular man), **Mexico** (a particular country), **Empire State Building** (a particular building).

An adjective derived from a proper noun is also capitalized. Examples: a **Shakespearean** play, a **Mexican** village.

Learn to CAPITALIZE the proper nouns and proper adjectives in these important categories:

a. Names of persons.

John Hancock, Marian Anderson, William Faulkner

b. Names of geographical places.

Europe, Pacific Ocean, United States, Ohio River, Mt. Washington, Atlantic City, Yellowstone National Park

DO NOT CAPITALIZE the second part of a hyphenated number: Example: Forty-second Street.

c. Names of sections of countries (especially of the United States) and their people.

New England, the South, the West, Northerner

DO NOT CAPITALIZE *north*, *south*, *east*, and *west* when used to indicate direction.

Go one mile south and then turn east.

d. Names of buildings, museums, churches, trains, ships, etc.

World Trade Center, Seattle Art Museum, Church of the Holy Family, Ambassador Hotel, Brighton Beach Express, S.S. Constitution

e. Names of institutions and organizations.

Sewanhaka High School, American Automobile Association, General Motors Corporation, Tuskegee Institute

f. Names of governmental subdivisions.

House of Representatives, Department of Agriculture, Bureau of Motor Vehicles, Boulder Police Department

g. Names of days, months, and holidays.

Monday, December, Labor Day

DO NOT CAPITALIZE the seasons: spring, summer, autumn (fall), winter.

h. Names of historical events, eras, and documents.

Battle of the Coral Sea, the Renaissance, the Declaration of Independence

i. Names of languages.
   English, French, Russian, Spanish, Hebrew

j. Names of nationalities.
   American, Japanese, Egyptian, Israeli

k. Names of religions.
   Christian, Roman Catholic, Protestant, Jewish, Mohammedan, Hindu

l. References to the Supreme Being.
   God, the Creator, the Almighty, the Lord, Heaven, Jehovah, Allah, Jesus Christ, Savior, His name
   "I will fear no evil: for Thou art with me."
   —Twenty-third Psalm

DO NOT CAPITALIZE references to pagan divinities—only their names.
   Zeus was the chief of the ancient Greek gods, and Jupiter was his Roman counterpart.

m. Titles preceding persons' names.
   Mr. Lombardi, Dr. Berg, Professor Holmes, General Lee, President Lincoln, Uncle Jack, Cousin Ruth

DO NOT CAPITALIZE titles used alone, except for very high government officials.
   The doctor came.
   Who is the president of your club?
   At the airport, the President was greeted by the Mayor.

n. Titles of parents and relatives not preceded by a possessive word (e.g., my, your, Frank's, etc.).
   I saw Mother with Uncle George.
   I saw my mother with my uncle.

EXCEPTION: If a name follows the title, capitalize the title, even when preceded by a possessive word.
   My Uncle George plays golf.

    o. Titles of books, plays, articles, poems, short stories, etc.

        DO NOT CAPITALIZE the following unless they stand first in the title: (1) the articles (*a, an, the*); (2) conjunctions (*and, or,* etc.); (3) short prepositions (*to, of, for,* etc.)—unless they end a title.

        The Old Man and the Sea, An Enemy of the People, "A Night at an Inn," "To a Mouse"

    p. Titles of newspapers and magazines.

        DO NOT CAPITALIZE the word *the* before the title of a newspaper or magazine, unless it begins a sentence.

        I read the *New York Times, Newsweek,* and the *National Geographic.*

    q. Titles of courses.

        This term I am taking English 8, Economics 1, Math 12, Physics 2, and French 6.

        DO NOT CAPITALIZE school subjects, except languages.

        This term I am taking English, economics, math, physics, and French.

    r. Titles of holy writings and their subdivisions.

        the Bible, the Old Testament, the New Testament, the Book of Ruth, the Gospel of St. Matthew, the Koran

    s. Brand names (but not the product)

        Electrolux vacuum cleaner, Ford sedan, Sunkist orange

3. CAPITALIZE the words *I* and *O.*

        Jane and I hope you will come.
        Hail to thee, O Caesar!

    DO NOT CAPITALIZE the word *oh*, except at the beginning of a sentence.

        "Destroyer and preserver; hear, oh, hear!"
                —Percy Bysshe Shelley

4. CAPITALIZE personifications (ideas or abstract objects treated as persons).

        "Oh Liberty! Liberty! what crimes are committed in thy name!"
                —Madame Roland

REVIEW EXERCISE ON CAPITALIZATION

Each of the following sentences contains an underlined expression. Below each sentence are four suggested answers. Decide which answer is correct. Be prepared to explain the reasons for your answers.

(1) I showed my <u>father your copy of the</u> *Reader's Digest.*
    1. Correct as is   3. father your copy of *The*
    2. Father your copy of the   4. Father your copy of *The*

(2) At what time did <u>the President summon his Doctor</u> to the White House?
    1. Correct as is
    2. The President summon his Doctor
    3. the president summon his doctor
    4. the President summon his doctor

(3) "My <u>Cousin Arthur," he said, "has</u> just left for Annapolis."
    1. Correct as is   3. cousin Arthur," he said, "Has
    2. cousin Arthur," he said, "has   4. Cousin Arthur," he said, "Has

(4) Is there a crosstown bus on <u>Thirty-Fourth Street?</u>
    1. Correct as is   3. Thirty-fourth Street?
    2. Thirty-Fourth street?   4. thirty-fourth street?

(5) The letter concluded with the words <u>"Yours very truly,</u> Salvatore De Vito."
    1. Correct as is   3. "yours very truly,
    2. "Yours Very Truly,   4. "yours very Truly,

(6) Dr. Berson teaches us <u>economics and American History.</u>
    1. Correct as is
    2. Economics and American History.
    3. economics and American history.
    4. economics and american history.

(7) "Until three years ago," explained Millie, <u>"My family lived in the South."</u>
    1. Correct as is
    2. "my family lived in the south."
    3. "my family lived in the South."
    4. "My family lived in the south."

(8) Before coming here, she had attended <u>High School in the city</u> of Denver.
    1. Correct as is
    2. high school in the city
    3. High School in the City
    4. high school in the City

(9) You can see wonderful botanical displays in Prospect <u>Park in the Spring.</u>
    1. Correct as is
    2. park in the spring.
    3. park in the Spring.
    4. Park in the spring.

(10) I earned my best marks in <u>chemistry 2 and Spanish 4.</u>
    1. Correct as is
    2. Chemistry 2 and Spanish 4.
    3. chemistry 2 and spanish 4.
    4. Chemistry 2 and spanish 4.

(11) "There are several fine national parks in the <u>west," said Uncle Ben.</u>
    1. Correct as is
    2. west," said uncle Ben.
    3. West," said uncle Ben.
    4. West," said Uncle Ben.

(12) Didn't you know that <u>Grandfather and Aunt Isabel</u> were coming for dinner?
    1. Correct as is
    2. grandfather and Aunt Isabel
    3. Grandfather and aunt Isabel
    4. grandfather and aunt Isabel

(13) We shall read <u>*The Call of the Wild* in our Literature class this spring.</u>
    1. Correct as is
    2. The *Call of the Wild* in our literature class this Spring.
    3. *The Call of the Wild* in our literature class this spring.
    4. *The Call Of The Wild* in our literature class this spring.

(14) "My speech teacher is a <u>Westerner," said Emily, "he</u> was raised in California."
    1. Correct as is
    2. Westerner," said Emily, "He
    3. westerner," said Emily. "He
    4. Westerner," said Emily. "He

(15) The turning point in <u>World War II was the battle</u> of Britain.
    1. Correct as is
    2. World War II was the Battle
    3. World war II was the Battle
    4. World War II was The Battle

(16) At Friday's assembly, Janet read <u>the Twenty-Third Psalm from the Bible.</u>
   1. Correct as is
   2. the Twenty-third Psalm from the Bible.
   3. The Twenty-Third Psalm from The Bible.
   4. the Twenty-Third Psalm from The Bible.

(17) "A tree that looks at God all day,
   <u>And lifts Her</u> leafy arms to pray."
   1. Correct as is   3. and lifts Her
   2. and lifts her   4. And lifts her

(18) Dad bought <u>Mother a General Electric refrigerator last summer.</u>
   1. Correct as is
   2. mother a General Electric Refrigerator last summer.
   3. Mother a General Electric refrigerator last Summer.
   4. mother a General Electric Refrigerator last Summer.

(19) Shall we learn about the <u>middle ages in European History I?</u>
   1. Correct as is
   2. Middle Ages in European history I?
   3. Middle Ages in European History I?
   4. middle ages in european history I?

(20) "Dear old Pete," began <u>the letter from my Cousin</u> Harvey, "You'll probably
   be surprised to get this letter."
   1. Correct as is
   2. "Dear Old Pete," began the letter from my cousin
   3. "Dear old Pete," began the letter from my cousin
   4. "Dear Old Pete," began the letter from my Cousin

Sample Examinations

COMPREHENSIVE EXAMINATION IN ENGLISH—JANUARY 1994 (1)

Directions for the Listening Section:

1. The teacher will read a passage aloud. Listen carefully. DO NOT WRITE ANYTHING.
2. Then the teacher will tell you to open your test booklet and read questions 1 through 10. At that time you may mark your tentative answers to questions 1 through 10 if you wish.
3. Next, the teacher will read the passage aloud a second time. *As you listen to the second reading*, WRITE THE NUMBER of the answer to each question.
4. After you have listened to the passage the second time, you will have up to 5 minutes to look over your answers.
5. The teacher is not permitted to answer questions about the passage.
6. After you have answered the listening questions, go right on to the rest of the examination.

Part I
Listening [10]

1. How does the speaker begin the passage? (1) by causing confusion (2) by creating suspense (3) by arousing fear (4) by generating suspicion

2. In the United States, official responsibility for restoring the wolf population depends on (1) local laws (2) each state legislature (3) a Federal act (4) private organizations

3. In which place do wolves no longer exist? (1) Spain (2) Italy (3) England (4) Germany

4. The speaker suggests that one principle of ecology focuses on the relationship of the (1) part to the whole (2) environment to science (3) old to the new (4) nation to the environment

5. The speaker feels that the reason wolves are sometimes portrayed as villains in literature is to (1) illustrate a moral (2) personify laziness (3) criticize authority (4) exemplify impatience

6. According to the speaker, wolves have learned that humans are (1) cowardly (2) shrewd (3) careless (4) dangerous

7. Who finally solves the problem of restoring wolves to Glacier National Park? (1) the wolves (2) the Congress (3) the National Park Service (4) the recovery team

8. The speaker's term "simple transplant" refers to (1) expanding the park's boundaries (2) relocating the wolf packs (3) selective breeding of wolves (4) abandoning natural recolonization

9. According to the speaker, wolves belong in Yellowstone Park because they (1) have lived there since 1926 (2) need large spaces to live in (3) have become too numerous in other parks (4) are part of the ecological community

10. What does the speaker say happens to people as a result of the absence of wolves?
(1) We feel safer.   (2) Our lives are less exciting.   (3) Our fairy tales change.
(4) We can hunt more easily.

Directions (11–30): Write the *number* of the word or phrase that most nearly expresses the meaning of the word printed in heavy black type.   [10]

11. **allure**   (1) charm   (2) secrecy   (3) sincerity   (4) judgment

12. **meager**   (1) faulty   (2) expensive   (3) inadequate   (4) measurable

13. **deflect**   (1) do over   (2) remove   (3) turn aside   (4) discuss

14. **slipshod**   (1) rough   (2) excessive   (3) glossy   (4) careless

15. **adage**   (1) essay   (2) poem   (3) proverb   (4) play

16. **avidly**   (1) rigidly   (2) eagerly   (3) colorfully   (4) impishly

17. **uncanny**   (1) without kindness   (2) beyond the normal   (3) without talent   (4) full of emotion

18. **saunter**   (1) pause   (2) bend   (3) slide   (4) stroll

19. **weather**   (1) endure   (2) regulate   (3) discover   (4) permit

20. **carnage**   (1) extreme frustration   (2) widespread theft   (3) massive slaughter
(4) deafening noise

21. The group was known for its **pacifism.**   (1) concern for the environment
(2) opposition to violence   (3) interest in religion   (4) views on education

22. The secretary **collated** the pages of the report.   (1) arranged   (2) typed
(3) duplicated   (4) proofread

23. The athlete's **tenacity** was amazing.   (1) poise   (2) luck   (3) determination
(4) strength

24. The newspaper reported that the committee's decision seemed **equitable.**   (1) unusual
(2) just   (3) predictable   (4) unavoidable

25. His chief role was that of **arbitrator.**   (1) developer   (2) organizer   (3) observer
(4) judge

26. The scouts were trained to **forage** as a survival skill.   (1) build a shelter   (2) identify
animal tracks   (3) search for food   (4) interpret weather signals

27. The speaker referred **obliquely** to the problem.   (1) objectively   (2) hesitantly
(3) indirectly   (4) sympathetically

28. The lecturer used **parables** to illustrate her point.   (1) charts   (2) stories   (3) slides
(4) statistics

29. A **nimble** mind is universally admired.   (1) logical   (2) trained   (3) sound
(4) quick

30. Some people believe that astrologers are **omniscient.** (1) possessed of universal knowledge (2) controlled by unseen forces (3) devoted to seeking perfection (4) capable of interpreting nature

Directions (31–40): In each of the following groups of words, only one of the words is misspelled. In *each* group, select the misspelled word and spell it correctly. [5]

31. erroneous livelihood explorred loathe meanness

32. banana argument parcel goverment rodeos

33. dryness foriegn running monkeys usable

34. guidence ceiling preparation mosquito pageant

35. ideally scarsity grateful sequence meadow

36. radios gauge devise feminine milage

37. negotiater recurring molecule placement symptom

38. vegeterian despise posture nuisance weary

39. bureaucrat efficiency officialy dilemma reinforce

40. armies illegible luxurious prespire surgeon

Directions (41–60): Below each of the following passages, there are several incomplete statements or questions about the passage. For *each*, select the word or expression that best completes the statement or answers the question *in accordance with the meaning of the passage*, and write its *number*. [20]

Passage A

On weekdays, when Mrs. Willoughby and her daughter, Miss Joanne, were alone, they took their lunch on trays in the drawing room, and after my mother had cleared up and washed the kitchen, the hour and a half till teatime was her own. My mother tells me that all morning she would plan what she might do with
5 it. She wanted to write to me; she wanted to write to her parents, and she must get a letter off to the Refugee Committee in London to find a sponsor for them; she wanted to take a bath; she wanted to walk in the fresh air; she wanted to study her English, for she found herself too exhausted at night after cooking, serving, and clearing up from dinner; she needed to sleep an hour, but my father had gone to
10 lie down upstairs and what she needed above all was to be alone. She sat at the kitchen table, aware of her leisure slipping away. She kept looking at the clock, calculating how much time she still had before preparing the tea tray. One afternoon, the door opened and Miss Joanne came through the kitchen, trailing grass and hay from the stables. She dropped a dirty blouse into the sink and went out
15 again, leaving both doors open. This caused a draft where my mother sat, and my mother got up and slammed the door behind the girl. Then she was sorry. She remembered how she had disliked the ill-natured maids in her mother's house, who fussed over their clean floors. She remembered that she owed these people her life. She went to the sink and washed Miss Joanne's blouse and starched it;

20   then, angry at herself for this servile act, she went to the china closet, took out
      Mrs. Willoughby's best Minton, and made herself some powerful Viennese coffee.
      She tasted the delicate fluted china between her lips, half afraid that Mrs. Wil-
      loughby might come in and catch her, half wishing that she would. My mother
      wanted to make herself known to the other woman.

                                                                      —Lore Segal

41. According to the narrator, what did her mother wish most to do in the afternoon?
    (1) read a book   (2) plan for the future   (3) have her tea   (4) enjoy some privacy

42. From the description in lines 1 through 12, the mother could best be described as
    feeling   (1) anxious   (2) enthusiastic   (3) incompetent   (4) important

43. Miss Joanne's actions reveal behavior that could be described as   (1) thoughtless
    (2) foolish   (3) stubborn   (4) impulsive

44. The passage implies that the mother's family had once been   (1) famous
    (2) influential   (3) charitable   (4) well-to-do

45. The phrase "servile act" in line 20 refers to   (1) disliking the maids   (2) slamming
    the door   (3) laundering the blouse   (4) making the coffee

46. The narrator develops the mother's character and personality by   (1) quoting her con-
    versations   (2) describing her work habits   (3) revealing her thoughts   (4) explaining
    her daydreams

47. The tone of this passage could best be described as   (1) sympathetic   (2) critical
    (3) resigned   (4) tolerant

Passage B

Thermometer Wine

      Always hung on its plaque
      on the porch like a mounted
      icicle, but was so old
      already the painted numbers
5   were peeling and hard to read.
      Only Daddy could tell
      the measurements — he'd known
      the instrument since a boy.
      At ten below it really
10   meant twenty, being slow
      with age, he said. At
      ten above it was roughly
      accurate, but on a hot day
      he added twenty to its reading.
15   I watched the red needle
      rise in the dog days and
      marveled how the tiny
      hair was both sensitive
      and significant.

20 The blood rose in that stem
    just a capillary of
    bright, as though the day
    were sipping through its ice
    straw that special wine,
25 and about to taste the
    color from the drop at
    the bottom that never clotted
    or dulled no matter how
    far up or down it wrote,
30 always chilled as snake or worm.

—— Robert Morgan

48. Which aspect of the thermometer is alluded to in the phrase "Always . . . icicle" (lines
    1 through 3)? (1) its size (2) its permanence (3) its worth (4) its accuracy

49. In line 16, the phrase "dog days" refers to a time when the temperature is (1) steady
    (2) unmeasurable (3) high (4) erratic

50. Which lines contain an example of personification? (1) lines 6 and 7 (2) lines 2
    and 3 (3) lines 15 and 16 (4) lines 22 through 24

51. The mercury in the thermometer is compared to each of the following *except* (1) a
    hair (2) an icicle (3) a capillary (4) wine

52. The narrator suggests that the "color from the drop at the bottom" (lines 26 and 27)
    might be tasted by the (1) narrator (2) father (3) day (4) needle

53. In which form is the poem written? (1) blank verse (2) free verse (3) couplets
    (4) quatrains

Passage C

The Big Tree (*Sequoia gigantea*) is nature's forest masterpiece and, as far as I
know, the greatest of living things. It belongs to an ancient stock, as its remains in
old rocks show, and has a strange air of other days about it, a thoroughbred look
inherited from the long ago, the *auld lang syne* of trees. Once the genus was
5   common, and with many species flourished in the now-desolate Arctic regions, in
the interior of North America, and in Europe; but in long eventful wanderings
from climate to climate only two species have survived the hardships they had to
encounter, the *gigantea* and *sempervirens*: the former now restricted to the western slopes of the Sierra, the other to the Coast Mountains, and both to California,
10 excepting a few groves of redwood which extend into Oregon.
The Pacific coast in general is the paradise of conifers. Here nearly all of them
are giants and display a beauty and magnificence unknown elsewhere. The climate is mild, the ground never freezes, and moisture and sunshine abound all the
year. Nevertheless, it is not easy to account for the colossal size of the sequoias.
15 The largest are about three hundred feet high and thirty feet in diameter. Who of
all the dwellers of the plains and prairies and fertile home forests of round-headed

oak and maple, hickory and elm, ever dreamed that earth could bear such growths? Sequoias are trees that the familiar pines and firs seem to know nothing about, lonely, silent, serene, with an appearance almost godlike, and so old that
20 thousands of them still living had already counted their years by tens of centuries when Columbus set sail from Spain, and were in the vigor of youth or middle age at the time of the birth of Jesus of Nazareth. As far as humanity is concerned, they are the same yesterday, today, and forever, emblems of permanence.

—John Muir

54. The use of the phrase "ancient stock" in line 2 suggests that sequoias (1) have a firmly established heritage (2) had no natural enemies (3) were originally imported (4) were probably planted by Native Americans

55. The author suggests that the survival of sequoias was greatly affected by (1) environmental difficulties (2) industrial expansion (3) cosmic forces (4) human settlements

56. The author characterizes the Pacific coast as being (1) rich in history (2) varied in climate (3) abundant in animal life (4) nurturing to some plants

57. The author characterizes the sequoias' exceptional growth as (1) mysterious (2) seasonal (3) completed (4) uncontrollable

58. The author suggests that the most probable reaction to seeing a giant sequoia would be (1) fear (2) disbelief (3) indifference (4) envy

59. In lines 15 through 18, the narrator makes his point through the use of (1) order of importance (2) an extended metaphor (3) a rhetorical question (4) cause and effect

60. In lines 22 and 23, the author suggests that people consider sequoias to be (1) vulnerable (2) endearing (3) beneficial (4) eternal

Part II

Directions: Write a well-organized essay of about 250 words on either *A* or *B*. [25]

A. Particular features of location or surroundings are often used to create atmosphere, which in turn helps to establish the reader's expectations about the characters and events in a work of literature. From the literature you have read, choose *two* works in which features of the location or surroundings provide an atmosphere that helps to establish the reader's expectations about the characters and events. For *each* work, describe the features of the location or surroundings that create atmosphere. Using specific references from *each* work, discuss the expectations that the atmosphere helps to establish and describe how those expectations are met by the characters and events in the work. Give titles and authors.

B. In some works of literature, a character who is weak or insecure early in the work becomes stronger or more confident later in the work. From the literature you have read, choose *two* works in which a character who is weak or insecure ultimately becomes stronger or more confident. For *each* work, identify the character. Using specific references from *each* work, show how the character demonstrates weakness or insecurity early in the work and how the same character demonstrates strength or confidence later in the work. Give titles and authors.

Part III

Directions: Answer *A* or *B* or *C*. [30]

A. Traditional concepts of "masculinity" and "femininity" are sometimes used to impose limitations on people. People may say, "That's not for girls (or boys)" or "Ladies don't do that" or "That's not manly," etc. In a narrative of about 250 words, relate an incident in which you or someone you know suffered from a limitation imposed because of traditional concepts of "masculinity" or "femininity." Discuss the effect of the incident on you or on the person involved. Use specific details.

B. A major responsibility of the President of the United States is to establish priorities for the nation. In a letter of about 250 words to the President, state which *two* priorities you believe he should have for the nation. Use specific reasons, examples, or details to explain why you believe those priorities should be at the top of the President's list. *Write only the body of the letter.*

C. Write a well-organized composition of about 250 words on *one* of the following topics:

The power of words	Right place, right time
Coming to the United States	Going metric
An athlete's life	Shades of gray

COMPREHENSIVE EXAMINATION IN ENGLISH—JUNE 1994 (1)

Directions for the Listening Section:

1. The teacher will read a passage aloud. Listen carefully. **DO NOT WRITE ANYTHING.**
2. Then the teacher will tell you to open your test booklet and read questions 1 through 10. At that time you may mark your tentative answers to questions 1 through 10 if you wish.
3. Next, the teacher will read the passage aloud a second time. *As you listen to the second reading*, WRITE THE NUMBER of the answer to each question.
4. After you have listened to the passage the second time, you will have up to 5 minutes to look over your answers.
5. The teacher is not permitted to answer questions about the passage.
6. After you have answered the listening questions, go right on to the rest of the examination.

Part I
Listening [10]

1. At the beginning of the passage, the speaker contrasts the accomplishments of his adulthood with the   (1) length of his life   (2) breadth of his experiences   (3) pleasures of his childhood   (4) poverty of his ancestors

2. To the Native Americans, everything that exists reveals characteristics of   (1) the earth   (2) their creator   (3) the family   (4) their tribe

3. According to the speaker, what development had he not foreseen?   (1) His culture would die.   (2) His family would separate.   (3) His religion would change.   (4) His skill would diminish.

4. How does the speaker describe his people's way of communicating with the Great Spirit?   (1) He portrays it as unrealistic.   (2) He depicts it as rigid.   (3) He compares it with that of other tribes.   (4) He contrasts it with other forms of worship.

5. During the speaker's childhood, transmission of knowledge depended upon   (1) the White man   (2) the oral tradition   (3) a written language   (4) the Great Spirit

6. According to the speaker, sign language was necessary for   (1) trade   (2) entertainment   (3) healing   (4) religion

7. The speaker probably describes the prairie as "unspoiled" to highlight the   (1) White man's later influence on the land   (2) expanse of the prairie   (3) discipline of his childhood   (4) friendliness of neighboring tribes

8. In confronting their losses, the Sioux regarded their god with an attitude of   (1) disappointment   (2) anger   (3) respect   (4) indifference

9. The autobiographical nature of this passage has the effect of   (1) hiding the truth   (2) objectifying memory   (3) exaggerating the past   (4) personalizing history

10. The speaker suggests that the survival of his people can be attributed to their (1) military skill   (2) religious beliefs   (3) tribal unity   (4) family ties

Directions (11–30): Write the *number* of the word or phrase that most nearly expresses the meaning of the word printed in heavy black type.   [10]

11. **placidly**   (1) peacefully   (2) powerfully   (3) purposefully   (4) protectively

12. **skeptical**   (1) sarcastic   (2) doubting   (3) aggressive   (4) critical

13. **deduce**   (1) combine efforts   (2) extend one's influence   (3) conclude by reasoning   (4) call to action

14. **perpetual**   (1) everlasting   (2) satisfied   (3) obliging   (4) devoted

15. **chafe**   (1) pursue   (2) trample   (3) irritate   (4) deceive

16. **foreboding**   (1) prediction of evil   (2) denial of mistakes   (3) total destruction   (4) tragic conclusion

17. **sheen**   (1) color   (2) luster   (3) texture   (4) design

18. **accost**   (1) accept   (2) rely   (3) explain   (4) confront

19. **adhere**   (1) argue forcefully   (2) hold tightly   (3) understand completely   (4) answer clearly

20. **revulsion**   (1) utter distaste   (2) deep sorrow   (3) self-pity   (4) overconfidence

21. They climbed **precariously** close to the crater of the volcano.   (1) dangerously   (2) unexpectedly   (3) excitingly   (4) unnecessarily

22. The client thought the decorator's work was **gaudy**.   (1) expensive   (2) showy   (3) unique   (4) shoddy

23. The actions of the visitors were **scandalous**.   (1) cowardly   (2) ridiculous   (3) shocking   (4) careless

24. The students thought the rules were **archaic**.   (1) unenforceable   (2) unreasonable   (3) old-fashioned   (4) confusing

25. His remarks **elicited** an immediate response.   (1) prevented   (2) begged for   (3) required   (4) drew forth

26. The audience appreciated the **brevity** of the speech.   (1) shortness   (2) honesty   (3) cleverness   (4) clarity

27. Farmers know that the **yield** will be affected by the weather.   (1) work required   (2) profit margin   (3) planting time   (4) amount produced

28. The garbage can was tipped over by a **marauding** dog.   (1) vicious   (2) raiding   (3) diseased   (4) homeless

29. The government **subsidizes** some aspects of farming.   (1) prohibits   (2) practices   (3) researches   (4) supports

30. She was interested in the **plight** of the survivors. (1) identities   (2) predicament   (3) reactions   (4) location

Directions (31–40): In each of the following groups of words, only one of the words is misspelled. In *each* group, select the misspelled word and spell it correctly.   [5]

31. adjustible calendar technique transmitted quadrant

32. cynical geology pennant naturaly expiration

33. applicant enviroment suppress mortgage novelist

34. piece sincerely official immature truthfullness

35. forecast ministry keenness poison defendent

36. misrule maxamize consultant referred absorb

37. mamoth recycle panorama mutineer mournful

38. laughable horrifying ernestly vegetable shaving

39. illegally forfeit sterile unrelieved labratory

40. stagnent roommate article remedy urban

Directions (41–60): Below each of the following passages, there are several incomplete statements or questions about the passage. For *each*, select the word or expression that best completes the statement or answers the question *in accordance with the meaning of the passage*, and write its *number*.   [20]

Passage A

Childhood, it has been said, is always partly a lie of poetry. When I was maybe eight years old, in the fall of the year, I would have to go out in the garden after school with damp burlap sacks and cover the long rows of cucumber and tomato plants, so they wouldn't freeze.

5   It was a hated, cold-handed job which had to be done every evening. I day-dreamed along in a halfhearted, distracted way, flopping the sacks onto the plants, sorry for myself and angry because I was alone at my boring work. No doubt my younger brother and sister were in the house and warm. Eating cookies.

But then a great strutting bird appeared out from the dry remnants of our
10   corn, black tail feathers flaring and a monstrous yellow-orange air sac pulsating from its white breast, its throat croaking with popping sounds like rust in a joint.

The bird looked to be stalking me with grave slow intensity, coming after me from a place I could not understand as real, and yet quite recognizable, the sort of terrifying creature which would sometimes spawn in the incoherent world of my
15   night dreams. In my story, now, I say it looked like death, come to say hello. Then, it was simply an apparition.

The moment demanded all my boyish courage, but I stood my ground, holding one of those wet sacks out before me like a shield, stepping slowly backwards, listening as the terrible creature croaked, its bright preposterous throat pulsating

20 and then the great bird flapped its wings in an angry way, raising a little commonplace dust.

It was the dust, I think, that did it, convincing me that this could not be a
dream. My fear collapsed, and I felt foolish as I understood this was a creature I
had heard my father talk about, a courting sage grouse; we called them prairie
25 chickens. This was only a bird, and not much interested in me at all. But for an
instant it had been both phantom and real, the thing I deserved, come to punish
me for my anger.

For that childhood moment I believed the world to be absolutely inhabited by
an otherness which was utterly demonic and natural, not of my own making. But
30 soon as that bird was enclosed in a story which defined it as a commonplace
prairie chicken, I was no longer frightened. It is a skill we learn early, the art of
inventing stories to explain away the fearful sacred strangeness of the world.
Storytelling and make-believe, like war and agriculture, are among the arts of self-
defense, and all of them are ways of enclosing otherness and claiming ownership.

— William Kittredge

41. In line 1, the statement that childhood "is always partly a lie of poetry" implies that
(1) we create fictions about our past (2) poetry is not honest (3) memories are
never realistic (4) poets understand children very well

42. For the narrator, thoughts of his brother and sister produced feelings of (1) warm-
heartedness (2) grief (3) relief (4) self-pity

43. The narrator's early impression of the bird was that it was (1) friendly (2) unreal
(3) awkward (4) ridiculous

44. What word best describes the child's feelings as conveyed in lines 25 through 27?
(1) frustration (2) surprise (3) guilt (4) greed

45. The words "sacred strangeness" (line 32) portray the narrator's attitude toward the
world as one of (1) antagonism (2) awe (3) trust (4) dismay

46. The narrator claims that storytelling is like war and agriculture because all (1) involve
hard work (2) require specific tools (3) depend on human intelligence (4) offer
protection from outside threats

Passage B

Poet in Winter

A small room with one table and one chair,
This man who writes, then cancels what he writes,
Tears up the sheet, runs fingers through his hair;
His violent longing makes a fiercer chill
5 Than the sensed tilting of his hemisphere
Toward the frozen solstice, and he fights
A strange, oncoming ice-age of the will.

For him love does not burn, but chains him so:
The unspoken words lie heavy on his tongue,
10   Thoughts are like granite hurled into soft snow;
He holds a winter landscape in his mind;
Known tracks, habitual roads are covered now
By a blank sameness; he is caught and wrung,
Twists in the eddy of a polar wind.

15   And yet that wind grasps only at the man
Thus damned to strive; one opening the door
Would see him there, and casually would scan
His bent head and the slowly scribbled page
That's hidden at the sound; the draught would fan
20   Fragments of verses to the littered floor
As a false snowstorm falls upon a stage.

—— Edward Lucie-Smith

47. In lines 4 through 7, the result of the man's "violent longing" is that he feels (1) determined (2) rejected (3) annoyed (4) insignificant

48. The first stanza suggests that the poet is writing about (1) abstract symbols (2) vague memories (3) intense emotions (4) deep convictions

49. In the second stanza, the man experiences love as (1) disappointing (2) enslaving (3) inflaming (4) bewildering

50. In the second stanza, the poet suggests that the condition of the man's mind is like (1) concealed terrain (2) an intricate maze (3) a hidden treasure (4) a smooth surface

51. Which lines most clearly suggest the man's lack of control? (1) lines 1 and 2 (2) lines 6 and 7 (3) lines 10 and 11 (4) lines 13 and 14

52. From the third stanza, what can be concluded about the man? (1) He does not want his work to be seen. (2) He is the only one affected by winter. (3) He is eager for suggestions from others. (4) He welcomes a chance to stop working briefly.

53. Which image does the poet use to unify the poem? (1) love (2) wind (3) roads (4) winter

Passage C

There is a tendency these days to defend whales and other endangered animals by pointing out their similarities to human beings. Cetaceans, we are told, are very intelligent. They possess a highly complex language and have developed sophisticated communications systems that transmit over long distances. They
5 form family groups, develop social structures and personal relationships, and express loyalty and affection toward one another. Much of their behavior seems to be recreational: they sing, they play. And so on.

These are not sentimental claims. Whales apparently do these things, at least as far as our sketchy information about their habits warrants such interpretations.
10 And for my money, any argument that helps to preserve these magnificent creatures can't be all bad.

I take exception to this approach not because it is wrong, but because it is wrongheaded and misleading. It is exclusive, anthropocentric, and does not recognize nature in its own right. It implies that whales and other creatures have value 15 only insofar as they reflect man himself and conform to his ideas of beauty and achievement. This attitude is not really far removed from that of the whalers themselves. To consume whales solely for their nourishment of human values is only a step from consuming them for meat. It is not only presumptuous and patronizing, but it is misleading and does both whales and men a grave disservice.
20 Whales have an inalienable right to exist, not because they resemble man *or* because they are useful to him, but simply because they do exist, because they have a proven fitness to the exactitudes of being on a global scale matched by few other species. If they deserve our admiration and respect, it is because, as Henry Beston put it, "They are other nations, caught with ourselves in the net of life and time, 25 fellow prisoners of the splendour and travail of life."

— Robert Finch

54. The purpose for the list of facts about whales in the first paragraph is most likely to (1) show the great range of whale behaviors (2) expand the reader's scientific knowledge (3) point out characteristics common to humans and whales (4) create sympathy for whales

55. In the second paragraph, the author suggests that our knowledge of whales is (1) very accurate (2) somewhat limited (3) constantly growing (4) merely guesswork

56. The author suggests that comparing whales and humans is undesirable because (1) it presumes humans are the measure of everything (2) whales and humans have such different habits (3) not enough is known about whales (4) whales are a much greater species

57. The author implies that the use of whales to support human values is (1) appropriate (2) exploitative (3) profitable (4) unlawful

58. The author's attitude toward whalers may be described as (1) patronizing (2) disinterested (3) disapproving (4) ridiculing

59. The image in lines 24 and 25, "caught with ourselves . . . fellow prisoners," suggests that (1) life is always cruel and dangerous (2) many things are beyond the control of a species (3) humans and whales are weak (4) humans and whales are dependent on each other

60. What change does the author seek to bring about?
(1) The knowledge about similarities among species will increase.
(2) Whales will no longer be used for food.
(3) People will cease netting and hunting of certain species.
(4) Humans will begin to respect nature for its own value.

Part II

Directions: Write a well-organized essay of about 250 words on either *A* or *B*.   [25]

A. In many works of literature, a female character has a significant influence, positive or negative, on another character. From the literature you have read, choose *two* works in which a female character has a significant influence on another character. For *each* work, identify the female character and the other character and state whether the influence was positive or negative. Using specific references from *each* work, explain how the female character influenced the other character. Give titles and authors.

B. In many works of literature, an important theme is an individual's achievement of self-knowledge as a result of undergoing an ordeal. This self-knowledge may be a recognition of the individual's own strengths, weaknesses, values, prejudices, aspirations, or fears. From the literature you have read, choose *two* works in which an individual achieves self-knowledge as a result of undergoing an ordeal. For *each* work, identify the individual and the self-knowledge he or she achieves. Using specific references from *each* work, explain how the ordeal led the individual to the self-knowledge. Give titles and authors.

Part III

Directions: Answer *A* or *B* or *C*.   [30]

A. A representative of a junior high school in your district has invited you to speak at the junior high graduation ceremonies on the topic "Getting Off to a Good Start in High School." Write a speech of about 250 words that you would give to the students, stating your recommendations for a successful start in high school. Use specific reasons, examples, or details to support your recommendations.

B. If you could choose a time and place in which to live, other than here and now, what would be your choice? In a composition of about 250 words, identify the time and place you would choose and explain why you would choose that time and place. Use specific reasons, examples, or details.

C. Write a well-organized composition of about 250 words on *one* of the following topics:

Music: a family affair	Information highway
A second chance	Today's explorers
Athletes as free agents: who benefits?	"It's a small world after all"

COMPREHENSIVE EXAMINATION IN ENGLISH—JANUARY 1995 (1)

Directions for the Listening Section

1. The teacher will read a passage aloud. Listen carefully. DO NOT WRITE ANYTHING.
2. Then the teacher will tell you to open your test booklet to page 2 and to read questions 1 through 10. At that time you may mark your tentative answers to questions 1 through 10 if you wish.
3. Next, the teacher will read the passage aloud a second time. *As you listen to the second reading*, WRITE THE NUMBER of the answer to each question in the appropriate space on the answer sheet.
4. After you have listened to the passage the second time, you will have up to 5 minutes to look over your answers.
5. The teacher is not permitted to answer questions about the passage.
6. After you have answered the listening questions, go right on to the rest of the examination.

Part I
Listening [10]

1. What does the speaker confess that she feared? (1) both everything and nothing (2) neither suffering nor failure (3) either going mad or dying (4) both fantasy and reality

2. The speaker would most likely have wanted to participate in activities that (1) pleased her parents (2) sparked her curiosity (3) were suggested by her friends (4) were not too dangerous

3. What does the speaker most likely mean when she describes her thoughts as "surging impulses that welled up"? (1) Sometimes her thoughts flowed quickly and were overwhelming. (2) She often forgot what she was thinking about. (3) Thinking wastes time so she did it as quickly as possible. (4) She collected her thoughts in a slow, methodical way.

4. The speaker indicates that she had a great desire for (1) faith (2) status (3) knowledge (4) friendship

5. The speaker implies that she did not want a life that was (1) without love (2) too public (3) chaotic (4) boring

6. Which word best describes what the speaker wanted her imagined book to be? (1) uncriticized (2) profitable (3) autobiographical (4) flawless

7. To what is the speaker referring when she compares her book to a tree and a grain of sand? (1) existence and immortality (2) love and annoyance (3) birth and growth (4) life and death

8. The speaker recognized that her secret longings were (1) questionable and vague (2) diverse and powerful (3) confusing and unexplainable (4) conflicting and troublesome

9. What does the speaker imply by describing murder as institutionalized and cruelty as systematic? (1) The current prison system promotes both murder and cruelty. (2) Both murder and cruelty will always exist. (3) Murder and cruelty have become too much a part of society. (4) The legal system treats murder and cruelty leniently.

10. The speaker's viewpoint at age 19 can best be described as (1) frightening (2) idealistic (3) vague (4) innovative

Directions (11-30): In the space provided on the separate answer sheet, write the *number* of the word or phrase that most nearly expresses the meaning of the word printed in heavy black type. [10]

11. **quip** (1) famous quotation (2) inspiring speech (3) interesting comparison (4) witty remark

12. **strife** (1) slur (2) conflict (3) discussion (4) scar

13. **consort** (1) speak for (2) rely on (3) associate with (4) make up

14. **filament** (1) thread (2) cloud (3) wreath (4) bulb

15. **haughty** (1) arrogant (2) sarcastic (3) particular (4) worthless

16. **emote** (1) display talent (2) exert pressure (3) express feeling (4) accept responsibility

17. **strenuous** (1) lengthy (2) dangerous (3) complicated (4) vigorous

18. **chronically** (1) actively (2) habitually (3) occasionally (4) foolishly

19. **inexplicable** (1) unconcerned (2) mysterious (3) forbidden (4) annoying

20. **hearten** (1) encourage (2) understand (3) reveal (4) adore

21. Before the sale, the manager's staff was **mobilized.** (1) carefully trained (2) increased in size (3) expected to work late (4) organized for action

22. During the Senator's **tenure**, taxes increased. (1) period of leadership (2) height of power (3) term of office (4) leave of absence

23. We found the runner **prostrate** at the finish line. (1) sitting down (2) lying flat (3) laughing loudly (4) arguing wildly

24. The workers complained that management's decision was **unilateral.** (1) hasty (2) unfair (3) self-serving (4) one-sided

25. Her purpose was to **intimidate** her listeners. (1) frighten (2) inspire (3) persuade (4) entertain

26. The mixture began to **calcify.** (1) bubble (2) evaporate (3) harden (4) discolor

27. He suffered from a strange **infirmity.** (1) temperament (2) weakness (3) anxiety (4) forgetfulness

28. A good quality in an employee is **perseverance.** (1) loyalty (2) honesty (3) patience (4) persistence

29. Carrying several packages at once can be **cumbersome.** (1) awkward (2) impossible (3) frustrating (4) dangerous

30. The student responded **flippantly** to the teacher's question. (1) with a lack of understanding (2) with a lack of enthusiasm (3) with a lack of seriousness (4) with a lack of clarity

Directions (31–40): In each of the following groups of words, only one of the words is misspelled. In *each* group, select the misspelled word and spell it correctly in the space provided on the separate answer sheet. [5]

31. unnecessary fiend paralel macaroni privilege

32. accommodation obituarry absorption bizarre syllable

33. disappointed caffeine illegible breatheing anonymous

34. matress immobile handkerchief happily planning

35. leisurely deceitful accidentaly capable ideally

36. inadviseable weighty relinquish echoes conservationist

37. pamphlet sieve abbreviate nuclear grusome

38. disciple wrinkle initiate scandelous treasurer

39. durable imigration prosperous horrify satisfactory

40. whistle succeed although sponsor concievable

Directions (41–60): Below each of the following passages, there are several incomplete statements or questions about the passage. For *each*, select the word or expression that best completes the statement or answers the question *in accordance with the meaning of the passage*, and write its *number* in the space provided on the separate answer sheet. [20]

Passage A

Meteors—those momentary streaks of light we see in the sky—have always been visible to humans. Today we know that each streak marks the death by incineration of a piece of rock usually no larger than a pea. But educated people did not always look at meteors this way. In 1718 Edmund Halley, the Astronomer Royal of Britain,
5 explained a bright meteor that was seen over much of Europe as the ignition of certain "inflammable sulphereous Vapours" in the atmosphere. Even Thomas Jefferson was not immune to a bias against objects coming from space. Told that two professors from Yale had confirmed such an event, he is supposed to have remarked, "I would prefer to believe that two Yankee professors would lie rather than that stones could fall from
10 heaven."

What seemed to be difficult for these men and their colleagues to accept was that the streak of light in the sky (a meteor) could turn into a stone on the ground (a meteorite). I would guess that this attitude was a holdover from the old idea that Earth was somehow special. To admit that rocks fell from the sky was to admit that Earth and

15   the rest of the Universe formed a seamless web—that our planet is neither isolated nor
     special.
          Two developments led to the acceptance of meteorites. One was the birth of modern
     chemistry in the late 18th century, and the consequent ability to analyze rocks that are
     supposed to have fallen from the sky and see whether they are different from their
20   neighbors. The other was a spectacular and well-documented meteorite fall near the
     town of L'Aigle, in northern France, on April 26, 1803. A commission of the French
     Academy of Sciences quickly traveled to the site and confirmed that the stones were
     not terrestrial in origin. With this "smoking gun," the artificial division between Earth
     and the rest of the Solar System vanished.

                                                                        —James Trefil

41. In the first sentence, which characteristic of meteors is described?   (1) They absorb
    light.   (2) They appear briefly.   (3) They appear only at night.   (4) They travel
    along the horizon.

42. In the 1700's, some people thought that meteors were   (1) bright clouds   (2) signs
    of the gods   (3) symbols of doom   (4) burning gases

43. The writer defines the terms "meteor" and "meteorite" in order to   (1) establish
    Jefferson's position   (2) justify the Yale professors' belief   (3) clarify a common
    misunderstanding   (4) provide scientific evidence

44. Jefferson's attitude toward meteorites seemed to be based on his belief in the
    (1) dependability of scientific methodology   (2) uniqueness of the planet Earth
    (3) existence of other planets   (4) distinction between science and faith

45. The current scientific explanation of meteorites supports the observations of
    (1) Edmund Halley   (2) Thomas Jefferson   (3) the Yale professors   (4) the medi-
    eval astronomers

46. As used in line 23, the term "smoking gun" means   (1) conclusive evidence   (2) an
    inexplicable event   (3) stubborn relief   (4) a mysterious weapon

47. The true nature of meteorites was established as a result of both a scientific break-
    through and   (1) a laboratory experiment   (2) a natural occurrence   (3) historical
    research   (4) international cooperation

Passage B

     Albany's Union Station was magical because it was more than itself, which is how
it is with any magical man, woman, or building. It was more than utilitarian. It was
also an idea, a state of mind, a minor architectural wonder that led you not only to the
trains but to the idea of trains.
5   It was magical from the beginning and it was meant to be. Those ceilings, fifty-two
feet high, that monumental concourse, were not casually designed. Space to move in
had nothing to do with the space that reached to the elegant roof. This was the work
of the Ozymandiastic minds of America's industrial captains: "Look on my works, ye
Mighty, and despair!"
10   Who was ever more powerful than the railroads? Not even the giants of the world

who rode them. William Jennings Bryan was among the first. His 1900 Presidential campaign train rolled through the station before the building was finished.

15 The station was finished a year later when Teddy Roosevelt came through from a hunting trip on Mount Marcy, changed trains, and went swiftly on to Buffalo to take the oath as President, William McKinley having just died from an assassin's bullet. Al Smith, FDR, Ike, and Adlai, heroes every one, arriving to cheering crowds, were stars of the moment but only human after all. The railroads were more than that.

20 When good American middle-class children of the first half of the twentieth century grew up, they went to Union Station and boarded a coach or, with luck, a Pullman, and rode into the awesome future.

What was a child of modest means and limited ways to make of that? The child knew railroads had magic all right because in his kitchen there hung a sepia print of a

25 grandfather and two grand-uncles standing beside Engine 151 on a clear day in the century's teens, and he knew the picture was holy. But once on the train what was the child to make of, say, the heavy silverware in the dining cars? What would he make of waiters with coats as white as the dining-car tablecloths? What of the elegant silver coffee service or the plush sofas and chairs in the Pullman car, one even that swiveled

30 like a drugstore stool so a sitter could look out of either window? What was the child to make of portly men with vests and watch chains and white mustaches, who smoked long dark cigars and read the *New York Sun* as the trees and the river sped by at sixty?

The stone exterior of Union Station opened onto a world where such people and things existed. From the first glimpse, the magical connection was established, and the

35 child could never enter through the doors again without the tissue of past awesomeness and present sophisticated anticipation congealing in an excited knot in the stomach. What next? Ah. What a splendid question.

—William Kennedy
(adapted)

48. In lines 1 and 2, what is the narrator saying about magical people or things? (1) They are often misunderstood. (2) They are larger than life. (3) They diminish our expectations. (4) They reflect our values.

49. The quotation from the poem "Ozymandias" (lines 8 and 9) suggests that the industrial captains thought of Union Station as (1) testimony to their own greatness (2) a reflection of their dedication to the people (3) the result of Americans' commitment to hard work (4) evidence of Americans' love of poetry

50. What aspect of Union Station is suggested by paragraphs 3 and 4? (1) its central location (2) its use for political rallies (3) its long delay in construction (4) its role in historical events

51. Which phrase conveys the attitude of the child's family toward the railroads? (1) "that monumental concourse . . ." (line 6) (2) ". . . heroes every one . . ." (line 17) (3) ". . . good American middle-class . . ." (line 20) (4) ". . . the picture was holy" (line 26)

52. Riding on the train provided the child with a glimpse of (1) a make-believe world (2) his ancestors' lifestyle (3) unfamiliar luxury (4) adult corruption

53. In line 38 ("What next . . . a splendid question"), the narrator suggests that the railroads represent (1) outdated technology (2) unusual courage (3) unfamiliar anxiety (4) unforeseeable possibilities

54. The passage conveys the narrator's feelings of (1) nostalgia (2) serenity (3) trust (4) acceptance

Passage C

Memorial Wreath

(For the more than 200,000
African-American soliders who
served in the Union Army during
the Civil War)

In this green month when resurrected flowers,
Like laughing children ignorant of death,
Brighten the couch of those who wake no more,
Love and remembrance blossom in our hearts
5 For you who bore the extreme sharp pang for us,
And bought our freedom with your lives.

And now,
Honoring your memory, with love we bring
These fiery roses, white-hot cotton flowers
10 And violets bluer than cool northern skies
You dreamed of in the burning prison fields
When liberty was only a faint north star,
Not a bright flower planted by your hands
Reaching up hardy nourished with your blood.
15 Fit gravefellows you are for Lincoln, Brown
and Douglass and Toussaint . . . all whose rapt eyes
Fashioned a new world in this wilderness.

American earth is richer for your bones;
Our hearts beat prouder for the blood we inherit.
—Dudley Randall

55. Which idea is repeated throughout the poem? (1) Children cannot comprehend the finality of death. (2) Civilians cannot appreciate what soldiers endure. (3) The Civil War was a futile exercise (4) The nation has benefited from the soldiers' sacrifice.

56. Which line alludes to those who died? (1) line 1 (2) line 2 (3) line 3 (4) line 4

57. Which phrase is a reference to death? (1) "this green month" (line 1) (2) "resurrected flowers" (line 1) (3) "extreme sharp pang" (line 5) (4) "these fiery roses" (line 9)

58. What image is suggested by the flowers in lines 9 and 10? (1) a parade (2) a grave (3) a well-kept cemetery (4) an American flag

59. What do lines 15 and 16 imply about the soldiers who are the subject of the poem? (1) They were noble figures. (2) Their deaths were inevitable. (3) They hoped to impress their leaders. (4) They were buried together.

60. In lines 16 and 17 ("all . . . world"), the poet suggests that the men mentioned in lines 15 and 16 were all (1) African Americans (2) visionaries (3) soldiers (4) presidents

Part II

Directions: Write a well-organized essay of about 250 words on either *A* or *B*. [25]

A. Reading about individuals whose way of life is dramatically different from our own often provides us with fresh insight into our own experiences and ideas. From the literature you have read, choose *two* works in which an individual's way of life is dramatically different from yours. For *each* work, identify the individual and describe the individual's way of life. Using specific references from *each* work, explain how reading about that way of life has provided you with fresh insight into your own experiences and ideas. Give titles and authors.

B. Some scenes from literature are especially memorable because of their tension, humor, or sadness. From the literature you have read, choose *two* works that contain a memorable scene. Using specific references from *each* work, discuss how the element of tension, humor, or sadness makes the scene memorable and explain how that memorable scene furthers your understanding of the work as a whole. Give titles and authors.

Part III

Directions: Answer *A* or *B* or *C*. [30]

A. Your local newspaper recently printed a report by a commission on mass transportation. The report suggested that the quality of life in large cities would be greatly improved by limiting the use of private automobiles. Write a letter of about 250 words to the editor of your local newspaper in which you either agree or disagree with the idea of limiting the use of private automobiles in large cities. Use specific reasons, examples, or details to support your opinion. *Write only the body of the letter.*

B. For educational and economic reasons, some politicians and educators have suggested that New York State adopt a system of year-round schooling, a system already in operation in some European and Asian countries. Write an editorial of about 250 words for your school newspaper in which you either agree or disagree with the idea of a system of year-round schooling for New York State. Use specific reasons, examples, or details to support your opinion.

C. Write a well-organized composition of about 250 words on *one* of the following topics:

A dream fulfilled   Health care for all
Music: the universal language   A culture of cultures
Sports in my life   Learning from failure

COMPREHENSIVE EXAMINATION IN ENGLISH—JUNE 1995 (1)

Directions for the Listening Section:

1. The teacher will read a passage aloud. Listen carefully. DO NOT WRITE ANY-THING.
2. Then the teacher will tell you to open your test booklet and read questions 1 through 10. At that time you may mark your tentative answers to questions 1 through 10 if you wish.
3. Next, the teacher will read the passage aloud a second time. *As you listen to the second reading*, WRITE THE NUMBER of the answer to each question.
4. After you have listened to the passage the second time, you will have up to 5 minutes to look over your answers.
5. The teacher is not permitted to answer questions about the passage.
6. After you have answered the listening questions, go right on to the rest of the exam-ination.

Part I

Listening [10]

1. For what does the speaker apologize?   (1) the behavior of his people in the past   (2) his intolerance toward the King   (3) his delay in coming forth with the truth   (4) the inconsistency of his own beliefs

2. The speaker views his "crime" as being   (1) avoidable   (2) honorable   (3) clever   (4) unintentional

3. According to the speaker, some parts of the Indian Penal Code were purposely intended to   (1) make certain punishments harsher   (2) disregard cultural traditions   (3) provoke fear in the population   (4) repress personal freedom

4. According to the speaker, laws cannot regulate   (1) feelings   (2) behavior   (3) ethics   (4) dreams

5. The speaker says that his attitude toward the British Government is based on its   (1) broken promises to the Indian people   (2) unsound economic policies   (3) damaging effect on his country   (4) prejudiced behavior toward minorities

6. The speaker says that some of the evidence used against him was   (1) provided by a traitor   (2) taken from his personal files   (3) falsified by the government   (4) written by him

7. The speaker indicates that evil is nourished by   (1) treason   (2) violence   (3) bitterness   (4) ignorance

8. According to the speaker, how must people face the penalty for non-cooperation?   (1) defiantly   (2) voluntarily   (3) hopefully   (4) cautiously

9. At the end of the passage, the speaker once again urges the judge to judge the   (1) government   (2) people   (3) law   (4) crime

10. When the speaker refers to actions as being "injurious to the public weal," he means those actions that are harmful to society's (1) well-being (2) morals (3) future (4) self-interest

Directions (11–30): Write the *number* of the word or phrase that most nearly expresses the meaning of the word printed in heavy black type. [10]

11. **jurisdiction** (1) policy (2) decision (3) protection (4) authority

12. **flux** (1) damage (2) change (3) distance (4) anger

13. **incoherent** (1) dull (2) lacking clarity (3) biased (4) hard to believe

14. **eccentric** (1) feeble (2) rude (3) ignorant (4) peculiar

15. **antagonize** (1) cause pain (2) question ability (3) create opposition (4) predict violence

16. **calamity** (1) dejection (2) misfortune (3) disbelief (4) poverty

17. **funereal** (1) dangerous (2) mysterious (3) gloomy (4) unreal

18. **zealous** (1) enthusiastic (2) wealthy (3) proud (4) skillful

19. **saddle** (1) discuss (2) convince (3) burden (4) remind

20. **ponder** (1) doubt (2) reject (3) establish (4) meditate

21. The students were **earnestly** involved in the project. (1) seriously (2) happily (3) reluctantly (4) independently

22. The student could not **perceive** the problem the way the teacher did. (1) recognize (2) rephrase (3) overcome (4) eliminate

23. The room was small and **unadorned.** (1) shabby (2) simple (3) sunny (4) spotless

24. He stared **impassively** through the bus window at the scene outside. (1) without expression (2) in confusion (3) with distrust (4) in amazement

25. For **aesthetic** reasons, she decided to change the design. (1) ethical (2) financial (3) artistic (4) legal

26. The shampoo advertisement promised that the user's hair would be **lustrous.** (1) fragrant (2) glossy (3) manageable (4) smooth

27. The group wanted to **ostracize** one of its members. (1) honor (2) support (3) banish (4) disqualify

28. The returning soldiers were reluctant to talk about their **exploits.** (1) orders (2) casualties (3) mistakes (4) feats

29. The little girl's sleep was **fitful.** (1) refreshing (2) irregular (3) brief (4) quiet

30. The prosecutor called the evidence **irrefutable.** (1) undeniable (2) illogical (3) inconsistent (4) unclear

Directions (31–40): In each of the following groups of words, only one of the words is misspelled. In *each* group, select the misspelled word and spell it correctly.   [5]

31. goalkeeper   conceive   boycot   grease   sandwich

32. clinical   incureable   bustle   deposit   technological

33. extraordinary   inquisative   tragedy   plentiful   obvious

34. cholesterol   missgiving   apprenticeship   negative   vowel

35. changable   academically   acknowledge   dissatisfied   hygiene

36. comission   rehearsal   eighth   safety   tourniquet

37. metropolitan   accuracy   minipulate   thief   skeleton

38. ascending   candidate   curtain   tomorrow   athelete

39. arrangement   scenery   deferred   symphony   edable

40. unneeded   orchestra   bachelor   dispise   competition

Directions (41–60): Below each of the following passages, there are several incomplete statements or questions about the passage. For *each*, select the word or expression that best completes the statement or answers the question *in accordance with the meaning of the passage*, and write its *number*.   [20]

Passage A

I thought about the island's history as I walked into the building and made my way to the room that was the center in my imagination of the Ellis Island experience: the Great Hall. It was in the Great Hall that everyone had waited — waiting, always, the great vocation of the dispossessed. The room was empty, except for me
5 and a handful of other visitors and the park ranger who showed us around. I felt myself grow insignificant in that room, with its huge semicircular windows, its air, even in abandonment, of solid and official authority.

I walked in the deathlike expansiveness of the room's disuse and tried to think of what it might have been like, filled and swarming. More than sixteen million
10 immigrants came through that room; approximately 250,000 were rejected. Not really a large proportion, but the implications for the rejected were dreadful. For some, there was nothing to go back to, or there was certain death; for others, who left as adventurers, to return would be to adopt in local memory the fool's role, and the failure's. No wonder that the island's history includes reports of three
15 thousand suicides.

Sometimes immigrants could pass through Ellis Island in mere hours, though for some the process took days. The particulars of the experience in the Great Hall were often influenced by the political events and attitudes on the mainland. In the 1890's and the first years of the new century, when cheap labor was needed, the

20 newly built receiving center took in its immigrants with comparatively little question. But as the century progressed, the economy worsened, the idea of genetic
"inferiority" became both scientifically respectable and popular, and World War I
made American fear of foreigners seem rooted in fact.

Immigration acts were passed; newcomers had to prove, besides moral cor-
25 rectness and financial solvency, their ability to read. Quota laws came into effect,
limiting the number of immigrants from southern and eastern Europe to less than
14 percent of the total quota. Intelligence tests were biased against all non-
English-speaking persons and medical examinations became increasingly strict,
until the machinery of immigration nearly collapsed under its own weight. The
30 Second Quota Law of 1924 provided that all immigrants be inspected and issued
visas at American consular offices in Europe, rendering the center almost
obsolete.

— Mary Gordon

41. At the time of the author's visit, the condition of the Great Hall reflected the results of
(1) waste   (2) indecision   (3) poverty   (4) neglect

42. The statistics in lines 9 and 10 show that the number of immigrants rejected at Ellis
Island   (1) was based on prejudice against eastern Europeans   (2) reflected the avail-
ability of cheap labor   (3) was comparatively low   (4) demonstrated the strict immigration policy

43. The author states that the rejection of the immigrants was pitiful because of the
(1) financial losses resulting from the journey   (2) fate many would face upon
returning home   (3) danger of epidemics on the return journey   (4) disruption of
family life

44. In lines 21 and 22, the author suggests that some people justified their prejudices against
immigrants by disguising their opinions as   (1) scientific theory   (2) economic policy
(3) political philosophy   (4) historical doctrine

45. What was a new admission requirement for immigrants arriving between World War I
and 1924?   (1) good health   (2) literacy   (3) an assured job   (4) a passport

46. According to the author, quotas were intended to   (1) increase the number of immigrants   (2) simplify the immigration process   (3) legalize limits on particular groups
(4) create ghettos in the cities

47. The author attributes the ultimate decline of Ellis Island as an immigration center to
the   (1) increase in the number of immigrants   (2) bias against non-European immigrants   (3) lack of adequate medical facilities   (4) screening of applicants in Europe

Passage B

ALTER EGOS

Two embroidered birds on silk
Made in China long ago
Perch on embroidered tree limbs
In bamboo frames on the wall.
5   One has long legs and a beak for fish,
The other has claws and keen eyes.
They face each other, unaware
That they share the same sky on the wall.

The fisher has patience he learned from lagoons,
10 He looks through reflections on shallow light
To see minnows shine in the sun.
He strikes while standing very still,
Then eats until they fill him,
And then he glides back home.

15 The hunter is wind in a storm as it blows,
He strikes by descent to his shadow below
On the prey that has seen its last light.
He knows the sound of a rabbit's cry
And the taste of its trembling fear.
20 He sleeps among stones in the clouds.

The two methods vary
But they're both birds of prey
And they both fill a space on the wall.
But the wall
25 Is just part
Of the house.

—— Robert Swift

48. The claws and keen eyes (line 6) are features of the   (1) fisher   (2) minnows   (3) hunter   (4) rabbit

49. Stanzas two and three contrast the birds' methods of attack and their   (1) habitat   (2) color   (3) size   (4) motivation

50. In line 17, the poet suggests that the fate of the hunter's prey is   (1) unknown   (2) inevitable   (3) commonplace   (4) justified

51. In lines 18 and 19, the poet portrays the bird as   (1) menacing   (2) sympathetic   (3) mournful   (4) willful

52. In line 20, the phrase "stones in the clouds" refers to   (1) hailstones   (2) cloud shapes   (3) mountaintops   (4) thunderstorms

53. Which lines support the metaphor suggested by the title?   (1) lines 1 through 4   (2) lines 12 through 14   (3) lines 18 and 19   (4) lines 21 through 23

Passage C

And as he neared thirty he became not a little depressed at the inroads that marriage, especially lately, had made upon his friendships. Groups of people had a disconcerting tendency to dissolve and disappear. The men from his own college — and it was upon them he had expended the most time and affection — were the
5 most elusive of all. Most of them were drawn deep into domesticity, two were dead, one lived abroad, one was in Hollywood writing continuities for pictures that Anson went faithfully to see.

Most of them, however, were permanent commuters with an intricate family life centering around some suburban country club, and it was from these that he
10 felt his estrangement most keenly.

In the early days of their married life they had all needed him; he gave them advice about their slim finances, he exorcised their doubts about the advisability of bringing a baby into two rooms and a bath, especially he stood for the great world outside. But now their financial troubles were in the past and the fearfully
15 expected child had evolved into an absorbing family. They were always glad to see old Anson, but they dressed up for him and tried to impress him with their present importance, and kept their troubles to themselves. They needed him no longer.

A few weeks before his thirtieth birthday the last of his early and intimate friends was married. Anson acted in his usual role of best man, gave his usual
20 silver tea-service, and went down to say his usual good-by.

—— F. Scott Fitzgerald

54. Anson views the effects of marriage on friendship as a (1) blessing (2) threat (3) necessary evil (4) financial drain

55. The passage implies that Anson went to the movies out of (1) loyalty (2) boredom (3) loneliness (4) necessity

56. According to the passage, Anson feels most alienated from those who (1) went abroad (2) went to Hollywood (3) lived in cities (4) commuted regularly

57. Based on lines 15 through 17, what might be the reason Anson's friends now keep "their troubles to themselves"? (1) They discuss their troubles with their wives. (2) They think their troubles are insignificant. (3) They are afraid of boring Anson. (4) They might appear less successful.

58. In the passage as a whole, Anson is most strongly affected by (1) financial worries (2) growing older (3) changing relationships (4) wives of friends

59. A major purpose of the passage is to describe (1) the sources of Anson's unhappiness (2) Anson's reaction to his last friend's marriage (3) the celebration of Anson's thirtieth birthday (4) Anson's feelings about himself

60. The last lines of the passage reinforce the tone of (1) anger (2) resignation (3) jealousy (4) fear

Part II

Directions: Write a well-organized essay of about 250 words on either *A* or *B*.   [25]

A. In some works of literature, family situations influence the actions or decisions of a family member. From the literature you have read, choose *two* works in which a family situation influences the actions or decisions of a family member. For *each* work, identify the family member. Using specific references from *each* work, describe the family situation and explain how that situation influences the actions or decisions of the family member. Give titles and authors.

B. Individuals in literature may pursue a goal either by using power wisely or by abusing power. From the literature you have read, choose *two* works in which an individual pursues a goal either by using power wisely or by abusing power. For *each* work, identify the individual and describe the goal the individual is pursuing. Using specific references from *each* work, explain how the individual either uses power wisely or abuses power to pursue the desired goal. Give titles and authors.

Part III

Directions: Answer *A* or *B* or *C*.   [30]

A. You are concerned that very few young people are involved in community service. In an article of about 250 words for your school newspaper, explain why young people should take an active part in serving their community. In your discussion, suggest some types of service young people can perform in your community and explain how such service would benefit both the individual and the community. Support your discussion with specific reasons, examples, or details.

B. Recent budget cuts have threatened extracurricular activities, such as sports, plays, and after-school clubs in your school. Your principal is soliciting student opinions on which extracurricular activities are essential to the educational program and student morale. In a letter of about 250 words to the principal, identify *one* extracurricular activity that you think is essential to the educational program and student morale and explain why that activity should be retained in your school. Support your opinion with specific reasons, examples, or details. *Write only the body of the letter.*

C. Write a well-organized composition of about 250 words on *one* of the following topics:

Ethics for the computer age	A tale for my grandchildren
Good losers, graceful winners	Women in the military
Art attack	It's your turn

COMPREHENSIVE EXAMINATION IN ENGLISH—JANUARY 1996 (1)

Directions for the Listening Section:

1. The teacher will read a passage aloud. Listen carefully. DO NOT WRITE ANYTHING.
2. Then the teacher will tell you to open your test booklet and read questions 1 through 10. At that time you may mark your tentative answers to questions 1 through 10 if you wish.
3. Next, the teacher will read the passage aloud a second time. *As you listen to the second reading*, WRITE THE NUMBER of the answer to each question.
4. After you have listened to the passage the second time, you will have up to 5 minutes to look over your answers.
5. The teacher is not permitted to answer questions about the passage.
6. After you have answered the listening questions, go right on to the rest of the examination.

Part I

Listening [10]

1. The contrast between the shelter and its surroundings serves to evoke a sense of (1) shame (2) awe (3) comfort (4) amusement

2. When the speaker says, "I never found my way back home," he most likely means that he (1) wandered from city to city (2) never left New York City (3) remained in the shelter (4) was changed by his experience

3. When the speaker comments that the children are guilty of "being born poor in a rich nation," his tone is (1) uncertain (2) objective (3) ironic (4) insensitive

4. The speaker implies that one common stereotype of homeless families is that the (1) families live only in large cities (2) fathers are absent (3) families have several children (4) fathers are uneducated

5. What is the speaker's attitude toward the nation's "culture heroes"? (1) disapproval (2) indifference (3) envy (4) sympathy

6. The message in the quotation from Thomas Merton is that people should (1) take pride in their achievements (2) defend the economy (3) acknowledge the truth (4) overcome their laziness

7. According to the speaker, the problem of homelessness in the United States is related to the (1) nation's failing economy (2) nation's refusal to act on its ideals (3) apathy of the homeless (4) increase in the number of immigrants

8. The speaker uses the term "long winter" to suggest a long period of (1) selfishness (2) recession (3) cold war (4) violence

9. The speaker suggests that good societies are characterized by (1) humility (2) education (3) wealth (4) compassion

10. What is the speaker's tone at the end of the passage? (1) nostalgia (2) optimism (3) anger (4) frustration

Directions (11–30): Write the *number* of the word or phrase that most nearly expresses the meaning of the word or words printed in heavy black type. [10]

11. **constrain** (1) confine (2) examine (3) plan (4) dispute

12. **impoverish** (1) invite discussion (2) make poor (3) suggest improvement (4) expect obedience

13. **verge** (1) meeting (2) occasion (3) edge (4) center

14. **inkling** (1) warning (2) proof (3) hope (4) hint

15. **ingrained** (1) firmly fixed (2) completely changed (3) poorly formed (4) secretly influenced

16. **diminutive** (1) dense (2) rough (3) small (4) flexible

17. **largely** (1) usually (2) mainly (3) luckily (4) surprisingly

18. **quarter** (1) take control (2) spend money (3) gather crops (4) provide housing

19. **taut** (1) cheap (2) narrow (3) tight (4) precise

20. **certitude** (1) aptitude (2) tolerance (3) power (4) confidence

21. They were **averse to** the plan. (1) opposed to (2) interested in (3) accustomed to (4) aware of

22. The corporation planned to **augment** its workforce. (1) relocate (2) replace (3) honor (4) increase

23. A **vendetta** developed between them. (1) fragile bond (2) workable compromise (3) bitter feud (4) distrustful silence

24. The commander was worried that some soldiers might be **impulsive.** (1) disloyal (2) rash (3) lonely (4) fearful

25. The children constructed a story that was quite **intricate.** (1) unbelievable (2) fascinating (3) repetitious (4) complex

26. He was criticized for his **muddled** ideas. (1) jumbled (2) outrageous (3) distasteful (4) outmoded

27. The employer's **autocratic** attitude annoyed the workers. (1) unpredictable (2) tyrannical (3) old-fashioned (4) indifferent

28. She never seemed to **squander** money. (1) win (2) find (3) hoard (4) waste

29. His **imperturbable** nature made him a good leader. (1) joyful (2) inquisitive (3) calm (4) charming

30. The mayor's **edict** resulted in a curfew for teenagers. (1) bias (2) ultimatum (3) order (4) campaign

Directions (31–40): In each of the following groups of words, only one of the words is misspelled. In *each* group, select the misspelled word and spell it correctly. [5]

31. dinasaur   manageable   reprieve   thirtieth   vinyl

32. dining   eighth   resourses   tremendous   familiar

33. spectacle   irreguler   consultant   forfeit   competent

34. tobacco   seizure   global   millitary   eligible

35. sapphire   marathon   aerobic   poisonous   applience

36. fulfill   flies   hospital   intelligence   marraige

37. capitalism   condemn   ambasador   privilege   vinegar

38. horrify   challenge   thankfulness   possibility   theives

39. practically   unnecessary   quarelsome   anchored   yield

40. unbearable   vehical   immature   nonsense   conscientious

Directions (41–60): Below each of the following passages, there are several incomplete statements or questions about the passage. For *each*, select the word or expression that best completes the statement or answers the question *in accordance with the meaning of the passage*, and write its *number*. [20]

Passage A

Ancient Egypt might justifiably be characterized as primarily a culture of graffiti. Seldom in the course of history can there have been a people so persistently devoted as the Egyptians to writing on walls, nor one who raised the practice to such a fine art. Obsessed as they were with ideas of immortality and eternity, each generation
5   strove to perpetuate their own names and deeds for all time in some way which would not be at the mercy of the kind of mischance that can wipe out all living witnesses to the memory of a man's greatness, or even his existence. In order to achieve this they developed written characters of matchless sculptural clarity with which they covered all their buildings and monuments from floor to ceiling.
10   Egyptian archaeology was never faced with the problems besetting the rediscovery of a lost site or civilization, for even the most short-sighted or indifferent traveler could scarcely remain unaware of the pyramids, the Sphinx, and the temples of Luxor and Karnak. They were already well known as tourist attractions and a source of mysterious fascination to the classical Greeks, who scribbled their names on the ancient
15   stones with all the assiduity of their modern counterparts. The hot, dry air of Egypt provides conditions which are particularly favorable to the survival of most materials, and scarcely any early people left such abundant remains, not only of their temples, tombs, and public works, but their furniture, equipment, jewels, clothes, and even their own bodies, ritually preserved against the resurrection day. Nearly every item
20   in this unparalleled wealth of material was inscribed with exquisite written symbols; the authentic voice of ancient Egypt was perpetuated in the hieroglyphs.

— Anne Ward

41. One characteristic of ancient Egyptians noted by the author was their (1) distrust of foreigners (2) mercy (3) determination (4) love of history

42. According to the author, the Egyptians' desire for immortality caused them to (1) develop a clear method of writing (2) build temples in areas they conquered (3) emphasize the importance of genealogy (4) study Greek mythology

43. What does this passage say about some contemporary tourists? (1) They remove ancient stones from temple sites. (2) They pray at Luxor and Karnak. (3) They scribble graffiti at ancient sites. (4) They are no longer interested in Egyptian tombs.

44. What distinguishes the ancient Egyptian civilization from other ancient civilizations? (1) The Egyptians left an unusually detailed legacy. (2) The Egyptian civilization lasted until modern times. (3) The Egyptians were not interested in religion. (4) The Egyptian culture had little historical influence.

45. According to the passage, Egyptian relics have survived because of (1) their beauty (2) their environment (3) the skill of archaeologists (4) the cooperation of the Greeks

46. The tone of the passage is best described as (1) inspiring (2) conversational (3) reflective (4) admiring

Passage B

The land is to be read as text. But where does one start? Do we learn the basics first: memorize the line and color of the land, then one future day be able to understand the movement of the clouds and the cries of birds in trees? Can we learn from a tree how to live? What message lies scrawled in the lobes and veins of leaves and
5 in the hollowed striations of bark?

There is a big sycamore just outside the yard at my house. Its branches vault and spread over the house, keeping it a few degrees cooler than the ambient temperature. That tree is a blessing. A dense layer of ivy covers its trunk. Last spring a family of blue jays set up house in it. I know this because they would tell me quite
10 emphatically that I was on their property. They would fly from tree to tree around the yard, scolding me.

In late summer the sycamore peels off large square chunks of bark, sprinkling them over the yard; they look and feel like paper. In the fall we rake bushels of its giant leaves and stand at its base looking up in awe at its bare spine — its clay-
15 colored bark and broad-shouldered branches outstretched over the neighborhood. In the deep of winter the bare tree stands stiff, inert but alive.

I might have a lot to learn from the sycamore — about endurance under the rhythm of weather and season, about acts congruent with the necessities of living, about hope in the teeth of winter. The great thing about the tree is that it is never not
20 itself. To the rigors of living it has clear and appropriate responses. I should hope to live like that.

It is a strange thing, this business of daily living, carrying our self-consciousness around us like a scarf, never noticing anything but ourselves echoing in the closed hollows of our minds. We wake and go about our lives, hardly remembering where
25 we are or where we come from. And then a voice like a bird's wakes us and we wonder at the world and our lives in it.

—Victor Soon

47. The metaphor in the first sentence suggests that nature (1) is the substance of literature (2) lacks basic structures (3) holds hidden meanings (4) brings life to education

48. Which metaphor is *not* found in the first paragraph? (1) The land is a book. (2) The land is a painting. (3) A tree is a teacher. (4) A leaf is a roadway.

49. The word "vault" (line 6) is used to suggest the tree's (1) weight (2) size (3) origin (4) location

50. The phrase "acts congruent with the necessities of living" (line 18) refers to life's (1) troubles (2) hopes (3) responsibilities (4) relationships

51. The fourth paragraph suggests that one quality of the sycamore is its (1) respect (2) love (3) sympathy (4) fortitude

52. Which line or lines contain the answer to the question in lines 3 and 4, "Can we learn from a tree how to live?" (1) "There is . . . house." (line 6) (2) "They would . . . me." (lines 10 and 11) (3) "To the rigors . . . responses." (line 20) (4) "We wake . . . from." (lines 24 and 25)

53. What does the last paragraph suggest? (1) Self-centeredness narrows our perspective. (2) Nature is self-conscious. (3) Daily living is a complex process. (4) Wild creatures understand the wonders of the world.

Passage C

Ethics

In ethics class so many years ago
our teacher asked this question every fall:
if there were a fire in a museum
which would you save, a Rembrandt painting
5   or an old woman who hadn't many
years left anyhow? Restless on hard chairs
caring little for pictures or old age
we'd opt one year for life, the next for art
and always half-heartedly. Sometimes
10 the woman borrowed my grandmother's face
leaving her usual kitchen to wander
some drafty, half-imagined museum.
One year, feeling clever, I replied
why not let the woman decide herself?
15 Linda, the teacher would report, eschews
the burdens of responsibility.
This fall in a real museum I stand
before a real Rembrandt, old woman,
or nearly so, myself. The colors

```
20    within this frame are darker than autumn,
      darker even than winter — the browns of earth,
      though earth's most radiant elements burn
      through the canvas. I know now that woman
      and painting and season are almost one
25    and all beyond saving by children.
```

— Linda Pastan

54. In lines 1 through 6, the narrator relates that every year the teacher starts the term by (1) asking a rhetorical question (2) arguing for the supremacy of art (3) posing the same dilemma to students (4) encouraging students to pity the elderly

55. The description of the woman (lines 5 and 6) is most probably included to (1) suggest why she visits the museum (2) set up a comparison of values (3) provide some idea of her ethics (4) clarify the needs of our society

56. In lines 9 through 12, the narrator indicates that she normally associates her grandmother with which environment? (1) a museum (2) a classroom (3) church (4) home

57. In lines 13 and 14, the narrator's reply suggests that she (1) did not like the teacher (2) was avoiding the need to make a decision (3) did not understand the question (4) understood the old woman's point of view

58. The comment in lines 15 and 16 reveals the attitude of the (1) teacher toward the narrator (2) narrator toward Linda (3) narrator toward the grandmother (4) teacher toward the old woman

59. Which statement best describes the situation in lines 17 through 19? (1) The narrator has undergone a frightening experience. (2) The narrator's grandmother is admiring the painting. (3) The narrator has an opportunity to reexamine her beliefs. (4) The narrator watches an old woman in the museum.

60. Lines 23 through 25 suggest that young people cannot save anything from the effects of (1) time (2) folly (3) fire (4) immorality

Part II

Directions: Write a well-organized essay of about 250 words on either *A* or *B*. [25]

A. In some works of literature, the author uses a symbol whose meaning contributes to a deeper understanding of the work. From the literature you have read, choose *two* works in which the author uses a symbol whose meaning adds to a deeper understanding of the work. For *each* work, identify the symbol. Using specific references from *each* work, explain the symbol's meaning in the work, and discuss how its meaning contributes to a deeper understanding of the work. Give titles and authors.

B. Sometimes two individuals in a work of literature develop a friendship that influences them both, despite their differences in age, background, experience, or personality. From the literature you have read, choose *two* works in which friendship influences two individuals who differ from each other in age, background, experience, or personality. For *each* work, identify both individuals. Using specific references from *each* work, explain how the individuals differ from each other and discuss how each is influenced by the friendship. Give titles and authors.

Part III

Directions: Answer *A* or *B* or *C*. [30]

A. Young people sometimes imitate dangerous actions they see on television or in the movies. Some people believe the entertainment industry should be held responsible for any harmful results of this imitative behavior. In a letter of about 250 words to the editor of your school newspaper, state your opinion about whether or not the entertainment industry should be held responsible when young people are harmed as a result of imitating dangerous actions they see on television or in the movies. Support your opinion with specific reasons, examples, or details. *Write only the body of the letter.*

B. In commemoration of Education Week, your community is honoring individuals who are effective "teachers," even though they do not teach in a classroom. Write a speech of about 250 words to be presented to the nominating committee, in which you identify an individual whom you believe to be an effective teacher, even though the person does not teach in a classroom. Using specific reasons, examples, or details, explain what this person taught you and what makes this individual an effective teacher.

C. Write a well-organized composition of about 250 words on *one* of the following topics:

Teamwork gets it done	The environment in crisis
My music, my world	Another language
Are books obsolete?	The right clothes

COMPREHENSIVE EXAMINATION IN ENGLISH—JUNE 1996 (1)

Directions for the Listening Section:

1. The teacher will read a passage aloud. Listen carefully. DO NOT WRITE ANY-THING.
2. Then the teacher will tell you to open your test booklet and read questions 1 through 10. At that time you may mark your tentative answers to questions 1 through 10 if you wish.
3. Next, the teacher will read the passage aloud a second time. *As you listen to the second reading*, WRITE THE NUMBER of the answer to each question.
4. After you have listened to the passage the second time, you will have up to 5 minutes to look over your answers.
5. The teacher is not permitted to answer questions about the passage.
6. After you have answered the listening questions, go right on to the rest of the examination.

Part I

Listening [10]

1. The rules the speaker mentions have to do primarily with   (1) personal conduct   (2) legal systems   (3) business procedures   (4) social customs

2. The quotation from Adlai Stevenson implies that real evil consists of   (1) associating with evil people   (2) being afraid of evildoers   (3) failing to recognize evildoing   (4) favoring evil over good

3. The speaker wonders whether Americans have replaced rules with   (1) party politics   (2) rash decisions   (3) vague excuses   (4) legal arguments

4. The speaker says having many "things" leads to a   (1) high standard of living   (2) determination to have more   (3) reluctance to share   (4) disrespect for standards

5. According to the speaker, what effect has need had on progress?   (1) It has slowed progress.   (2) It has negated progress.   (3) It has shaped progress.   (4) It has stimulated progress.

6. The speaker uses the expression "evil . . . wore the face of good" to suggest that progress may   (1) banish hardships   (2) promote laziness   (3) mask dangers   (4) encourage selfishness

7. What common idea does the speaker seem to be illustrating?   (1) Always be prepared.   (2) Too much of a good thing is not good.   (3) Hard work always pays off.   (4) Opportunity knocks but once.

8. The speaker indicates that Americans think differently about fire and atomic fission because of the   (1) kind of power each generates   (2) way society values each   (3) ecological impact each has   (4) level of their experience with each

9. What is the speaker's belief about work? (1) Work is essential. (2) Work is inescapable. (3) Work is old-fashioned. (4) Work is exhilarating.

10. What does the speaker suggest is lacking in American society? (1) good labor practices (2) adequate resources (3) a sense of direction (4) a drive to excel

Directions (11–30): Write the *number* of the word or phrase that most nearly expresses the meaning of the word or words printed in heavy black type. [10]

11. **tantalize** (1) disgust (2) remind (3) tangle (4) tease

12. **ingeniously** (1) carefully (2) cleverly (3) hesitantly (4) quickly

13. **citation** (1) summons to court (2) work of art (3) call to arms (4) division of labor

14. **buoyant** (1) visible at night (2) free from danger (3) capable of floating (4) about to burst

15. **knoll** (1) small hill (2) deep lake (3) narrow path (4) tall tree

16. **indentured** (1) marked by dishonesty (2) taken by force (3) freed by law (4) bound by contract

17. **enigmatic** (1) mysterious (2) changeable (3) false (4) teasing

18. **arduous** (1) difficult (2) satisfying (3) complex (4) disgraceful

19. **foil** (1) modify (2) ignore (3) frustrate (4) imitate

20. **captivate** (1) understand (2) revive (3) reward (4) charm

21. Her **vivaciousness** was a factor in her winning the contest. (1) intelligence (2) liveliness (3) maturity (4) resourcefulness

22. His attitude toward his colleague was **paternal**. (1) fatherly (2) trusting (3) helpful (4) friendly

23. The painter combined the paint and the **solvent**. (1) tinting agent (2) thickening agent (3) hardening agent (4) dissolving agent

24. The mayor suggested that the document be **notarized**. (1) revised (2) authenticated (3) duplicated (4) distributed

25. The senior accepted the **laurels** graciously. (1) opportunities (2) challenges (3) suggestions (4) honors

26. The candidate's **forthright** manner was appealing to everyone. (1) dignified (2) straightforward (3) casual (4) modest

27. The end of the war was **imminent**. (1) longed for (2) unlikely (3) near (4) unpredictable

28. With some **trepidation**, the student went to the office. (1) annyoance (2) haste (3) fear (4) determination

29. The comedian was **impervious to** the comments from the audience.   (1) discouraged by   (2) unaffected by   (3) amused by   (4) angered by

30. The defendant tended to **equivocate** during the cross-examination.   (1) respond evasively   (2) gesture dramatically   (3) lecture forcefully   (4) argue loudly

Directions (31–40): In each of the following groups of words, only one of the words is misspelled. In *each* group, select the misspelled word and spell it correctly.   [5]

31. horrified   ignorence   hospitality   joyous   shining

32. romanticism   retention   restaurant   restoration   requirment

33. potentially   innocent   orphenage   reliable   advantage

34. luscious   disapear   tendency   speech   broccoli

35. moderater   disciple   yacht   statue   remnant

36. moraly   niece   believe   judicial   precede

37. withholding   fierce   alternative   piracey   accuracy

38. traitor   turkeys   cheiftain   eligible   useful

39. exclusive   atribute   sentimental   parallel   recession

40. truly   viewpoint   variation   physician   millionare

Directions (41–60): Below each of the following passages, there are several incomplete statements or questions about the passage. For *each*, select the word or expression that best completes the statement or answers the question *in accordance with the meaning of the passage*, and write its *number*. [20]

Passage A

Since very early in the history of human beings when cultures began to evolve with different ways of doing things and different understandings of the world, groups have interacted with one another across cultural boundaries. Whether through conquest, trade and travel, or meeting one another along common bor-
5   ders, peoples have always exchanged cultural information, along with other resources, in a complex web of relationships that has shaped human history. The cultural information has flowed in both directions, even when the political, military and economic might has been concentrated on one side of the relationship. The influence of the conquered on the conqueror is often denied or ignored in
10   the subsequent tellings of the story by the victor, but it is documented throughout history.
Encoded within the beliefs, customs, language, arts, and other expressions of each culture is basic information about its history, what the world is like, how it works, what is of value in it, and how people should live in relation to each other
15   and to the environment. This information is often specific and subtle — how

close it is appropriate to stand to someone you are addressing, or when it is appropriate to play a particular tune, or what colors go together.

Each culture is the product of human intelligence — among many other qualities — applied to the problems and opportunities of living in the world and
20 passed down through the generations. Just as the hawk is not judged a better
species than the mouse, so it makes no sense to view one culture as better or
worse than another, regardless of inequities in economic or military might or
technological accomplishment. Each occupies a particular niche in the system of
world cultures, and each survives with its mix of particular wisdom and folly.

— John W. Suter

41. According to lines 1 through 3, culture is a reflection of a society's   (1) age
    (2) beliefs   (3) geography   (4) language

42. According to the passage, what happens when one group conquers another?   (1) The
    loser's culture is destroyed.   (2) The winner's culture loses respect.   (3) A cultural
    exchange occurs.   (4) A simpler culture emerges.

43. In lines 9 through 11, the author implies that a victor may give a version of history
    that is   (1) verifiable   (2) apologetic   (3) uninformed   (4) self-serving

44. In the passage, the author implies that in some cultures a person could offend another
    person by   (1) refusing native food   (2) asking directions of strangers   (3) coming
    too near the person when speaking   (4) speaking English only

45. When the author identifies culture as the "product of human intelligence" (line 18),
    he is implying that   (1) only intelligent societies survive   (2) primitive societies have
    no recognizable culture   (3) each society has reached the same conclusions about life
    (4) people construct their own societies

46. In lines 20 through 23, the author most probably makes reference to a hawk and a
    mouse because they seem to represent   (1) two nonthreatening animals   (2) animals
    respected in many cultures   (3) apparent differences in status   (4) observable differ-
    ences in intelligence

47. In lines 23 and 24, the author implies that no culture has progressed to the point of
    (1) being without faults   (2) admitting its mistakes   (3) rejecting improvement
    (4) accepting other cultures

Passage B

Morning Song

Sun on his face wakes him.
The boy makes his way down
through the spidery dark
of stairs to his breakfast
5   of cereal in a blue bowl.
He carries to the barn
a pie plate heaped

with vegetable scraps
for the three-legged deer.
10 As a fawn it stood still
and alone in high hay
while the red tractor
spiraled steadily inward,
mowing its precise swaths.
15 "I lived" is the song
the boy hears as the deer
hobbles toward him.
In the barn's huge gloom
light falls through cracks
20 the way swordblades
pierce a magician's box.

— Gregory Orr

48. In lines 2 and 3, the poet suggests that the boy's movements are   (1) cautious   (2) strong   (3) swift   (4) clumsy

49. The figurative language used in line 3 suggests the   (1) disrepair of the house   (2) effect of the shadows   (3) poverty of the family   (4) memories of the boy

50. In lines 10 and 11, what quality of the fawn is suggested?   (1) vulnerability   (2) stubbornness   (3) fear   (4) playfulness

51. One purpose of lines 10 through 14 is to   (1) switch the point of view   (2) describe the boy   (3) provide a flashback   (4) foreshadow an event

52. Lines 13 and 14 serve to contrast the immobility of the deer with the   (1) mechanical nature of farming   (2) savagery of nature   (3) kindness of the boy   (4) relentless advance of the mower

53. The "song" referred to in line 15 is one of   (1) regret   (2) triumph   (3) love   (4) bravery

54. Which statement most accurately describes the interior of the barn?   (1) Sunlight penetrates the structure.   (2) The timber walls need repair.   (3) The air circulates slowly.   (4) Dampness rises from the floor.

Passage C

The freeze-up on Black Bear Lake is a prelude to winter. The freeze-up is a prelude to hardship. The freeze-up is a prelude to loneliness. It begins on a November evening as a filigreed fingering of ice along the shoreline. It greets me in the morning as a rim of ice around the boat hull and a skim of ice atop the
5 water buckets. Some nights the ice forms halfway across the lake; but, come morning, it shatters into a trillion thin shards beneath waves and wind. The

freeze-up takes its time. The freeze-up is implacable. There is no stopping it. The freeze-up is an event as important in nature as the solstices, equinoxes, full moon and eclipses. It affects the living patterns of many fish and wildlife species. And
10 it dramatically changes my life-style on this Adirondack lake where I live alone in the log cabin I built myself.

Motoring down the lake in my small aluminum outboard boat, I "feel" how heavy the water has become, how dark, how turgid. The propeller seems to be churning syrup and the boat handles sluggishly. At a few degrees above freezing,
15 water is actually denser than at 32 degrees. God help you if you fall out of the boat. If the shock doesn't kill you outright, the cold water will do so within three minutes.

I remember one rainy, blustery night during my first winter at Black Bear Lake when I had jumped into my boat at the empty public landing, my poncho
20 waving wildly in the wind. By mistake, I had left the gearshift in forward, something I almost never do. Fumbling with the flapping poncho, I forgot my usual routine to check if the engine was in neutral. I stood, straddling the seat, and pulled the starting rope. The engine roared into life, the boat lurched forward, then careened sideways. I fell heavily upon the gunwale, narrowly missed losing
25 my balance and dumping over backward into the lake. Getting the boat under control once more, I started to tremble. Imagining a frantic lunge for shore, the entanglement with my poncho underwater, the circular chase by a runaway motorboat, I resolved to be more careful in boats during freeze-up.

— Anne La Bastille

55. The effect of lines 1 and 2 is achieved by the narrator's use of what literary device?
(1) contrast   (2) symbolism   (3) definition   (4) repetition

56. The narrator associates the freeze-up with   (1) difficulty and isolation   (2) observation and judgment   (3) conflict and resolution   (4) challenge and accomplishment

57. As used in line 3, the phrase "filigreed fingering" suggests that the ice is
(1) widespread   (2) threatening   (3) enticing   (4) delicate

58. The phrases "rim of ice" and "skim of ice" (line 4) suggest that the freeze-up
(1) occurs only in sheltered areas   (2) moderates overnight   (3) is in its initial stage
(4) affects only remote locales

59. The narrator did not check the engine because   (1) she was pressed for time   (2) she had little experience with boats   (3) an animal caught her attention   (4) her clothing caused a distraction

60. The narrator's attitude toward the freeze-up could best be described as
(1) affectionate   (2) respectful   (3) bitter   (4) defensive

Part II

Directions: Write a well-organized essay of about 250 words on either *A* <u>or</u> *B*.   [25]

A. Many works of literature are set in a world troubled by war, prejudice, poverty, or natural disaster; yet they offer the reader reassurance or hope. From the literature you have read, choose *two* works that offer reassurance or hope in connection with some troubling situation. Using specific references from *each* work, describe the troubling situation and explain how the work offers the reader reassurance or hope. Give titles and authors.

B. Sometimes the relationship between two individuals in a work of literature changes because one individual underestimates the strength, charm, or intelligence of another individual. From the literature you have read, choose *two* works in which the relationship between two individuals changes because one of the individuals underestimates the other. For *each* work, identify the individuals. Using specific references from *each* work, explain how one individual underestimates the other, and discuss how the relationship between the individuals changes as a result of the underestimation. Give titles and authors.

Part III

Directions: Answer *A* <u>or</u> *B* <u>or</u> *C*.   [30]

A. The student council in your school wishes to give special recognition to the "quiet heroes" in your community. These people whose good deeds or brave struggles go largely unnoticed. In a letter of about 250 words to the president of the student council, identify one person in your community whom you consider to be a "quiet hero." Using specific reasons, examples, or details, explain why that person deserves special recognition. *Write only the body of the letter.*

B. Your high school guidance department is preparing a publication to help students make appropriate career choices and has asked students to contribute their ideas to the series. In a composition of about 250 words, discuss a career you know about. Describe its significant features, the personal qualities needed, and the education or training necessary for success in the career. Use specific reasons, examples, or details.

C. Write a well-organized composition of about 250 words on *one* of the following topics:

Running is . . .	The rain forest: lungs of the planet
Breaking down barriers	Left-handed in a right-handed world
Pride in craftsmanship	A lesson from history

COMPREHENSIVE EXAMINATION IN ENGLISH—JANUARY 1997 (1)

Directions for the Listening Section:

1. The teacher will read a passage aloud. Listen carefully. DO NOT WRITE ANYTHING.
2. Then the teacher will tell you to open your test booklet and read questions 1 through 10. At that time you may mark your tentative answers to questions 1 through 10 if you wish.
3. Next, the teacher will read the passage aloud a second time. *As you listen to the second reading*, WRITE THE NUMBER of the answer to each question.
4. After you have listened to the passage the second time, you will have up to 5 minutes to look over your answers.
5. The teacher is not permitted to answer questions about the passage.
6. After you have answered the listening questions, go right on to the rest of the examination.

Part I

Listening [10]

1. In her opening lines, the speaker attributes her smooth entrance into her profession to (1) an encouraging editor (2) a lack of competition (3) guidance from friends (4) women writers of the past

2. According to the speaker, writing was considered a suitable occupation for women because it (1) generated additional income for the family (2) brought fame to the family (3) caused little strain on the family (4) provided entertainment for the family

3. Who does the speaker imply is the girl in the bedroom? (1) a family member (2) a female friend (3) the speaker herself (4) an imaginary writer

4. The speaker says she became a journalist when (1) an editor offered her a job (2) she sent an article to an editor (3) she applied for an advertised position (4) a friend submitted her writing to a publisher

5. As recalled by the speaker, what form did her early writings take? (1) book reviews (2) poems (3) novels (4) mystery stories

6. The speaker portrays the Angel in the House as being (1) honest (2) self-reliant (3) inquisitive (4) self-sacrificing

7. In describing the angel as 'pure,'' the speaker most likely means the angel is (1) young (2) frivolous (3) virtuous (4) plain

8. In "killing" the angel, the speaker was trying to preserve her own (1) status (2) integrity (3) sanity (4) history

9. In spite of the name Angel in the House, the speaker's angel is really (1) an obstacle (2) a traitor (3) a flirt (4) a coward

10. The Angel in the House most nearly represents the (1) poetic muse (2) spirit of other women writers (3) author's approaching death (4) ideal woman of that time

Directions (11–30): Write the *number* of the word or phrase that most nearly expresses the meaning of the word printed in heavy black type. [10]

11. **endorsement** (1) obedience (2) approval (3) resignation (4) compromise

12. **corrosive** (1) slowly destructive (2) highly prejudiced (3) generally distrustful (4) rather ignorant

13. **articulate** (1) prepare carefully (2) express clearly (3) divide equally (4) undertake eagerly

14. **buckle** (1) roughen (2) shake (3) bend (4) scorch

15. **assert** (1) regret (2) declare (3) endure (4) escape

16. **verbatim** (1) in writing (2) with explanation (3) as a summary (4) word for word

17. **civility** (1) cleverness (2) mercy (3) obedience (4) politeness

18. **hypothesis** (1) accepted policy (2) logical conclusion (3) tentative assumption (4) firm principle

19. **intrepid** (1) honorable (2) experienced (3) sensitive (4) brave

20. **leniently** (1) mildly (2) cautiously (3) successfully (4) thoughtfully

21. The report was very **concise.** (1) unusual (2) brief (3) scholarly (4) important

22. Her **adversary** was quite self-confident. (1) guide (2) attorney (3) opponent (4) subordinate

23. The agreement remained **intact** despite the situation. (1) acceptable (2) influential (3) productive (4) untouched

24. The worker **adamantly** refused to obey instructions. (1) generally (2) rarely (3) stubbornly (4) angrily

25. A verbal agreement **constituted** the contract between the partners. (1) formed (2) altered (3) refined (4) canceled

26. The office of the corporate president reflected great **affluence.** (1) taste (2) individuality (3) disorder (4) prosperity

27. The new senator **exploited** his political power. (1) took advantage of (2) tried out (3) clung to (4) bragged loudly about

28. He could not be **coerced** into taking action. (1) tricked (2) shamed (3) forced (4) bribed

29. She was given an award for being the most **congenial** participant in the contest. (1) talented (2) friendly (3) beautiful (4) clever

30. The negotiators worked **fruitlessly** toward their objective. (1) impatiently   (2) half-heartedly   (3) unsuccessfully   (4) painfully

Directions (31–40): In each of the following groups of words, only one of the words is misspelled. In *each* group, select the misspelled word and spell it correctly.   [5]

31. countrys   injurious   camouflage   seizure   formulas

32. prevalent   irregular   accelaration   retail   judicious

33. unnecessary   misunderstand   silhouette   acquired   happyness

34. bachelor   accumulated   fuchsia   challanging   piloted

35. underneath   retreive   hereditary   undesirable   congratulatory

36. totality   explanation   occurred   forgotten   pianoes

37. unneeded   diseased   commited   tangible   perceived

38. disturbance   aweful   allotted   dissimilar   calendar

39. cylinder   conceivably   barely   dissappointed   scissors

40. arguement   harmonious   witness   performance   academy

Directions (41–60): Below each of the following passages, there are several incomplete statements or questions about the passage. For *each*, select the word or expression that best completes the statement or answers the question *in accordance with the meaning of the passage*, and write its *number*. [20]

Passage A

In March 1943 I was sent by the Navy to a small town in north Texas. I was to begin learning to fly there — not at a proper naval establishment but at a civilian flying school. It wasn't much of a school: its staff was a couple of local crop-dusters, and its airport was a pasture on the edge of town, which we shared with the sheep.
5   It had no runway, only grass, which the sheep kept trimmed. It was not even flat — it sank in the middle, and rose steeply at the far side, where it ended in a grove of scrubby trees. At the corner of the field by the road was a small hangar, and a shed that was called the Flight Office; beside the hangar four or five Piper Cubs were parked. That was all the equipment there was, except for a windsock, once red and
10   yellow but faded now to an almost invisible gray, which drooped on a staff near the fence. There was nothing impressive or even substantial-looking about the place; but I took my first flight there, and soloed there, and I have the same sort of blurred affection for it that I have for other beginnings — for the first date, the first car, the first job.
15   First flight: what images remain? I am in the rear seat of a Cub, and my instructor is taxiing to the takeoff position. The wheels of the plane are small, and it rides very low, so that I seem to be sitting almost on the ground, and I feel every bump

and hollow of the field as we taxi. The wings flap with the bumps, and the whole machine seems too small, too fragile, too casually put together to be trusted.

20   The instructor turns into the wind and runs up the engine, and I feel the quick life of the plane. It begins to roll, bumpily at first, as though we are still taxiing. The nose is high, I can't see around it, and I have a panicky feeling that we are rushing toward something — a tree or a sheep or another plane; and then the flow of air begins to lift the wings, the tail comes up, and the plane moves with a new grace,

25 dancing, touching the rough field lightly, and then not touching it, skimming the grass, which is still so close that I can see each blade, and I am flying, lifted and carried by the streaming air.

    At the end of the field the grove of trees is first a wall, a dark limit; and then it sinks and slides, foreshortening to a green island passing below us; the plane banks,

30 and I can see the town — but *below* me, all roofs and treetops — and beyond it there is distance, more and more distance, blue-hazy and flat and empty stretching away to the indistinct remote horizon. The world is enormous: the size of the earth increases around me, and so does the size of the air; space expands, is a tall dome filled with a pale clean light, into which we are climbing.

35   Below me the houses, each in its own place, look small and vulnerable perched on the largeness of the earth. I stare down at first like a voyeur, looking into other people's lives. A truck drives along a road and turns into a yard; a woman is hanging out clothes; she stops and runs to the truck. Should I be watching? Does she feel me there above her life? The world below exposes itself to me — I am flying,

40 I can see everything!

                                            — Samuel Hynes

41. The narrator suggests that he learned to fly in order to   (1) respond to parental pressure (2) satisfy youthful curiosity   (3) fulfill military orders   (4) achieve a childhood dream

42. In lines 12 and 13, the expression "blurred affection" suggests a feeling of (1) nostalgia   (2) anger   (3) inspiration   (4) depression

43. What is the meaning of the question "what images remain?" (line 15)?   (1) How much of the old airport is still there?   (2) What do I remember about the flight? (3) What is the point of looking back?   (4) Was it real, or did I imagine it?

44. In the second paragraph, the description of the plane conveys the narrator's feelings of (1) humility   (2) admiration   (3) frustration   (4) anxiety

45. In lines 30 through 34, the description conveys an impression of   (1) infinite space (2) blinding speed   (3) dizzying height   (4) brilliant light

46. In lines 36 and 37, the narrator implies that a "voyeur" is someone who   (1) threatens (2) flies   (3) snoops   (4) chases

47. In lines 39 and 40, the phrase "I am flying, I can see everything!" implies a sense of (1) defiance   (2) thoughtfulness   (3) contempt   (4) exhilaration

Passage B

Rain

<pre>
     Old-timers are saying it's never
     been so dry, but one of them disagrees,
     remembering a drought so bad you could cross
     the San Juan River downtown in your dress
5   oxfords and never get them wet.
     I dream, at dawn, the rustle
     of wind through leaves of aspen
     and scrub oak into rain drumming
     on the roof, dripping from the eaves,
10   the quilt covering my head into grey skies,
     mist like a cool hand on my forehead.
     Awakening, I scan the stony, turquoise
     sky for clouds, interstices to crack
     the blank days of endless blue.
15   Earth as dust, an unnerving heat at 2 PM
     high in the mountains, the hot,
     dry wind blowing grit in the teeth.
     I want to beat my fists in the dusty
     road, a sob in the throat. What if
20   it's our fault? Stripped of the comfort
     of other droughts, cyclical, caused by
     the world we're part of, have we
     brought this one on ourselves? Scorching
     the earth's deep green, burning
25   the sky a risk we took and lost?
     We did all this and now: there's nothing
     we can do to make it rain.
                    — Holly St. John Bergon
</pre>

48. In lines 6 through 9, the dream of rain is triggered by the (1) pattering of squirrels on the roof (2) sound of the wind in the trees (3) greyness of the sky at dawn (4) coolness of the night air

49. In lines 12 through 14, the words "stony," "blank," and "endless" suggest the (1) silent acceptance of fate (2) slow passage of time (3) uneventfulness of the day (4) relentlessness of the drought

50. In lines 18 and 19, the narrator expresses feelings of (1) exhaustion (2) hostility (3) despair (4) terror

51. In line 20, the poet suggests that the "comfort" of other droughts is the knowledge that (1) other droughts did no harm (2) people used to welcome the variety in weather (3) people used to prefer dry weather (4) other droughts were part of nature's pattern

52. What emotion is conveyed in lines 19 through 25? (1) awe (2) guilt (3) resignation (4) scorn

53. In lines 26 and 27, the narrator is concerned with the idea of the (1) limitations of human power (2) inevitability of drought (3) vulnerability of human beings (4) universality of suffering

54. What is ironic about the poem? (1) It is set in the present but refers to the past. (2) It asks questions but never answers them. (3) It uses description but avoids comparison. (4) Its title is "Rain" but it is about drought.

Passage C

The first impressions one has of William Randolph Hearst's kingdom are not actually of his buildings (almost too overwhelming to enter right away) but of the elaborate, statue-strewn marginalia surrounding them. Hearst never saw a rose garden that he did not think would be improved by a marble statue of Europa gal-
5 loping bare-bottomed on a bull through it. And after seeing Hearst's swimming pools you realize, humbly, that you have never really seen a swimming pool before.
The Neptune Pool is built on a promontory overlooking the Pacific, a huge oval tank holding some 350,000 gallons of water, surrounded by concentric circles of Greco-Roman marble columns, a nice place to shoot a new movie version of "Julius
10 Caesar." But the indoor pool beneath the tennis courts (which have glass skylights along the net lines to provide interior lighting) is even more spectacular. The pool is entirely surrounded by gold-leaf and blue mosaic tiles that are also set into the walls and ceilings to double their image in the water. Electrified alabaster lamps bloom along the pool's edges where swimmers once climbed in and out on carved
15 marble ladders.
But by now, the visitor accepts carved marble swimming pool ladders as being both reasonable and even necessary. We have mentally quickened our stride to keep up with Hearst's appetites, income and audacity. This is someone who ordered more than one ancient oak tree (whose branches covered a complete acre with
20 shade) uprooted and replanted. When he died, an entire Spanish monastery lay in a warehouse, in individual stones waiting to be reassembled.
Hearst in his lifetime ran newspapers, sat briefly in Congress, was held respon-sible in the main for starting the Spanish-American War, tried to become President and was seemingly everywhere in the country at once, inspiring fear, hatred and
25 loyalty. (As his columnist Ambrose Bierce once wrote, "Nobody but God loves him and he knows it.") But there never seemed to be a day in Hearst's life when he did not also buy something, once jotting "I'll take everything — WRH" on the top of an art dealer's catalogue. Hearst was a compulsive shopper and all the world was his mall.

— Phyllis Theroux

55. According to the passage, a visitor to Hearst's estate is first impressed by the (1) beauty of the buildings (2) ornateness of the grounds (3) tranquillity of the setting (4) number of swimming pools

56. In lines 3 through 5, the reference to a garden and statue has the effect of (1) celebrating Hearst's knowledge of flowers (2) explaining Hearst's source of wealth (3) suggesting Hearst's love of animals (4) ridiculing Hearst's use of statues

57. In line 11, the author states that the indoor pool "is even more spectacular" than the (1) Neptune Pool (2) Pacific (3) tennis courts (4) skylights

58. In lines 20 and 21, the reference to the monastery implies that Hearst had (1) bought the monastery (2) destroyed the monastery (3) become religious (4) lost interest in swimming pools

59. The effect of lines 22 through 25 is to (1) highlight Hearst's constant success (2) reveal Hearst's lack of a personal life (3) list Hearst's varied experiences (4) demonstrate Hearst's drive for perfection

60. The anecdote about the art catalogue illustrates Hearst's (1) good taste (2) busy schedule (3) knowledge (4) extravagance

Part II

Directions: Write a well-organized essay of about 250 words on either *A* or *B*. [25]

A. In some works of literature, an individual's behavior is the result of being troubled by an event or situation from the past. From the literature you have read, choose *two* works in which an individual's behavior is a result of being troubled by the past. For *each* work, identify the individual and describe the event or situation from the past that troubles the individual. Using specific references from *each* work, tell how the individual's behavior is affected by the troubling event or situation. Give titles and authors.

B. Although some characters in literature serve an important function because they change, others serve an important function because they do *not* change. From the literature you have read, choose *two* works in which a character does *not* change but still serves an important function. For *each* work, identify the character. Using specific references from the work, discuss the character's function in the work and explain the significance of having this character remain the same throughout the work. Give titles and authors.

Part III

Directions: Answer *A* or *B* or *C*. [30]

A. Your school is going to hire a new principal. You are a member of the committee that will be interviewing candidates for this position. The committee chairperson has asked each member to identify one school-related issue each candidate should address in the interview. In a letter of about 250 words to the committee chairperson, identify the issue that you want the candidate to address and explain why you think the issue is important. Use specific reasons, examples, or details. *Write only the body of the letter.*

B. You have been invited to be a guest writer for the music column of your local newspaper and have decided to use this opportunity to introduce your readers to music that you feel should have a wider audience. Choose *two* musical works that you believe should have a wider audience. In an article of about 250 words for your local newspaper, identify the *two* musical works and discuss the elements that make *each* work worthy of having a wider audience. Use specific reasons, examples, or details.

C. Write a well-organized composition of about 250 words on *one* of the following topics:

Big city/small neighborhood   The parent I hope to be
Life without television   A matter of trust
Danger: second-hand smoke   Hometown teams

COMPREHENSIVE EXAMINATION IN ENGLISH—JUNE 1997 (1)

Directions for the Listening Section:

1. The teacher will read a passage aloud. Listen carefully. DO NOT WRITE ANYTHING.
2. Then the teacher will tell you to open your test booklet and read questions 1 through 10. At that time you may mark your tentative answers to questions 1 through 10 if you wish.
3. Next, the teacher will read the passage aloud a second time. *As you listen to the second reading*, WRITE THE NUMBER of the answer to each question.
4. After you have listened to the passage the second time, you will have up to 5 minutes to look over your answers.
5. The teacher is not permitted to answer questions about the passage.
6. After you have answered the listening questions, go right on to the rest of the examination.

Part I

Listening [10]

1. King Harold's soldiers were exhausted when they arrived at the battle site because they (1) had climbed steep terrain (2) had to take a roundabout route (3) were wearing heavy armor (4) were returning from another battle

2. Which statement best describes King Harold's army just prior to the battle? (1) The army was as well trained as the enemy. (2) The army was untested in battle. (3) The army was greatly reduced in size. (4) The army was fully equipped for battle.

3. The description of the Norman troops suggests that they (1) objected to unnecessary waste (2) had an advantage in the forthcoming battle (3) were unable to wage inland war (4) were eager to seize the hill

4. Who broke off the negotiations that could have prevented the battle? (1) the Danish general (2) the peasant leaders (3) King Harold (4) Duke William

5. To what does the speaker attribute the fact that the battle "was already lost"? (1) an important invention (2) superiority of numbers and weapons (3) discord among the troops (4) the placement of the opposing armies

6. At the beginning of the battle, which men occupied the front line of King Harold's army? (1) expert archers (2) armed peasants (3) men on horseback (4) trained soldiers

7. What did fighting on horseback represent to King Harold's lords? (1) deception (2) tradition (3) nobility (4) cowardice

8. What strategy did the Normans use to protect their advancing cavalry? (1) a predawn attack (2) an arrow strike (3) defensive camouflage (4) troop division

COMPREHENSIVE EXAMINATION IN ENGLISH—JUNE 1997 (2)

9. What tactical mistake did the Saxons make? (1) They retreated under the shield wall. (2) They left the front line weakened. (3) They followed the retreating Normans. (4) They hurled their weapons too early.

10. What was the "device of crucial significance" that contributed to the Norman victory? (1) the stirrup (2) the arrow (3) the shield (4) the spear

Directions (11–30): Write the *number* of the word or phrase that most nearly expresses the meaning of the word printed in heavy black type. [10]

11. **compulsion** (1) ongoing depression (2) erratic pulse (3) strong impulse (4) deceptive calmness

12. **laden** (1) optimistic (2) burdened (3) constant (4) criminal

13. **unconditionally** (1) absolutely (2) voluntarily (3) honestly (4) knowingly

14. **dire** (1) dreadful (2) unexplainable (3) disorganized (4) embarrassing

15. **mandate** (1) liberate (2) abolish (3) acknowledge (4) command

16. **audacity** (1) excitement (2) expectation (3) annoyance (4) boldness

17. **reprieve** (1) temporary relief (2) appropriate punishment (3) unlawful escape (4) immediate revenge

18. **impeach** (1) libel (2) accuse (3) defeat (4) punish

19. **conversely** (1) on the contrary (2) as a matter of fact (3) on the whole (4) in addition to

20. **transpire** (1) fade (2) compromise (3) occur (4) hurry

21. The suspect **fabricated** the story. (1) created (2) ridiculed (3) denied (4) explained

22. According to the critics, the artist's work was **pedestrian**. (1) ridiculous (2) childish (3) disturbing (4) ordinary

23. The sailor waited **apprehensively** for news about his shipmates. (1) with uneasiness (2) with curiosity (3) with boredom (4) with grief

24. The professor voiced her opinion **emphatically**. (1) reluctantly (2) diplomatically (3) forcefully (4) immediately

25. The new supervisor worked hard to eliminate the workers' **tedium**. (1) laziness (2) boredom (3) insecurity (4) regret

26. The writer was asked to **append** a list of resources. (1) explain (2) summarize (3) number (4) attach

27. As a result of numerous accidents, the construction site was under **scrutiny**. (1) careful examination (2) extensive repair (3) justifiable attack (4) continuous patrol

28. The speaker's conclusion was **plausible.** (1) clever (2) believable (3) straightforward (4) troubling

29. The new administration wanted to **consolidate** several assistance programs. (1) create (2) change (3) cancel (4) combine

30. The architect proved to be **inept.** (1) lazy (2) unfit (3) careless (4) uninspired

Directions (31–40): In each of the following groups of words, only one of the words is misspelled. In *each* group, select the misspelled word and spell it correctly. [5]

31. enrolment grease enliven goalkeeper qualify

32. dissatisfied whistle abundant ballet intellectuel

33. antenna cieling controlled disguise physician

34. noticeable nineteenth definitely conscioussness renounce

35. enemies incompetent allergick ecstasy spaghetti

36. apology calendar unmistakable salarys preexisting

37. fierce chaperoned fragrence rodeos simultaneous

38. weird truly disappear fullfill assets

39. attendence accuracy manageable license unneeded

40. nuclear vacination actress sacrifice disapproval

Directions (41–60): Below each of the following passages, there are several incomplete statements or questions about the passage. For *each*, select the word or expression that best completes the statement or answers the question *in accordance with the meaning of the passage*, and write its *number*. [20]

Passage A

We weren't doing anything. We hadn't hurt anybody, and we didn't want to. We were on holiday. We had studied maps of the city and taken hundreds of photographs. We had walked ourselves dizzy and stared at the other visitors and stammered out our barely Berlitz versions of a beautiful language. We had mar-
5 veled at the convenient frequency of the Metro and devoured vegetarian crêpes from a sidewalk concession. Among ourselves, we extolled the seductive intelligence and sensual style of this Paris, this magical place to celebrate the two hundredth anniversary of the French Revolution, this obvious place to sit back with a good glass of wine and think about a world lit by longings for Liberty, Equality,
10 Fraternity.

It was raining. It was dark. It was late. We hurried along, punch-drunk with happiness and fatigue. Behind us, the Cathedral of the Sacred Heart glowed ivory and gorgeous in a flattering wash of artificial, mellow light.

15   These last hours of our last full day in Paris seemed to roll and slide into pleasure and surprise. I was happy. I was thinking that, as a matter of fact, the more
things change, the more things change.

    I was thinking that if we, all of us black, all of us women, all of us deriving
from connected varieties of peasant/immigrant/persecuted histories of struggle
and significant triumph, if we could find and trust each other enough to travel
20   together into a land where none of us belonged, nothing on Earth was impossible anymore.

    But then we tried to get a cab to stop for us, and we failed. We tried again,
and then again. One driver actually stopped and then, suddenly, he sped away,
almost taking with him the arm of one of my companions who had been about to
25   open the door to his taxi.

    This was a miserable conclusion to a day of so much tourist privilege and
delight, a day of feeling powerful because to be a sightseer is to be completely
welcome among strangers. And that's the trick of it: No one will say "no" to freely
given admiration and respect. But now we had asked for something in return—a
30   taxi. And with that single, ordinary request, the problems of our identity, our
problems of power, reappeared and trashed our holiday confidence and joy.

— June Jordan

41. The meaning of the phrase "barely Berlitz versions" (line 4) is enhanced by what other
word?   (1) "dizzy" (line 3)   (2) "stared" (line 3)   (3) "visitors" (line 3)
(4) "stammered" (line 4)

42. According to lines 6 through 10, what does Paris symbolize for the narrator?
(1) courage   (2) fashion   (3) romance   (4) freedom

43. In the second paragraph, the narrator's description of the cathedral and its surroundings
emphasizes the contrast between   (1) sadness and cheer   (2) space and time
(3) light and dark   (4) stability and change

44. In lines 17 through 21, the narrator expresses pleasure at her realization that she and
her companions   (1) had become best friends   (2) could learn French so easily
(3) could feel comfortable in a strange land   (4) were celebrating an anniversary

45. In the fifth paragraph, what does the narrator imply about the cab drivers?   (1) They
were prejudiced.   (2) They were reckless.   (3) They were dishonest.   (4) They were
irresponsible.

46. Which statement best describes the narrator's feelings about her last hours in Paris?
(1) She was perplexed.   (2) She was frightened.   (3) She was disheartened.   (4) She
was angry.

47. The incident with the cab drivers was foreshadowed in which line or lines?
(1) line 1   (2) lines 11 and 12   (3) lines 14 and 15   (4) lines 17 and 18

Passage B

The Gift

To pull the metal splinter from my palm
my father recited a story in a low voice.
I watched his lovely face and not the blade.
Before the story ended he'd removed
5   the iron sliver I thought I'd die from.

I can't remember the tale
but hear his voice still, a well
of dark water, a prayer.
And I recall his hands,
10   two measures of tenderness
he laid against my face,
the flames of discipline
he raised above my head.

Had you entered that afternoon
15   you would have thought you saw a man
planting something in a boy's palm,
a silver tear, a tiny flame.
Had you followed that boy
you would have arrived here,
20   where I bend over my wife's right hand.

Look how I shave her thumbnail down
so carefully she feels no pain.
Watch as I lift the splinter out.
I was seven when my father
25   took my hand like this,
and I did not hold that shard
between my fingers and think,
Metal that will bury me,
christen it Little Assassin,
30   Ore Going Deep for My Heart.
And I did not lift up my wound and cry,
Death visited here!
I did what a child does
when he's given something to keep.
35   I kissed my father.

— Li-Young Lee

48. What feeling do the father's actions instill in the boy? (1) bravery (2) optimism (3) wonder (4) reassurance

49. The words "lovely" (line 3), "prayer" (line 8), and "tenderness" (line 10) suggest that as a child, the narrator viewed his father with an attitude of (1) sympathy (2) adoration (3) astonishment (4) pride

50. What feelings are revealed in lines 26 through 32? (1) triumph and relief (2) fear and regret (3) peace and contentment (4) anger and confusion

51. To what does the title of the poem most likely refer? (1) a legacy of gentleness (2) a capacity for storytelling (3) an aptitude for healing (4) a desire to help others

52. The narrator's memory of his father's actions is triggered by the situation described in (1) line 3 (2) line 7 (3) line 9 (4) line 20

53. What is ironic about this poem? (1) The father began a story but never finished it. (2) An incident from childhood was reenacted in adulthood. (3) The boy was injured but he did not cry. (4) The act of removing was also an act of giving.

Passage C

For many fish species, survival means fellowship with others of their kind. The way they stick together and the varied behaviors they exhibit have delighted, perplexed, and amused observers for centuries. Some species gather in groups of no more than half a dozen and may be sociable for only a few days or weeks a
5   year. Others spend almost their entire lives swimming in formation with thousands of their fellows, packed together so tightly that they nearly rub fins as they swim.

To coordinate their activities, fishes communicate in many and sometimes most unusual ways. Some rely on sight and distinctive body-color patterns. Most
10 have special sense organs on their skins that can "hear" the movement of their cohorts through the water around them. Others talk to one another in private languages of clicks, grunts and growls. And still others communicate with electric pulses that they generate in highly specialized muscles.

Different kinds of fish schools can be both similar to and different from other
15 kinds of animal groups. Many animal societies are collections of close relatives, and members of many mammal groups — such as lion prides and certain monkey troops — are at least as closely related as cousins.

Among fishes, though, familial relationships are looser. Unlike birds (and some solitary or pair-forming fish species) who feed or shelter their young, and
20 mammals, who suckle them, schooling fishes abandon eggs and larvae to float away on the currents. This drifting makes it unlikely that the fish in large schools are closely related to one another, and the lack of interaction between parents and offspring makes it equally unlikely that they themselves can tell whether they are related or not.

— Joseph S. Levine

54. According to the passage, the reason some fish congregate is for (1) territorial expansion (2) self-preservation (3) familial relationships (4) hunting efficiency

55. The phrase "half a dozen" (line 4) refers to the number of (1) observers (2) groups (3) species (4) individuals

56. In line 4, the word "sociable" is probably used to mean that the fish (1) find mates (2) live together (3) migrate annually (4) make friends

57. According to the passage, fish groups differ in (1) location (2) feeding habits (3) swimming patterns (4) size

58. The statement "To coordinate . . . most unusual ways" (lines 8 and 9) is supported in the paragraph through the use of (1) reasons (2) anecdotes (3) examples (4) definitions

59. According to the passage, communications among fish sometimes relies on (1) visual recognition (2) natural selection (3) family relationships (4) physical contact

60. In which way are some pair-forming fishes like birds? (1) Both build homes. (2) Both care for their offspring. (3) Neither interacts with parents. (4) Neither fears mammals.

Part II

Directions: Write a well-organized essay of about 250 words on either *A* or *B*. [25]

A. Some works of literature deal with a conflict between parent and child. Sometimes the conflict is beneficial to the relationship; sometimes it is harmful to the relationship. From the literature you have read, choose *two* works in which a parent and child come into conflict. For *each* work, identify the parent and child. Using specific references from *each* work, describe the conflict between the parent and child and discuss whether the effect of the conflict on their relationship is beneficial or harmful. Give titles and authors.

B. In some works of literature, an individual suffers but does not give in to despair because of some inner strength or support from others. From the literature you have read, choose *two* works in which an individual suffers yet does not despair. For *each* work, identify the individual and tell what causes the individual's suffering. Using specific references from *each* work, explain how the individual's inner strength or the support from others keeps the individual from giving in to despair. Give titles and authors.

Part III

Directions: Answer *A* <u>or</u> *B* <u>or</u> *C*.   [30]

A. A recent letter to the editor of your local newspaper stated that afterschool athletic programs have little value. In a letter of about 250 words to the editor of the local newspaper, state whether you agree or disagree with the statement that afterschool athletic programs have little value. Support your opinion with specific reasons, examples, or details. *Write only the body of the letter.*

B. More and more frequently, commercial or industrial interests come into conflict with environmental interests. Select one specific issue or situation in your region that reflects this conflict. In a 250-word article for your school newspaper, describe the issue or situation and present the arguments on *both* sides of the conflict. Use specific reasons, examples, or details to support your discussion.

C. Write a well-organized composition of about 250 words on *one* of the following topics:

The fall of a hero	What I really learned in school
Organ transplants	Lost in cyberspace
Body piercing: art or vulgarity	Keeping the peace

COMPREHENSIVE EXAMINATION IN ENGLISH—JANUARY 1998 (1)

Directions for the Listening Section:

1. The teacher will read a passage aloud. Listen carefully. DO NOT WRITE ANYTHING.
2. Then the teacher will tell you to open your test booklet and read questions 1 through 10. At that time you may mark your tentative answers to questions 1 through 10 if you wish.
3. Next, the teacher will read the passage aloud a second time. *As you listen to the second reading,* WRITE THE NUMBER of the answer to each question.
4. After you have listened to the passage the second time, you wil have up to 5 minutes to look over your answers.
5. The teacher is not permitted to answer questions about the passage.
6. After you have answered the listening questions, go right on to the rest of the examination.

Part I

Listening [10]

1. The speaker believes his recommendation to stop watching television is (1) reasonable (2) impractical (3) optional (4) innovative

2. According to the speaker, television gives apparent approval to (1) materialistic values (2) violent activity (3) foul language (4) rude behavior

3. The speaker mentions *Mister Rogers* and *Sesame Street* to support his idea that
   (1) even nonviolent programs can have negative effects
   (2) most television programs contain violence
   (3) acceptable children's programs exist
   (4) children prefer television to kindergarten

4. The speaker compares political campaigns to (1) soap operas (2) sports events (3) concerts (4) commercials

5. The speaker criticizes televised debates as being (1) boring (2) biased (3) superficial (4) unrehearsed

6. The speaker indicates that the quality of televised debates is dependent upon
   (1) audience expectation
   (2) government guidelines
   (3) candidates' qualifications
   (4) corporate funding

7. According to the speaker, brightly colored moving images have the power to
   (1) educate (2) annoy (3) stupefy (4) excite

8. According to the speaker, television has changed viewers' ability to communicate because it encourages them to
   (1) use both words and symbols
   (2) rely heavily on visual cues
   (3) expect quick, easy answers
   (4) expand their vocabulary

9. According to the speaker, one effect of minimizing the spoken word in communication is to
   (1) decrease attention span
   (2) hinder reading ability
   (3) weaken social relationships
   (4) limit abstract thought

10. The speaker offers "reasoning, logic, and putting ideas together" as elements of
    (1) clear thinking
    (2) visual communication
    (3) critical monitoring
    (4) improved programming

Directions (11–30): Write the *number* of the word or phrase that most nearly expresses the meaning of the word or words printed in heavy black type. [10]

11. **attired** (1) decorated (2) clothed (3) conspicuous (4) proud

12. **bait** (1) injure (2) betray (3) control (4) tease

13. **buttress** (1) fasten (2) support (3) collide (4) analyze

14. **consensus** (1) contract (2) attitude (3) agreement (4) goal

15. **daub** (1) repair (2) smear (3) mount (4) joke

16. **cajole** (1) demand (2) please (3) assist (4) coax

17. **imperative** (1) urgent (2) reasonable (3) recommended (4) appropriate

18. **derivation** (1) repetition (2) completion (3) origin (4) context

19. **brash** (1) reliable (2) foolhardy (3) expensive (4) scarce

20. **sardonic** (1) brief (2) cynical (3) hidden (4) injurious

21. The missing man was found in a **hermitage** just outside the village. (1) suburb (2) church (3) hideaway (4) hangout

22. The performance was described as a praiseworthy **spoof.** (1) tragedy (2) musical (3) opera (4) takeoff

23. The new student displayed **an aptitude** for woodworking. (1) a talent (2) an enthusiasm (3) an ambition (4) a disregard

24. The official was reluctant to **abdicate** his duties. (1) add to (2) fulfill (3) give up (4) question

25. The strangers **sacked** the village. (1) looted (2) discovered (3) burned (4) rescued

26. The young girl walked **jauntily** toward the bus stop. (1) in a fearful manner (2) in a secretive manner (3) in a careful manner (4) in a lively manner

27. His friends were surprised by his **fainthearted** behavior. (1) silly (2) cowardly (3) impolite (4) mysterious

28. After the storm, the campers' tent was **sodden.** (1) saturated (2) soiled (3) flattened (4) buried

29. Her behavior was often described as **genteel.** (1) timid (2) sneaky (3) refined (4) haughty

30. The student director looked **dapper** in his new suit. (1) uncomfortable (2) neat (3) wealthy (4) funny

Directions (31–40): In each of the following groups of words, only one of the words is misspelled. In *each* group, select the misspelled word and spell it correctly. [5]

31. revealled subscription tourist poison mournful

32. allegiance nieghboring convenience ancient excellence

33. iceing budget busiest copies perceive

34. pharmacy generosity alcohol appologetic opponent

35. extreme specimen changeable vegatation tariff

36. ecology vulgar acheing theoretical frugal

37. negotiation immature approximatly donor inadequate

38. correspond magnificent volcano hazy integrety

39. macaroni despise abbreviation reconize bureaucracy

40. vinegar terestrial peaceful merriment conscience

Directions (41–60): Below each of the following passages, there are several incomplete statements or questions about the passage. For *each*, select the word or expression that best completes the statement or answers the question *in accordance with the meaning of the passage*, and write its *number* on the separate answer sheet. [20]

Passage A

A reverence for facts was difficult to express in the newswriting forms available to reporters through much of the nineteenth century. Facts found their true voice only with the arrival of the "inverted pyramid" in the second half of the nineteenth century. During the American Civil War in particular, journalists, rushing to trans-

5   mit their most newsworthy information over often unreliable telegraph lines, had
begun to develop the habit of compressing the most crucial facts into short,
paragraph-long dispatches, often destined for the top of a column of news.

     From here it was not a long distance to reserving the first paragraph of their
stories, the "lead," for the most newsworthy facts and then organizing supporting
10 material in descending order of newsworthiness. (The news value of the facts
stacked in these stories, like the width of an inverted pyramid, grows smaller as
you read down.) Theodore Dreiser recalled being introduced to this style, including the "who, what, how, when, and where" lead, with his first job in journalism
at the *Chicago Globe* in 1892. "News is information," his copy editor would pro-
15 claim. "People want it quick, sharp, clear—do you hear?"

     The inverted pyramid organizes stories not around ideas or chronologies but
around facts. It weighs and shuffles the various pieces of information, focusing
with remarkable single-mindedness on their relative news value.

     This style of newswriting took decades to establish its dominance.
20 Newspapers continued to dawdle over an engaging tale.

     Much information continued to be placed in newspapers first come, first
served—the dispatches arrayed, as they were in the *New York Tribune's* initial
coverage of Lincoln's assassination, in the order in which they arrived. However,
more and more reports of breaking news began to assume the form of this
25 upside-down pyramid of facts.

     When words are herded into any rigid format—from news ballad to two-
minute videotape report—their ability to re-create events in their fullness may
suffer. The demands of format—especially when enforced under deadline pressure—undoubtedly contribute to the journalist's habit of, in Norman Mailer's
30 words, "munching nuances like peanuts." In the sixteenth and seventeenth centuries, newsmakers found their sentences transformed into verse; in the twentieth century they find their statements chopped into fifteen-second "sound-
bites." The inverted pyramid is no more accommodating a host to nuances than
other news forms. Facts—a quotation here, a number there—shine through
35 these hierarchical columns of information, but the temporal, historical, atmo-
spheric, or ideological connections between these facts are often weakened,
occasionally severed.

                            — Mitchell Stephens

41. According to the author, the "inverted pyramid" (line 3) originated from the limitations of (1) readers (2) writers (3) technology (4) transportation

42. In line 8, the phrase "it was not a long distance" refers to the (1) prompt emergence
of short news stories (2) expected growth in dispatches (3) uneventful transition to
the 20th century (4) quick evolution of the lead

43. The "news value" of facts (line 10) refers to their (1) length (2) significance
(3) angle (4) clarity

44. The anecdote about Theodore Dreiser suggests that copy editors felt that the inverted pyramid (1) encouraged formula writing (2) met the time constraints of editing (3) suited readers' need for information (4) helped writers meet deadlines

45. The reference to the stories of Lincoln's assassination illustrates the practice of printing news stories in order of their (1) occurrence (2) popularity (3) frequency (4) arrival

46. According to the author, when words are "herded into any rigid format" (line 26), they may limit a story's (1) completeness (2) objectivity (3) language (4) imagery

47. In lines 35 and 36, the phrase "temporal . . . connections" helps to explain what previous word in the passage? (1) "herded" (line 26) (2) "format" (line 26) (3) "peanuts" (line 30) (4) "nuances" (line 33)

Passage B

The Tortoise In Eternity

Within my house of patterned horn
I sleep in such a bed
As men may keep before they're born
And after they are dead.

5   Sticks and stones may break their bones,
And words may make them bleed;
There is not one of them who owns
An armour to his need.

Tougher than hide or lozenged bark,
10   Snow-storm and thunder proof,
And quick with sun, and thick with dark,
Is this my darling roof.

Men's troubled dreams of death and birth
Pulse mother-o'-pearl to black;
15   I bear the rainbow bubble Earth
Square on my scornful back.

                                             — Elinor Wylie

48. In line 1, the phrase "patterned horn" refers to (1) grass (2) metal (3) shell (4) plastic

49. In the first stanza, the narrator's bed is compared to a womb and a (1) cradle (2) grave (3) house (4) blanket

50. In line 6, the poet implies that humans may suffer   (1) moral failure   (2) physical injury   (3) intellectual limitations   (4) emotional pain

51. In the third stanza, what characteristic of the narrator does the description of the "darling roof" (line 12) emphasize?   (1) self-sufficiency   (2) vanity   (3) self-mockery   (4) determination

52. In lines 13 and 14, the narrator describes men's dreams as a continuous   (1) search for riches   (2) shifting from hope to despair   (3) journey from innocence to knowledge   (4) preparation for eternity

53. In line 16, the nararator describes her back as "scornful" because she feels superior to   (1) the Earth's beauty   (2) people   (3) mother-o'-pearl   (4) other tortoises

54. The narrator develops the ideas in lines 13 through 16 mainly through the use of (1) contrast   (2) repetition   (3) cliché   (4) onomatopoeia

Passage C

The pair of children looked Asian, two or three years old, their glossy heads like lacquered bowls bobbing in the sunlight. Kneeling at the wide-open window, they pulled white tissues from a box and sent them wafting down on the breeze. A flimsy-looking iron gate reached to their stomachs, but every few seconds they
5 popped up to lean out over it, clapping their hands as the tissues caught on the branches of trees, wrapped around a lamp post, and fluttered leisurely to the concrete below like great snowflakes.

Not a soul in sight. Della watched from across the street, a floor above them—the fifth; they would not see her if she waved. If she called out, the sound
10 could startle them, make them lose their balance. She shut her eyes and curled her hands into fists as one child leaned way out, the tops of the bars pressing into his legs. The police? It was her first day here; she didn't even know the opposite building's address. And the time it would take, the heavy footsteps clattering up the stairs . . . . Meanwhile they would fall and she would relive this moment all
15 the years to come, remembering herself watching at the window of the empty bedroom in her new apartment, her new life, thinking about how she would remember herself at the window, watching . . . .

Just then a dark-haired woman appeared from the invisible spaces of the apartment across the street, plucked each child from the windowsill, and
20 snatched up the box of tissues. Shut the window, thought Della, but the woman receded into the invisible spaces.

— Lynne Sharon Schwartz

55. In lines 1 and 2, the description of the children's heads ("their . . . sunlight") helps call attention to their   (1) faces   (2) ages   (3) movements   (4) needs

56. The description of the falling tissues in lines 5 through 7 is reinforced by the use of (1) personification   (2) alliteration   (3) hyperbole   (4) simile

57. Which line or lines *first* foreshadow the possibility of danger?
    (1) lines 1 and 2 ("The . . . sunlight")
    (2) line 2 ("Kneeling . . . window")
    (3) lines 5 and 6 ("clapping . . . trees")
    (4) lines 6 and 7 ("fluttered . . . snowflakes")

58. What organizational technique does the author use to describe Della's indecision about helping the children? (1) comparison (2) chronological order (3) cause and effect (4) classification

59. What omission is suggested by the ellipsis in line 14? (1) further activities of the children (2) further actions taken by Della (3) other reasons to call the police (4) other details about the arrival of the police

60. In lines 18 through 20, the abruptness of the dark-haired woman's actions is conveyed by the use of (1) strong verbs (2) repeated phrases (3) vivid adjectives (4) short sentences

Part II

Directions: Write a well-organized essay of about 250 words on either *A* <u>or</u> *B*. [25]

A. President John F. Kennedy once stated: "Our problems are manmade; therefore, they may be solved by man. . . . No problem of human destiny is beyond human beings." From the literature you have read, choose *two* works in which an individual solves a problem that is manmade. For *each* work, identify the individual and the manmade problem. Using specific references from *each* work, show how the individual solves the problem that is manmade. Give titles and authors.

B. One mark of good fiction is characters who are portrayed in all their human complexity. That is, they display contradictory and inconsistent behaviors often displayed by real people; for example, bravery and cowardice, tenderness and cruelty, humor and pathos. From the fiction you have read, choose *two* works in which a character is portrayed in all his or her human complexity. For *each* work, identify the character. Using specific references from *each* work, describe the character and show how the character is portrayed in all his or her human complexity. Give titles and authors.

Part III

Directions: Answer *A* <u>or</u> *B* <u>or</u> *C*. [30]

A. The staff of your school newspaper is soliciting ideas for new activities that would give students a sense of pride in themselves and their school. Write an article of about 250 words to be published in the school newspaper suggesting *one* activity that does *not* already exist in your school and that you believe would help to give students a sense of pride in themselves and their school. Support your suggestion with specific reasons, examples, or details.

B. A local radio station has announced an essay contest in which the winner will spend one day with a prominent person of his or her choice from the field of entertainment, sports, business, or politics. Write an essay of about 250 words in which you identify the prominent person from the field of entertainment, sports, business, or politics with whom you would like to spend a day. Use specific reasons, examples, or details to explain why you chose this person.

C. Write a well-organized composition of about 250 words on *one* of the following topics:

A lost art	Home on the web
Against the tide	Celebrity endorsements
If rocks could talk	Lyrics with a lesson

Index